D1080124

THE TECHNIQUE OF BOBBIN LACE

Dedication

To my Mother

THE TECHNIQUE OF BOBBIN LACE

❖

Pamela Nottingham

B T Batsford Ltd   London

© Pamela Nottingham 1976
First published 1976
Second impression 1977
Third impression 1977
Fourth impression 1978
Fifth impression 1979
Sixth impression 1980
Seventh impression 1981
Eighth impression 1982
Ninth impression 1983
Tenth impression 1984
Eleventh impression 1985
Twelfth impression 1987
Thirteenth impression 1989

All rights reserved. No part of this publication may be
reproduced in any form, or by any means, without permission
from the publisher.

Filmset by Servis Filmsetting Ltd, Manchester

Printed and bound in Great Britain by
Anchor Press Ltd, Tiptree, Essex
for the publishers B T Batsford Ltd
4 Fitzhardinge Street, London W1H 0AH

ISBN 0 7134 3230 6

Contents

Introduction

In recent years there has been a great revival in the art of pillow lace making. No longer is it considered to be an occupation for elderly folk; today a vast number of young people are attending classes all over the country, and pillow lace making will continue to live as a leisure pursuit to be enjoyed by many.

This book sets out to answer the need for a collection of lace patterns arranged progressively. Full instructions are given in order that the student may work alone, but occasional help from other lace makers or attendance at classes will reduce the time it takes to master basic stitches and patterns.

There are five chapters in the book, with more than 70 prickings, offering a variety of patterns with many uses. The first chapter is a general introduction, and the second describes the making of Torchon lace. Students are advised to work and understand these before attempting the traditional English Bedfordshire and Bucks Point laces.

In Chapters 3 and 4 patterns have been selected for particular techniques, and a student will benefit from working through the series, gradually acquiring additional knowledge which will prove invaluable when it comes to working old traditional patterns. Chapter 3 on Bedfordshire lace includes instruction for the adaptation of patterns, the making of new designs for mats, motifs and collars, and gives suggestions for the interpretation and use of old and damaged patterns. Chapter 4 explains Bucks Point with several straightforward patterns; many prickings have corners, with diagrams and/or instructions for their execution. The intricacy of Point lace, and perhaps the mystery which surrounds the working, result from a complicated method of designing. This is described along with instructions for designing corners for straight edgings. An easy method of making circular motifs is included and finally advice is given on the working of more elaborate patterns.

A fifth chapter gives encouragement to those who wish to adapt the craft to the form of simple braids and trims for modern use. All patterns are straightforward and require only a limited knowledge of the craft. For the enthusiast who wishes to develop new ideas, the chief requirements are a sound understanding of Bedfordshire and Torchon laces and a willingness to experiment. Old techniques may be adapted for use with modern threads in a bold, exciting manner and truly original work produced.

Much confusion has arisen in the past because stitches, terms and even the names of laces vary from one district to the next. Common terms are used as far as possible and each one is explained clearly as it arises in the context of practical lace making. Surely it is easier to learn a new technique in a particular lace situation than to read an isolated written description. Once fully understood it can be applied to other patterns.

I express thanks to all my lace students, for through them I hope to have developed a logical approach to teaching the craft, which I have tried to incorporate in this book; also to Miss S.E. Dawson who introduced me to the craft and has willingly given advice and help ever since. I am very grateful to Patricia Philpott who has taken the photographs, and to Freda Bullock who has helped to check the script. I appreciate very much the encouragement and help that I have received from my husband, Arthur Johnson, and I owe to him many thanks for his patience and skill in producing all the diagrams.

1 ⸭ Equipment, preparation and other useful information

EQUIPMENT

Lace Pillows

Traditionally pillows vary in size and shape according to the country of origin and the type of lace to be made. There are two important requirements of a pillow: first that it should be very hard in order that the pins remain firm and upright, and second that it must allow for the bobbins to fall on a slight slope in order that the threads are kept taut and the tension of the lace maintained. Three types of pillow in common use are the French pillow, the round or rectangular flat pillow and the bolster:

French pillow   This consists of a small padded roller set in towards the back of a fairly flat pillow. It is used for making edgings as work can continue indefinitely as the roller is rotated.

To make a French pillow follow carefully diagrams 1*a*, 1*b* and 1*c*. Wooden boards, approximately 9mm thick, are cut and assembled as shown in diagram 1*a* and 1*b*. The roller is padded with lengths of straw, fabric is bound round tightly, and a second cover is tacked and sewn on to the roller frame. A double thickness of linen is fastened across the back

D 1

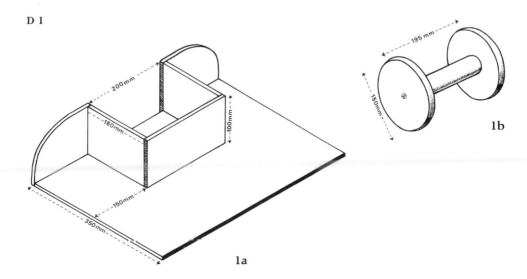

200 mm

160 mm

100 mm

150 mm

350 mm

1a

195 mm

160 mm

1b

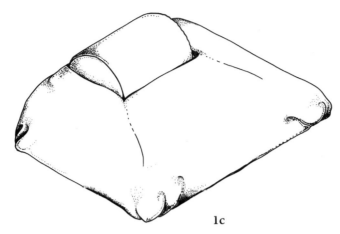

1c

of the pillow frame, forming a box into which the roller is dropped to revolve freely. Hessian or tailor's canvas is pulled tightly and tacked over the frame and stuffed with chopped straw or wadding until smooth and firm. A second cover may be added. A large hat pin stuck through the back of the roller and the linen prevents movement when the pillow is in use.

Flat pillow   This is the easiest type to make. It has the advantage that the inexperienced worker can spread out the bobbins for easy use, but the disadvantage that continuous edgings cannot be worked readily. It is particularly useful when making collars, mats, motifs or short lengths.

To make a rectangular pillow take a piece of plywood approximately 350mm × 400mm (14in. × 16in.) and remove the sharp corners with sandpaper. Make a bag the same size as the board leaving one end open (diagram 2). Slide in the board – it should fit very closely – and stuff one side only with finely chopped straw. It is important to pack the straw tightly to achieve a hard pillow. Oversew the remaining side. When working, raise the end of the pillow to give the necessary slope towards the lace maker.

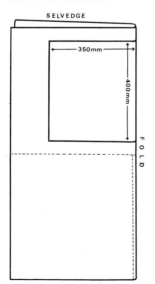

SELVEDGE

350mm

400mm

FOLD

D 2

Bolster pillow   A new one should be purchased. An old one is rarely worth the expense as it is often soft around the centre from years of use, and would need to be pulled apart and re-stuffed. A good bolster should have a minimum diameter of 275mm (11in.); the length is unimportant – usually about 450mm (18in.). The short South Bucks bobbins or continental bobbins are ideal on this type of pillow but the beaded bobbins are difficult to manage unless the bolster has a far larger diameter giving a flatter working area and less immediate slope.

In order to use a bolster pillow successfully the lace maker must adopt a method of keeping it in position to prevent it from rolling. An old fashioned pillow stand – no longer easy to find – is excellent, but a rectangular open-topped box or frame with suitable size semi-circles cut from opposite sides will support it adequately. Alternatively the lace maker may sit with the pillow on her knees supported against a table.

A cover which can be removed for occasional laundering is advisable and is best made in strong cotton or linen fabric. Dark green or blue drill is restful to the eyes and enhances the general appearance of any pillow. Take a piece of fabric 300mm (12in.) longer than the pillow – if the pillow is very large adjust this length accordingly – and seam it into a cylinder slightly larger than the pillow. Make 25mm (1in.) hems at both ends and thread with tape, put the pillow inside and draw up the tapes, tie with a bow and tuck the ends inside. With the exception of Honiton lace which requires a special pillow and bobbins, a bolster can be used for all types of lace.

Straw or hay chopped finely is without doubt the best filling for a pillow, but must be packed in very well to give a hard surface. Sawdust and bran are too heavy and within weeks 'bed' down, making the surface soft and unable to support the pins. Polystyrene soon becomes pitted and will not bend to give sufficient slope, even the flat pillow falls towards the edges.

Cover Cloths

These are required to cover part of the pillow when working, and to cover the whole pillow when not in use. Preferably they should be dark green or blue rectangles hemmed on all sides, at least the width of the pillow but not necessarily quite as long, depending on fabric available. Only one cloth is required for a French pillow and this is to cover the pillow when not in use.

Bobbins

Each country has its own style of lace bobbin, all possessing the three requirements to make it an efficient tool: a slim neck on which the thread is wound; sufficient weight to keep the thread taut to make lace of clear design and even tension; and a shape which is easy to handle. Continental bobbins and those small South Bucks bobbins fashioned in the Chiltern

Hills are plain, the weight lying in the thickness of the wood; but the slim bobbins made in the north of Buckinghamshire, in Bedfordshire and Northamptonshire are of wood and bone, highly decorated with pewter and copper wire and weighted by a ring of beads attached to the end of the bobbin with wire (diagram 3). Today they have become collectors' items, but it is possible to purchase plastic bobbins or have the old bobbins copied in wood.

Always use bobbins of the same type, i.e. all South Bucks or all beaded. If possible, select those of the same size and weight. The beads on the bobbins are for weight and to prevent the bobbins from rolling and it is impossible to use this type unbeaded. The wire holding the beads must be secure and tidy; loose ends get caught in other bobbins causing annoyance and delay.

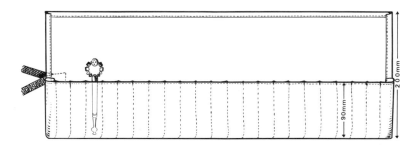

In order to keep bobbins tidy and ready for use a bobbin case can be made (diagram 4). A pair of bobbins may be kept in each compartment and the top folded over for safety. When rolled up it can be fastened with tapes.

Pins

Lace pins are made of brass so that they will not rust in the pillow. Fine lace using thin thread and prickings with the holes close together requires a finer pin than the coarser varieties. Short pins about 25mm (1in.) long are preferable as they do not bend as readily as longer ones. A few berry pins and/or hat pins are useful to hold bobbins to the sides of the pillow when not in use.

Thread

Linen thread is the most suitable as it will withstand years of wear and use. Today fine linen thread is no longer manufactured. Old thread may be satisfactory but if it has been kept in adverse conditions it can be rotten and useless. As bobbin lacemaking is a combination of weaving and twisting threads, a highly twisted thread is unsuitable. For fine work a two-cord thread is preferable. Man-made fibres should be used with caution as a resilient thread does not produce a clear and accurate pattern.

Patterns

The pattern or pricking, as it is more often called, consists of fine holes pricked into a piece of parchment or thick glazed card, with Indian ink guide lines added afterwards. It takes many hours to produce hand made lace and so it is surely worth preparing an accurate pattern.

Patterns may be copied from a book of lace instruction, borrowed from lace makers, found in antique shops or worked out on graph paper. In order to make prickings the following are required:

Pin vice   Obtainable from a tool or craft shop.

Sewing needles   Sharps 8 9 10. Remember the higher the size number the finer the needle. For general work no.8 is satisfactory.

Pricking board   A piece of thick cork, or two cork table mats, or a piece of polystyrene.

Drawing pins.

Pricking card   Thick glazed card is essential to hold the pins in position and so achieve clear accurate lace.

PREPARATION
To Wind Bobbins

When beginning a pattern the bobbins are used in pairs, a knot is never found in lace and the thread between the bobbins must be free from knots. If the lace thread is on a skein it is advisable to wind it on to a spool and then use it from the spool to wind it on to bobbins. Hold a bobbin in the left hand and the thread in the right, and wind over and away in a clock-

D 5

wise direction (diagram 5). Wind evenly as much thread as possible on to this bobbin. Cut the thread. Take a second bobbin in the left hand and wind half of the thread from the first bobbin back on to the second. As soon as the direction of winding has been established it is easier to transfer the bobbin to the right hand, turn the bobbin to wind on the thread which can be guided by the thumb and forefinger of the left hand. Although so much winding seems tedious it is necessary as fine lace thread will twist and tangle if any length is left unwound.

Make a hitch on the thread of each bobbin to prevent unwinding

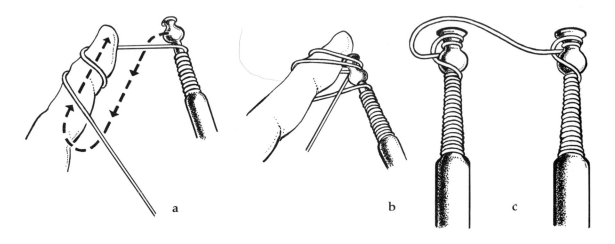

D 6

(diagrams **6***a*, **6***b* and **6***c*). Allow about 150mm (6in.) of thread between the bobbins. Temporarily wind the thread round the neck of one of the bobbins, place in a bobbin case or secure three or four pairs together with a rubber band.

When using bobbins cut from a previous piece of lace, knot them together in pairs, remove the hitch from one bobbin and wind the thread including the knot back on to this bobbin. Avoid winding back exactly the same amount on each bobbin. Replace the hitch. Instruction will be given later on the removal of knots.

To Prepare Prickings
A   To make a pattern using graph paper   On the graph paper mark where the holes are to be pricked using a sharp pointed hard pencil according to instructions given.
B   To copy a pricking from a book   Fasten the tracing paper firmly over the pattern and mark in each dot using a sharp pencil.
C   To make a 'rubbing' from a pattern   This method is suitable only for coarse lace, usually Beds-Maltese or plaited laces, and permission should be sought from the owner of the pattern. Frequent rubbing of a pattern will cause the holes to be misplaced on the original, but there is the advantage that a pattern may be copied when time is limited and that the original is not damaged by inaccurate pricking. To 'rub' a pattern lay it with the wrong, unmarked, side uppermost on a firm flat surface. Place a sheet of airmail or bank paper on top and holding it firmly at one end stroke or rub with a piece of heelball always moving in the same direction. The prick marks will appear on the paper and these can be pricked on to card. Patterns with a one direction design will appear reversed.

To Make the Pricking

Cut a piece of card approximately the same size as the pattern to be copied, over it place the pattern, and fix these firmly on to the pricking board using drawing pins at the four corners only. Screw the needle into the pin vice, allowing only 12mm ($\frac{1}{2}$in.) to protrude at the end. It may be necessary to use a small pair of pliers to screw it sufficiently tightly to hold the needle when pricking. Hold the pin vice and needle in a vertical position and keep the board flat on the table. A slanting pin vice or tilted board will damage the original and produce an inaccurate and useless copy.

Prick through the holes or the markings accurately. Prick diagonally across the pattern in the direction of working, using a ruler as a guide line. When pricking through a paper the needle should touch the ruler each time to ensure straight lines. The footside holes (i.e. the straight row to one side and the full length of the pattern) should be pricked along a ruler after completing the rest of the pattern. When the pricking is thought to be complete, lift the pattern, card being pricked, and drawing pins *altogether* and hold them up to the light when any missed holes are readily seen. Replace on the board and rectify any omissions.

Draw in any markings first with pencil in case of errors. When correct, mark in Indian ink, other markings may rub off and discolour the work. Only take one copy at one time. More will cause the holes on the original and the top copy to be enlarged and the cards may slip out of position.

When pricking through another pattern it is sometimes noticed that a hole is out of position or even missing, *never* rectify this when pricking. Miss out any doubtful holes and put them in by eye afterwards on the copy only. *Never* alter or in any way change the original.

To Prepare or 'Dress' the Pillow

The pattern should be pinned firmly at four corners on to the pillow. Extra pins along the sides of the pricking are unnecessary and will catch the threads and break them. Allow a couple of inches of pricking to show and cover the lower part of the pillow with a cloth. This will hug the pillow more closely if a piece is folded under so that a fold rather than the actual selvedge or hem is to the edge. To fasten in position use one pin only at each edge of the pillow. Either use a pincushion fastened towards the back right hand side or stick pins into the pillow in the same position ready for use.

ADDITIONAL INFORMATION

Pins

Avoid touching the thread with the fingers. To facilitate putting in pins, hold the pair of bobbins to the left of the pin in the left hand with the necks well raised. This lifts the threads and the pin holes can be more easily seen.

Pins at the edges of the lace should slope outwards and in the centre of the work slightly backwards.

Pins must be kept in the pricking for the complete length on the edges and for two to three inches in the centre.

Threads

The length of the thread between the bobbin and the work should rarely exceed three inches in length.

To lengthen a thread hold the bobbin in the right hand horizontally across the pillow. Carefully turn the bobbin towards the worker, at the same time pulling firmly and more thread will be unwound.

To shorten a thread hold the bobbin in the left hand horizontally and with a pin in the right hand loosen the hitch. Keeping the pin through the hitch loop wind the bobbin towards the worker, at the same time pulling to keep the thread taut.

To join broken threads is impossible when the break occurs actually in the lace. Either the lace must be undone until at least 12mm ($\frac{1}{2}$in.) of thread is released, or some mending must be done when the lace is removed from the pillow. The latter is not very satisfactory but is carried out as

D 7

follows. With a clove hitch (diagram **7**), hitch the end of the thread hanging from the bobbin on to the pin, and stick the pin into the pillow close to the back or side of the pricking. Allow the thread to fall into position and continue working. It is successful in a patch of cloth, which can with care be darned into net but it is impossible in half stitch.

To join broken threads use a weaver's knot. This is particularly useful when only a short end is hanging from the lace.

The weaver's knot   Cross the two ends to be joined with the end from the bobbin lying horizontally under the vertical thread from the lace. Take the vertical thread and bend it back under the horizontal thread (diagram

a   D 8   b

8A). Take the horizontal thread behind the loop threads, across the top under itself but not down through the loop (diagram **8B**). Ease it gently until tight, keeping it flat on the pillow.

To get rid of knots in cloth stitch when the knot is on one of the passive threads, twist the thread with the next thread once and then take it back over the work, loop it round a pin put to the side of the pricking for that purpose and bring it back into work, twist again and continue. If the knot is on the weaver make a faulty stitch to transfer the knot to a passive thread. When work is complete the two ends may be cut close to the lace. *This method may be used in cloth stitch only.*

In all other circumstances pin up another bobbin to the side of the pricking as previously described and allow it to fall alongside the bobbin with the knotted thread. Fasten the two bobbins together with a rubber band and continue using the double thread as one for 25mm (1in.) or so depending on the pattern. Discard the bobbin with the knotted thread before the knot is reached. This may be cut off and re-used to get rid of the next knot. When possible it is better to get rid of a knot when it is still several centimetres (inches) from the lace.

Moving Lace on the Pillow

It is necessary to move the lace being made if the piece of work, e.g. a collar, will not fit completely on the pillow. It also is necessary when making an edging with corners, or when working on a flat pillow.

There are two methods of doing this: the first to be explained is tedious requiring considerable patience and skill. It is commonly known as 'setting up' a pattern. In method one the threads must be pinned to the cover cloth in small groups to avoid confusion later. The cover cloth must be folded up over the bobbins and raised so that it supports completely the weight of the bobbins. Pin it to the pillow. Remove all the pins in the pricking, checking that the cloth is fully supporting the bobbins and that the threads are not being pulled. Raise the lace and bobbins up the pillow and re-pin in position near the top of the pricking. It is necessary to replace all the pins in several pattern repeats and to pin the edges for a greater distance to the pillow behind the pricking.

In order to move lace by the second method, cut pieces of felt 50mm (2in.) wide and 75, 65, 50, 40 and 25mm (3, 2½, 2, 1½ and 1in.) long. Arrange these in order on top of each other to form a raised centre and gradual slope at either end. Sew them together, and lay under the lower part of the pattern. Continue to make lace until pins are in the pricking over the centre of the raised part of the felt. The pins will be in the felt and not deeply in the pillow. Support the bobbins as previously described. Remove the pins that are *behind* the felt. Lift the pricking, felt and bobbins to the top of the pillow. Replace more pins as necessary. Refasten the pricking to the pillow and make another pricking that can be pinned below, pattern matching. Continue to make lace and when the felt is free, place it in position for re-use. This method is especially useful on flat pillows and bolsters when working a corner, and it is necessary to turn the lace to continue.

To Join Lace

Work the pattern until it exactly matches up to the beginning of the lace. Making sure that there are no twists in the length of lace, pin the beginning on to the pricking immediately below the lace already worked. All the pins should be in position for at least 25mm (1in.) depending on the lace. Remove the pin at the edge of the lace recently pinned in position, and insert a fine crochet hook through the hole between the threads. Carefully pull through one thread of the pair which would normally work that hole, and pass the other bobbin of the pair through the loop made. Pull both tightly and knot them together using a reef knot.

Reef knot   Take the left thread over the right and twist through. Take the

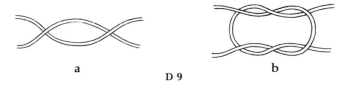

a   D 9   b

right thread and pass it over the left and twist through (see diagrams **9A** and **9B**). Secure the footside first and then the headside and gradually fasten off all the threads between.

To Cut off Bobbins

When the lace has been completed it is possible to cut the threads so that the bobbins are taken from the pillow with the threads already knotted together. The method is quickly learned when seen but following written instruction is more difficult.

Hold a pair of bobbins in the left hand. Take a pair of blunt loose bladed scissors, hold with the thumb and third finger in normal fashion and place – blades closed – horizontally under the two threads. Twist the thread behind and over as shown in diagram **10A**. Move the pair of scissors through 90 degrees until parallel with the threads and to the right of them as shown in diagram **10B**. Open the points and grasp the threads above (diagram **10C**). A loose bladed pair of scissors allows the threads to be held without being cut. Pull the blades down through the loop on the scissors, at the same time taking the bobbins in the left hand upwards which helps the loop off the end of the blades (diagram **10D**]. Then cut with the blades and allow one bobbin to fall from the hand, this automatically tightens the knot.

Basic Stitches

Instructions are now given for the length shown in photograph **2** which illustrates three basic stitches: cloth stitch, half stitch, and cloth stitch and twist; and the use of the latter to make a narrow beading which demonstrates the method used to obtain the straight edge on one side of a lace edging or both sides of an insertion.

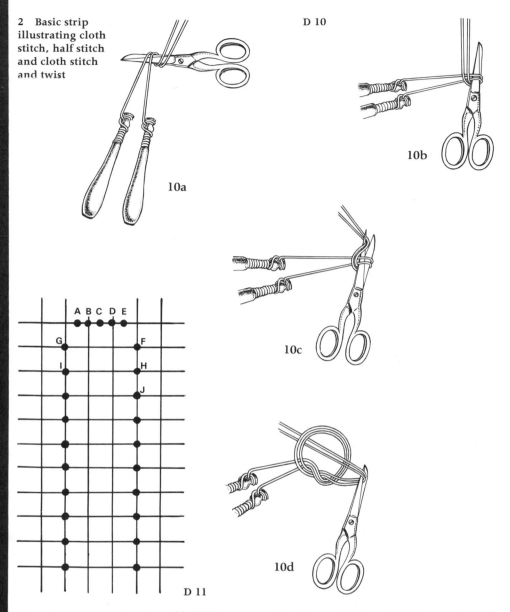

2   Basic strip illustrating cloth stitch, half stitch and cloth stitch and twist

D 10

10a

10b

10c

10d

D 11

Requirements   6 pairs of bobbins wound with no.50 Swedish linen thread for pricking based on 10 squares to 25mm (1in.), or no.80 thread for a pricking based on 10 squares to 20mm. A pricking which is worked out on graph paper as shown in diagram 11. It is unnecessary to mark the letters on the pricking, they will be referred to in the text.

Prepare the pillow and stick up pins in holes A to F. Hang one pair of bobbins round each pin. The pair hanging at F is known as the weaver – sometimes referred to as the leader or worker. Very temporarily a student may like to mark them with bands or coloured threads wound round the bobbins. Bobbins are always used in pairs and two pairs are used to make a stitch.

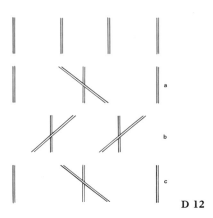

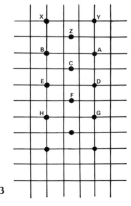

D 12   D 13

Cloth stitch – also known as whole stitch   Refer to diagram **12**. Using the pairs hanging from **E** and **F** make a cloth stitch as follows. Count the threads from left to right from **1** to **4**. The figures refer to the positions only and not to the bobbins so that they must be recounted before each move,

a Using the left hand lift **2** over **3**.
b Using both hands lift **2** over **1** and **4** over **3** *at the same time*.
c Using the left hand lift **2** over **3**.

The pairs have now changed position, the weaver having passed through the passive pair from **E**. Discard the right hand pair to the right of the pillow.

Work another cloth stitch using the weaver and the pair from **D**. Discard the right hand pair and in turn work cloth stitch with pairs from **C**, **B** and **A**. The weaver is now at the left hand side of the work. Twist the weaver twice by placing the right hand thread over the left and repeating this move. Put in a pin at **G** to the right of the weaver pair. The weaver is ready to work back to **H**.

Work a cloth stitch with the weaver and pair from **A**. Discard this pair to the left of the pillow. Make a cloth stitch with the weaver and pair from **B**. Discard to the left and continue. The stitch and twists are always worked with the same basic movements, regardless of the direction of weaving. At the end of each row hold the weaver firmly and 'stroke' the bobbins to improve the tension. Practise until a length can be worked rhythmically and automatically without referring to the instructions.

Cloth stitch and twist – also known as whole stitch and twist   This is a variation of cloth stitch and will in this case be used at the edges of the work only. To make the stitch, work a cloth stitch and twist each pair once (diagram **12**: **abcb**).

To continue the practice strip, begin with the pin in position and the weaver at the end of the row. Work cloth stitch and twist with the weaver and first pair. Cloth stitch through the next three pairs, twist the weaver once and cloth stitch and twist the weaver and last pair together. Twist the weaver once more and put in the pin. Continue until it can be worked quickly without referring to instructions.

Half stitch – also known as lattice stitch   The weaver changes in every row and only one thread travels across the work. Therefore it is advisable to remove anything used to identify the weaver.

Begin with the pin in position and the weaver at the end of the row. Refer to diagram **12**. Take the weaver and the first pair and make a half stitch as follows:

a lift 2 over 3

b lift 2 over 1, and 4 over 3, and stop.

These two moves make a half stitch. Discard a pair and using the next pair make another half stitch. Continue across the work and at the end of the row, twist the weaver (i.e. the last pair of which only one thread has actually travelled all the way across) once more. Put up the pin inside this pair as usual. Work several rows, notice that the threads no longer hang straight down singly but are crossed in pairs.

Half stitch is weak at the edges and will become untidy and lose its shape with wear and laundering. Work cloth stitch and twist at the ends of the rows before and after the pin.

Note that cloth stitch and twist is the same as two half stitches.

Braid

In order to work the braid another pricking must be made as in diagram **13**. Cut the pricking close to the first holes, and cut the pricking on the pillow close to the last row of holes and match them. Pin to the pillow. It is impracticable to try to work through a double thickness of card. Continue with practice stitches until X and Y have been worked, and work a cloth stitch and twist after the last pin. Take the two middle pairs and make a cloth stitch and twist. Put up a pin between the pairs at Z. Cover the pin with cloth stitch and twist using the same pairs. The braid will give the worker practice in working the straight edge which is known as the *footside*.

To work the braid   Work pin A (the footside pin) on the right side of the lace. Take the third pair from the right and work cloth stitch and twist twice to the right to get to the outside edge. Twist the outside pair once more. Put up pin A inside of two pairs (i.e. between the two pairs worked through). Ignore the outer pair, and work cloth stitch and twist to cover the pin. This sequence of stitches is always used on the footside in Torchon lace.

Work pin B in the same manner. Take the third pair from the left hand edge and work cloth stitch and twist twice to get to the outside edge, and twist the outer pair once more. Put up pin B inside of two pairs. Ignore the outer pair and work cloth stitch and twist to cover the pin. In order to make a working pattern take the two middle pairs and work cloth stitch and twist, put up pin C, and cover with cloth stitch and twist. Take the third pair from the right and work out as described for pin A in order to work pin D. Take the third pair from the left and work out to pin E. Work pin F as for pin C.

Continue until written instruction is unnecessary.

3   Torchon laces

2 ❖ Torchon Lace

Torchon lace is the easiest to make, and it gives a student a good general idea of technique. All Torchon patterns are geometric and can be worked out on graph paper. At first a student will copy patterns, but later should be able to make her own quite easily from lace or photographs, or work out her own designs. The patterns described here are progressive and students are recommended to work a pattern until a good understanding is gained before attempting the next.

EXPLANATION OF TERMS USED

To cover the pin   After putting in the pin make another stitch with the same pairs to enclose the pin. Normally the same stitch will be used before and after the pin.

To hang pairs on a pin   Hang pairs of bobbins on the pin so that pairs fall inside each other, thus outside bobbins either side will be the same pair and the two centre bobbins will be the same pair.

To hang pairs on a pin in order   As this implies, the pairs will hang side by side, two bobbins of the same pair being next to each other.

The footside   This is the straight edge on to which the fabric is attached. English lace makers work the footside on the right hand side of the lace but Continental lace makers work the footside on the left hand side. A footside is worked both sides when making an insertion. When using a Continental pricking and photograph all that is necessary is to turn them both round and work with the footside on the right.

Torchon footside method has been described fully for the working of the braid. When instructions request that the next footside pin be done it is necessary to work as follows. Take third pair from outside edge and cloth stitch and twist twice to the edge. Twist the outer pair once more. Pin inside two pairs. Ignore the outer pair, cloth stitch and twist to cover the pin.

The head or heading   This is the patterned side of the lace, on the left hand side of the pricking when making lace.

The ground   This is the net or mesh and in Torchon lace may be worked in a variety of ways.

Passive threads   Those threads which hang straight on the pillow, e.g. the threads which hang down in a patch of cloth, or the pair which lies alongside the footside. Incidentally, when lace needs to be gathered this pair can be pulled to reduce the length of the lace as required.

Direction of working   With the exception of passive threads and weavers all the pairs move diagonally in Torchon lace. Pairs enter a patch of cloth or half stitch diagonally, and pairs move diagonally in the ground. In ground, work the hole farthest away first, and move diagonally towards the worker. Normally it is easier to work from the footside as explained in instructions, but there are occasions when it is necessary to work left to right but *always* from a distant point to a nearer one.

Thread   The thickness of the thread depends on the distance apart of the holes. The following threads are recommended:

Swedish linen thread no.35 suitable for 8 squares to 25mm grid.
D.M.C. *Coton Perle* no.12 suitable for 8 squares to 25mm grid.
Anchor Pearl Cotton no.12 suitable for 8 squares to 25mm grid.
Swedish linen thread no.50 suitable for 10 squares to 25mm grid.
D.M.C. *Cordonnet Special* no. 100 suitable for 10 squares to 25mm grid.
D.M.C. *Cordonnet Special* no. 150 suitable for 10 squares to 20mm grid.
D.M.C. *Retors D'Alsace* no.30 suitable for 10 squares to 20mm grid.
Sewing cotton no.40 or no.50 suitable for 10 squares to 20mm grid.

FAN PATTERN

Refer to diagram 14 and photograph 4. Prepare pricking 1 and wind 11 pairs of bobbins. Hang two pairs of bobbins on pin A1, and one pair on each of pins B, C, D, E and F. Hang four pairs on pin G in order from right to left.

To work the ground   Using the two pairs hanging from A1, twist the two right hand bobbins three times. Cloth stitch and twist to cover the pin, give one extra twist to the outside (right hand) pair, and discard. Take the inner (left hand) pair and the pair from B, and work cloth stitch and twist but do *not* put up a pin. Discard the right hand pair.

Take the other pair and pair from C, and make a half stitch. Put up pin 2 in the centre of these pairs, and cover with another half stitch. Discard the right hand pair. Take the other pair, and pair from D and make a half stitch. Place pin 3 in position in the centre of these pairs, and cover with another half stitch. Discard the right hand pair. Continue using the pair from E for pin 4 and the pair from F for pin 5. Remove support pins B, C, D, E and F.

This is the simplest form of Torchon ground, and in this pattern the rows are always worked diagonally from the footside.

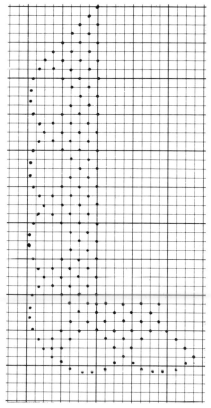

D 14

4   Fan and corner

Pricking 1

To continue, work footside pin 6. Using the pair from the footside (i.e. third pair from the edge) and the next pair hanging from 3, work a half stitch; put up pin 7, cover with a half stitch. Discard the right hand pair, and using the pair from 4 work a half stitch, put up pin 8, half stitch. Discard the right hand pair and work pin 9 using the pair from 5. Similarly complete pins 10, 11, 12, 13 and 14. Remember to take the third pair to work out to complete the footside pins 10 and 13.

The triangle of ground is complete and pairs hang from 5, 9, 12 and 14, and will come into the fan diagonally, one pair at each pin.

To work the fan   Begin at G, using the left hand pair as weaver, cloth stitch to the right through the other three pairs hanging on this pin, and through the next pair hanging from 5. Put up pin 15 between these two pairs, and twist the weaver twice. The weaver is the pair to the right of pin 15, and when pulled can be seen to be the pair which has travelled across the work.

Using the weaver pair, work cloth stitch to the left through all pairs. Twist the weaver pair twice, and put up pin 16 to the right of it. Weave back to the right through the four passive pairs and through the pair hanging from 9. Put up pin 17 between the last two pairs; the pair to the right of the pin is the weaver pair and must be twisted twice. Note that the same pair remains as weaver pair throughout the fan. Using the weaver pair work back to the left through all pairs, twist the weaver pair twice and put up pin 18.

Continue to pin 22 bringing in extra pairs at pins 19 and 21. From pin 22 work back to the right through all the passive fan pairs except one (i.e. through six pairs). Twist the weaver pair twice, put up pin 23 and work back to pin 24. Notice that the pair brought in at pin 21 has been left out after that pin. From pin 24 work back to pin 25 through one passive pair less than the previous row (i.e. through five pairs).

Work back to pin 26 and to pin 27 again through one pair less than in the previous row (i.e. through four pairs). Work back to pin 28, but do not cover it. It is easier to find the weaver pair if it is at the extreme left of the work. Twist pairs hanging from 21, 23, 25 and 27 once each.

Return to the ground   Work pin 1 as a normal footside pin, and continue, using the instructions given above, remembering to work diagonally and not to complete the last pin-hole on each diagonal row of ground as it is needed for the fan.

Variations   See photograph 4:

1 and 2 Cloth stitch.
3   Cloth stitch and twist on the edge as in the braid.
4   Half stitch with cloth stitch and twist on the outside edge before and after the pin.
5   After pin 21 has been put up, twist the passive pairs once each and continue weaving normally.

6   In the cloth fan the weavers are twisted in the same position in each row, the number of twists arranged to get the desired effect.

Corner   See diagram **15**. Complete the pattern as far as the diagonal corner line – indicated by a broken line. Pin Y is the corner pin on the footside, and is worked normally using the third pair from the edge – hanging from 14. Pin Z is the corner pin to link the fans. Take the fan weavers from pin 28, and weave to the left through the three fan pairs, put up pin Z and weave back to the outside edge which will be the beginning of the next fan. Turn the pillow and complete the fan. Study the ground carefully as the footside pin Y in the corner has been worked, and the pair from the bottom of the fan and the pair from Y will work pin 2. Complete the diagonal row of ground, pins 3, 4 and 5.

CIRCULAR MAT

This may be made in the same way, the fan is larger but the arrangement of the ground and footside is the same. To make the pricking, trace the pattern (pricking **2**) and prick through three sheets of paper. Draw a circle with a radius of 55mm on another sheet of paper and match the pricked papers to make a circle. Make a pricking on card. Hang two pairs on pin A and one pair each on pins B, C, D, E, F, G, and four pairs on H in order from right to left.

    Begin at A and work the diagonal ground rows until five footside pins and rows of ground have been worked. Take the left hand pair at H and weaver, and begin the fan.

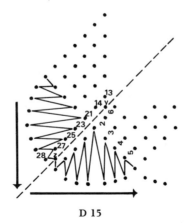

D 15

Pricking 2

SPIDER AND FAN PATTERN

Refer to diagram **16** and photograph **5**. Prepare pricking 3 and 13 pairs of bobbins. Hang two pairs on A1 and one pair on each of B, C and D, and four pairs on each of E and F in order from right to left.

To begin Work the first row of ground from A1 to 5 as in the fan pattern using pairs from E at pins 4 and 5.

To work the fan The fan is smaller than in the previous pattern but the principle is the same. Begin at F using the left hand pair as weaver pair

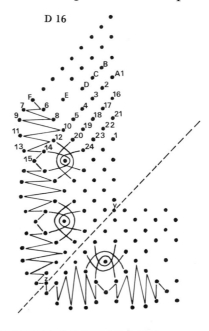

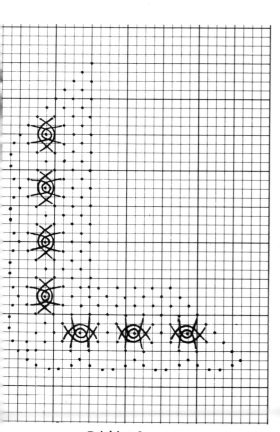

Pricking 3

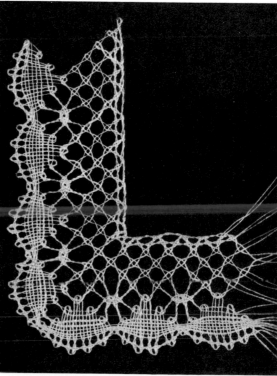

5 Spider and fan

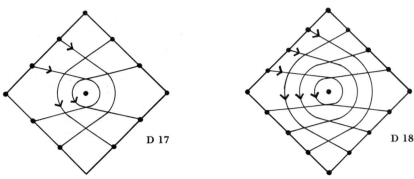

D 17   D 18

and cloth stitch to the right through the other three pairs hanging on this pin and through the next pair hanging from E. Put up pin 6. Complete the fan bringing in the other pair from E at pin 8 and the pair from 5 at pin 10. Remove support pins B, C, D and E. Remember to twist the pairs hanging from pins 10, 12 and 14.

To work the ground   Work from pins 16 to 24. Pins 16 and 21 are footside pins worked by taking the third pair from the edge out to the edge and the other pins are Torchon ground worked in half stitch, pin, half stitch.

Torchon spider   The spider is worked with the four pairs from 14, 12, 20 and 24. Each of these pairs must be twisted three times. Each has one twist already and requires two more. Refer to diagram **17**. Take the second pair and weave with cloth stitch through pairs three and four. Take the first pair and weave through the next two pairs with cloth stitch. Note that the pairs have crossed through each other evenly. Put up pin 25 between the two centre pairs, and pull all the pairs to achieve firm twisted legs.

Repeat the movements for the first half of the spider, i.e., take the second pair and weave with cloth stitch through pairs three and four; take the first pair and weave through the next two pairs with cloth stitch; twist each pair three times, and pull to improve the tension as the pairs are brought into the pattern. Aim to keep the 'body' flat. A pattern repeat is complete. Work pin 1 as a footside pin and continue.

Corner   This is worked in the same way as the corner of the simple fan pattern. Complete the pattern as far as the diagonal corner line, work pins Y and Z, turn the pillow and continue.

Note that spiders can be worked with many more pairs. Diagram **18** illustrates the spider with three pairs entering on each side. It is worked as follows. Take the third pair (i.e. the left hand pair nearest the centre) and weave with cloth stitch through all three pairs coming from the right. Take the second pair, and weave with cloth stitch through the next three pairs which are those from the right. Notice that the second pair has followed the first but *not* overtaken it. Take the first pair, weave through three pairs with cloth stitch, and again notice that the first pair has followed the other pairs from the left, but not overtaken, so that they lie evenly through each other. Put up the pin between the centre pairs, and repeat the moves to complete the spider body.

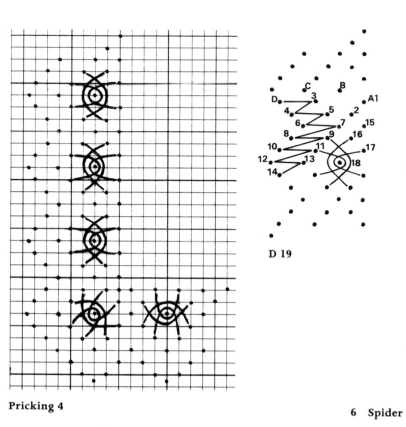

Pricking 4

D 19

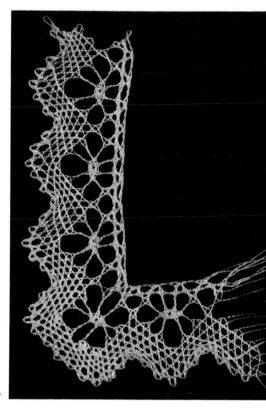

6 Spider

SPIDER PATTERN

Refer to diagram **19** and photograph **6**. Prepare pricking **4** and 12 pairs of bobbins. Eleven pairs are required for the straight edging and an extra pair for the corner. Hang two pairs on A1, four pairs on each of B and C in order from right to left, and one pair on D.

To begin Work pins A1 and 2 using pairs as required from B.

To work the half stitch edge This is worked completely in half stitch with cloth stitch and twist before and after the pins on the outside (left side) edge. Take the pair from D as weaver pair, and work through all the pairs hanging from C, and one pair hanging from B. Put up pin 3 to the left of the weaver pair. Take the weaver pair back through all five pairs to the outside edge and pin 4. Remove support pin C. Weave back through the five pairs in the half stitch trail, and through one more pair hanging from B. Put up pin 5. Work to pin 6 through the six pairs in the trail, and back through these pairs and the pair from 2 to pin 7. Remove support pin B. Continue the half stitch trail leaving out pairs after pins 7, 9 and 11, as was done in the fan, as far as pin 14. Do *not* cover this pin, as it will be easier to find the weaver pair at the extreme left side of the work.

To work footside and ground Work pins 15, 16 and 17.

To work the spider Use pairs from 11, 9, 16 and 17, and complete the spider around pin 18. Remember the twists on the legs, before and after the body.

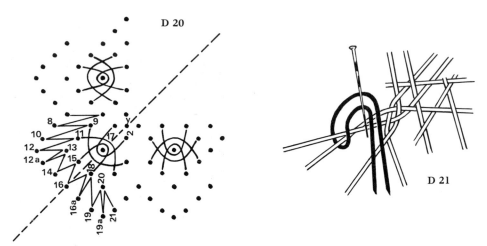

Order of working Patterns are usually worked in sections for ease of understanding and speed of working. It should be noticed that a complete pattern of trail is worked at one time, and then pins 15, 16 and 17, which release the pairs for the right hand side of the spider. When the spider has been worked, pins 1 and 2 must be worked to lead again into the trail.

Corner See diagram **20**. Work the spider before the corner and begin the trail in the usual manner, stopping when pin 8 is in position.

From the diagram it can be seen that the pairs for the spider's legs hang from different pins and to avoid a weak trail an extra pair is joined in after pin 8. Take the extra pair and put one bobbin under the weaver pair, bring the loop up and round the pin allowing the pair to fall inside and to the right of one thread of the half stitch trail – see diagram **21**. Continue to pin 14. Work pins 15, 16 and Y.

The spider cannot be worked with the usual pairs as only one pair is available on the right hand side. The pair from Y is *not* used. All four pairs must be found before the diagonal corner line is reached and the half stitch trail worked to this position also.

Half stitch trail There are more pins on the outside than the inside edge and to achieve an even result the pin-holes 13, 18 and 20 must be used twice. On the second occasion the weaver pair is put round the pin already in position. At first, work the trail as far as pin 16. Remember that pin 13 is the top point and nothing is left out after this pin.

Spider This is worked with pairs from 15, 11, 9 and 17. When it is complete turn the pillow and complete the half stitch trail as far as 21. Use the right hand side leg of the spider and the third pair from the foot-side corner pin to work half stitch pin 2, half stitch.

The corner is complete and normal working can proceed. To remove the extra pair take the weaver pair at 21, and cloth stitch and twist through the first two pairs of the trail. Take the two centre threads of the four worked through, tie them together in a reef knot, and turn them back over the work. Cross the other two threads and they will lie as the outside passive pair. Later the threads put back over the work may be cut off or for extra strength darned into the half stitch trail.

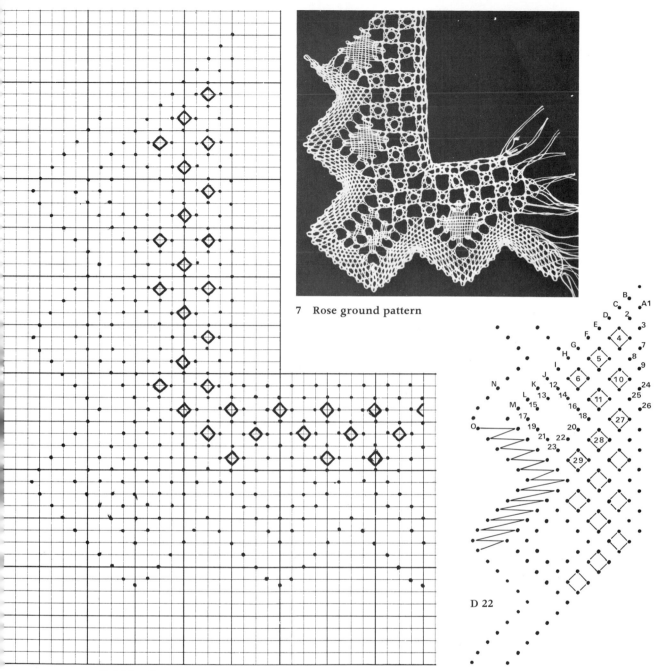

7   Rose ground pattern

D 22

Pricking 5

ROSE GROUND PATTERN

Refer to diagram **22** and photograph **7**. Prepare pricking **5** and 19 pairs of bobbins. Hang two pairs on A1 one pair on each of pins B, C, D, E, F, G, H, I, J, K, L and M, four pairs on pin N in order from right to left, and one pair on pin O.

To work footside and rose ground   Work pins A1, 2 and 3.

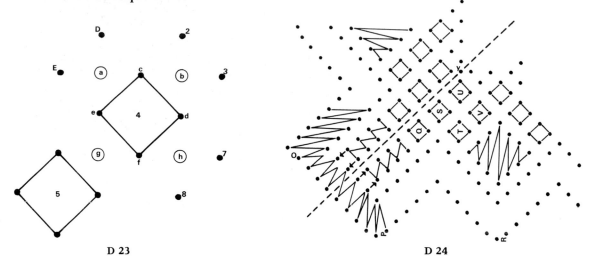

D 23   D 24

Rose ground is worked in units of four pins (diagram **23**) and is lettered in stitches a to h. Pairs come into the 'diamond' of holes from pins E and D, and 2 and 3. The pairs from each side make a cloth stitch and twist at a and b, but *no* pins are put up.

The centre pairs work half stitch, pin c, half stitch; the right hand pairs work half stitch, pin d, half stitch; the left hand pairs work half stitch, pin e, half stitch; and the centre pairs work half stitch, pin f, half stitch. The pairs hanging from pins e and f and from d and f make cloth stitch and twist at g and h, but *no* pins are put up. Remove support pins B, C, D and E.

Referring back to diagram **22**, work unit 5. The two pairs coming in from the right hand side already have cloth stitch and twist on them from g, and another is unnecessary. The pairs from the left (F and G) require the cloth stitch and twist. Work unit 6. Return to the footside and work pins 7, 8 and 9. Work unit 10, remembering to cloth stitch and twist pairs from 8 and 9 before beginning. Work unit 11.

Complete the cloth stitch diamond   Return to the footside and work pins 24, 25 and 26. Work units 27, 28 and 29.

Work the half stitch trail   It is worked in the same manner as the previous pattern. Pairs from cloth diamond must be twisted before entering the half stitch trail.

Corner   Complete the pattern as far as the diagonal corner line – see diagram **24**. It is impossible to work a cloth diamond, and two narrow strips are worked instead. Work pin Y in the usual way, and the first of the cloth strips. Work the half stitch trail from O to P using pins twice where indicated, taking in pairs before the diagonal corner line and leaving them out afterwards as shown by arrows. Turn the pillow and work rose ground unit Q. Work the half stitch trail to R. Work rose ground units S, T, U, V and the cloth diamond.

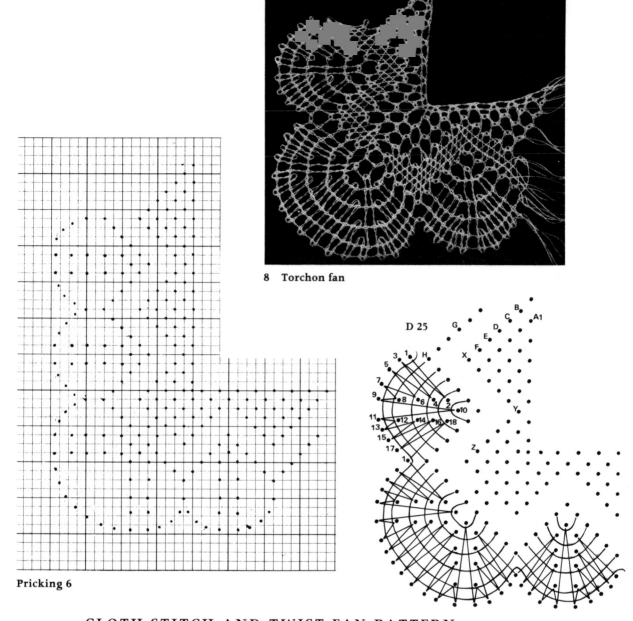

8 Torchon fan

Pricking 6

CLOTH STITCH AND TWIST FAN PATTERN

Refer to diagram **25** and photograph **8**. Prepare pricking 6 and 15 pairs of bobbins. Hang two pairs of bobbins on A1, one pair on each of B, C, D, E, F and H, five pairs on G in order, and two pairs on I.

The footside and ground This is worked normally until five footside pins are in position. Instead of working the ground pins with half stitch before and after the pin, in this pattern, for variety, cloth stitch and twist before and after the pin has been used.

The half stitch trail Using the pair from H as weaver, work in half stitch through the pairs hanging from G, and put up a pin at X. Complete the half stitch trail as far as Y, leaving out a pair after each pin on the left hand side, and bringing in one at each pin on the right hand side. Cloth stitch and twist has been put before and after the pin at ends of rows.

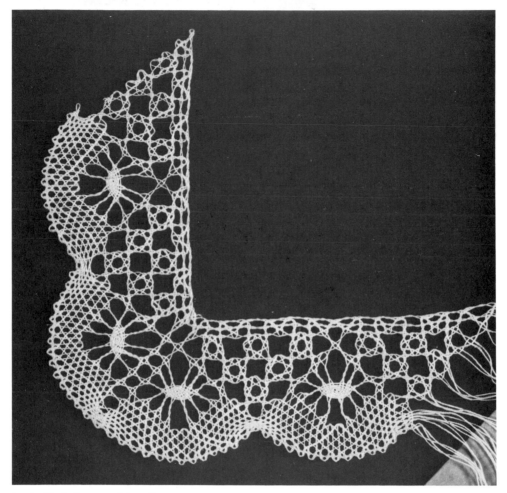

9   Half stitch curved heading

To work the fan   This is worked in cloth stitch and twist. Take the pairs on 1 and cover the pin with cloth stitch and twist and continue with cloth stitch and twist through the next four pairs to the right. Put up pin 2 with the weaver to the right of it. Twist the weaver once more and work back to the left through all pairs to the outside edge, twist the weaver once more, and put up pin 3. Work back through four pairs (one less than the previous row) and put up pin 4. Continue, leaving out one pair after each pin, as far as pin 9. The weaver works through six pairs to pin 10, and back through the same six pairs to the edge and pin 11. The lace will look more attractive if two twists are put on the weaver for these two long rows. The weaver travels through two pairs to pin 12, back to pin 13, then through an extra pair each time for pins 14, 16 and 18, and is left at pin 1.
To complete one repeat pattern   Work the half stitch trail from Y to Z, bringing in one pair at each pin on the left, and leaving out one pair after each pin on the right hand side.

Corner   The illustration shows the method of working the corner fan.
Trail   Note that the half stitch trail is broken on the corner diagonal –
and restarted when the pillow has been turned.

TO MAKE TORCHON PATTERNS FROM LACE

As soon as the method of making Torchon lace is fully understood, and
when the various stitches and their execution are recognized, the making
of patterns is straightforward. Torchon lace is worked at an angle of
45 degrees from the footside, and can be worked out on normal graph
paper. At first it may be easier to plot the holes on a paper with lines far
apart as it will be easier to see, and then transfer it to the required finer
grid afterwards. Work on tracing paper fastened over grids on pages
213–215.

To begin the pattern   Mark alternate intersections along a straight line
for the footside. Then count the number of ground stitches on the longest
diagonal row and mark the intersections on the graph paper. Mark in dots
for the obvious pattern features – cloth diamonds, spiders, other distinct
shapes. Fill in the ground – a ruler may help to keep the rows of dots in
the right place. Remember that rose ground will appear as squares on the
lace but is marked in diamonds on the pricking. Curves on the heading
will be drawn in by eye and the dots marked as required. If one curve is
worked out successfully the others may be traced or pricked from it to
achieve an accurate edge. It is worth remembering that the only occasions
on which dots will be drawn in that are not on a diagonal are as follows:
headside curve, centre of a spider, the six dots which make up the hole in
the centre of a patch of cloth, or for a raised spot.

Before transferring the pattern on to pricking card it is worth drawing
in the path of the weaver as this confirms that the correct number of holes
have been marked.

Refer to photograph **9** and work out the pricking. On page 39 working
diagram **26** will confirm the accuracy of your work.

To make corners for Torchon patterns   Take a small mirror with a straight
unframed edge and, holding it vertically, move it at an angle of 45 degrees
from the footside along the lace until an attractive corner is seen. With a
knowledge of Torchon patterns one can decide if it is possible to work it
in a straightforward manner. For practice place a mirror on the patterns
given earlier and note where the corner line was taken and how the corner
was achieved.

In most patterns it is possible to have a complete pattern unit before
the corner and this will be repeated afterwards. There are always *two*
rows of holes, one before and one after the diagonal corner line – *never*
one row on the actual diagonal. Working the last row before the diagonal
corner line the threads are travelling out and down to the head. When the
pillow has been turned it will be found that threads travel down and
towards the footside. An extra pin-hole is always needed for neatness and

goes in the corner on the footside. No hole will fall in that position because holes are either side but not on the diagonal. The usual method for working this hole (usually referred to as Y) has been explained in instructions for earlier patterns. A patch of cloth or half stitch cannot extend over the corner diagonal as the pillow is turned and the direction of working is changed. If there is a complete break through the pattern at the corner it is usual to add extra pin-holes as required to achieve a neat arrangement of threads on the heading. If there is a continuous half stitch trail the pin holes are used twice when necessary.

Refer back to photograph **9** and prepare a pricking for the corner. The working diagram is not given for the corner but the corner line is shown in diagram **26** on page 39.

Patterns with directional designs   If the pattern has a definite directional design it is necessary to reverse the pattern in the centre of each side. A mirror held at right angles to the footside will show a suitable place for doing this. When a corner is designed using a mirror it will automatically appear in reverse and the centre reverse will compensate for this. Lace in photograph **10** shows this arrangement and pricking **7** is given alongside. Detailed working for the head is explained by diagram **27A** and **27B**. The pair from d become the weaver, and work in cloth stitch through pairs from c and b and through the pair from a in cloth stitch and twist. The weaver has to be twisted on the outward journey to achieve the even result.

TO BEGIN WORKING A PATTERN

This frequently puzzles the inexperienced worker but is quite simple once a basic understanding of the working of lace has been gained. In order to explain the principles involved reference will be made to diagram **26**.

1   Decide on the diagonal row of ground that is to be worked first. When possible choose a row that leads into the beginning of a patch of cloth, or half stitch, or a spider. Put up the footside pin A1 on this row, and hang two pairs on this pin, twist the right hand threads three times and make a cloth stitch and twist round the pin. This forms a closely twisted loop around the pin and eventually threads may be pulled through and knotted off if a complete edging is required.

The two pairs hanging from this pin would normally be the footside pairs with the pin put up inside them but on this occasion the pin has to hold them in position for a firm start to the row.

2   In Torchon ground pairs enter the ground, and work ground stitches diagonally. A row of support pins may be placed on the row *behind* the row to be worked, and one pair of bobbins hung on each of these pins B to I. In reality the threads would hang from these pins had the lace already been worked.

3   In a diamond of cloth it is obvious that a pair will come in diagonally for each hole. On the heading when working a pattern with a trail, a fan,

D 26

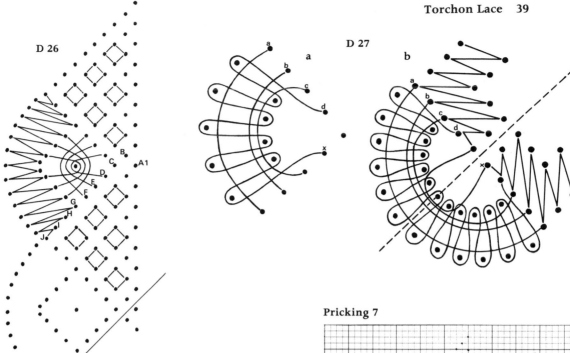

D 27

a

b

10 Reversal pattern

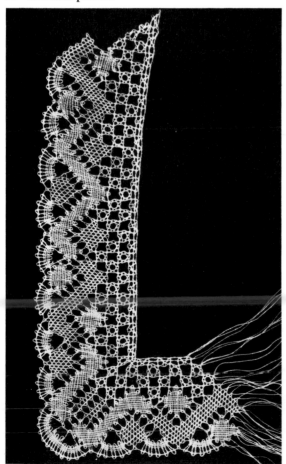

Pricking 7

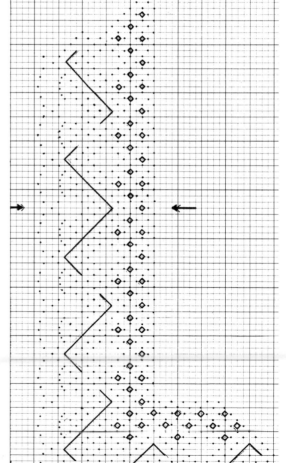

or other shape, the pairs will enter one to each hole on the right hand side and the curve on the left hand side will contain all the pairs. By experience or by trial the worker has to estimate the number of pairs required to fill up the edging satisfactorily. It is quite usual to try this out, and adjust the number of pairs required as the effect can be seen. These pairs are hung up on a pin at J, and to achieve a flat heading they are hung in order.

4   As soon as the first row has been worked, the support pins are removed giving a neat beginning, particularly important if the lace is to be joined later.

To estimate the number of pairs required for a pattern   On Torchon lace pricking choose the longest diagonal row of holes, and count two pairs for the first pin-hole and one pair for each of the other holes. If there is a cloth or half stitch fan or other pattern effect, extra pairs will be required and these must be counted as follows: one weaver pair, and sufficient passives to make the lace attractive.

SQUARE MATS

These are straightforward to work and when understood are easy to design. A mat is worked in four triangular sections (diagram 28). Section 1 is worked with the head on the left hand side as usual. When every pin

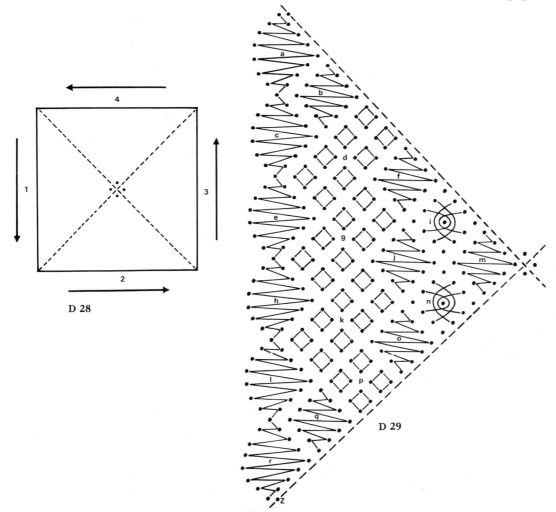

D 28

D 29

has been put up the pillow is turned as for a corner, and the next section is worked. Again turning the pillow, sections 3 and 4 are worked in turn.

Prepare pricking **8**, and use working diagram **29**. Mark the pin holes on to squared paper, and prick on to card. To mark in the rose ground and direction of the weaver, turn the pattern for each section. Prepare 28 pairs of bobbins – see photograph **11**. Hang four pairs on to the top pin of the fan a in order from right to left, and one pair on each of the other pins of the previous diagonal row.

The fan   Work the fan using the left hand side pair as weaver, the outside edge will look more attractive if the cloth stitch and twist variation is used there. Work the cloth diamond b. Work fan c. Work the eight units of rose ground d, and then fan e.

Continue working diagonally in blocks, f, g, h, etc., until the last fan r has been completed. Take the weaver to pin Z and back to the outside edge and then turn the pillow. Complete the next section using the pairs hanging as for a normal corner. Work the other two sections turning the pillow each time. A similar mat is shown completed in photograph **12**. Instructions for ending off neatly have been given on page 18.

Pricking 8

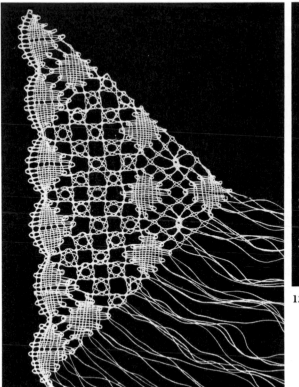

11   Mat triangle

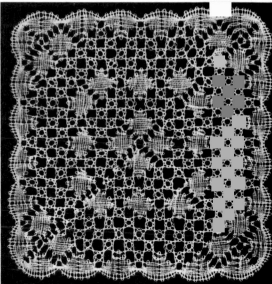

12   Whole mat

THE SAMPLER

Refer to pricking **9**, diagrams **30** and **31**, and photograph **13(a)**. The sampler shows the method of making an insertion with a footside on both sides. It also gives a very strong beginning and end for the strip of lace made, which is useful when neat ends are required, for example at the edge of a trolley cloth or chair back when there is no fabric to mask the edge of the lace. Prepare pricking **9** and 20 pairs of bobbins. The same arrangement of holes is pricked at both ends.

To begin   Refer to diagram **30**. Hang three pairs on the edge pin 1, and two pairs on each of the other pins A, B, C, D, E, F, G and H. Beginning at the outside edge twist each pair three times. Note that these are not actual pairs of bobbins as they were wound, but simply the bobbins falling next to each other on the pillow.

Take the extreme right hand pair and work cloth stitch and twist through the first pair and then cloth stitch to the left until the last pair is reached, twist the weaver once, and work cloth stitch and twist with the last pair. Put up pin 2 inside these two pairs. Remove pin A. As usual ignore the outer pair and work back in cloth stitch as far as the last two

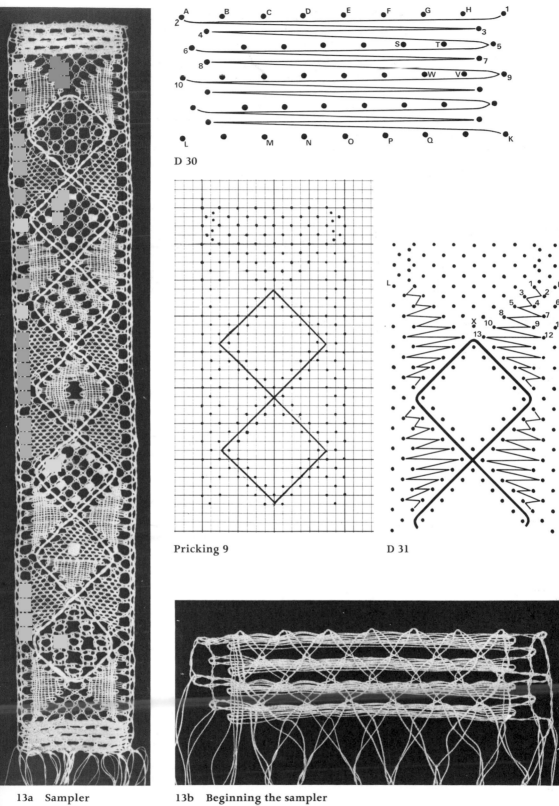

D 30

Pricking 9

D 31

13a   Sampler

13b   Beginning the sampler

pairs. Do not use these. Put up pin 3 inside the weaver, twist the weaver twice and take it back still in cloth stitch to the left side as far as the last two pairs. Do not use these; put up pin 4 and twist the weaver twice. Work in cloth stitch to the right as far as the last two pairs. Twist the weaver and the next passive pair once each and work them in cloth stitch and twist. Put up pin 5 and cover with cloth stitch and twist. The pairs hanging from pins B, C, D, E, F, G and H are linked diagonally with half stitch, pin, half stitch in the row in a line with pins 5 and 6. For example, the pairs hanging from pins H and G will work pin T, and the other pair from G with the pair from F will work pin S, and so on.

To continue   Take the weaver hanging round pin 5 and work to the left in cloth stitch as far as the last two pairs. Twist the weaver and the next passive pair once each, and work them in cloth stitch and twist.

Put up pin 6 and cover with cloth stitch and twist. Pins 7 and 8 are worked in the same way as pins 3 and 4. From pin 8 the weaver is taken back through to the right in cloth stitch as far as the last two pairs. The weaver and next passive pair are twisted once and the outside edge pair is twisted three times. The weaver works cloth stitch and twist through these two pairs, and pin 9 is put up inside two pairs as for a normal footside. The outside pair is ignored and the pin covered with the other two pairs.

At this stage the row of pin holes in line with 9 and 10 must be worked again in half stitch, pin, half stitch. For example the pairs from pins 7 and T work pin V, and the pairs from pins T and S work pin W, and so on.

The weaver is worked back to the left hand side and pin 10 worked as pin 9. Pin 10 is in the same position as pin 2, and if the instructions are repeated from this pin as far as pin 9 the lace will be complete as far as K. Remember to cover pin K with cloth stitch and twist. The third pair from the edge will be taken out to work pin L.

The pin-holes at M, N, O, P and Q will be worked with the appropriate pairs in half stitch, pin, half stitch. It can be seen that the other two pin-holes are at the top of the triangles of cloth stitch. Now refer to diagram 31. The ground or net stitches between the two triangles must be completed next.

To work the triangle   To work pin 1 use the pair falling diagonally from the left and the pair hanging from above, and work a cloth stitch. Put up pin 1 and cover it with a cloth stitch. The right hand pair of bobbins becomes the weaver and make a cloth stitch with the next pair to the right. Put up pin 2 and using the weaver work back through the two passive pairs and through one more from the ground stitches. Put up pin 3 and work back with the weaver through *two* pairs only to pin 4. Notice that the other pair must be released to make a footside pin at 6. Put up pin 4 and work back to pin 5.

At this point leave the triangle and work pin 6 as a normal footside pin. Return to the triangle and take the weaver from pin 5 through all the passive pairs hanging in the triangle (i.e. three pairs) and through one more pair coming in from the footside. Put up pin 7.

Work to pin 8, and back to pin 9, remembering that one pair has been released after pin 7 to complete pin 11. Work pins 10 and 11 and remember to bring in one of the footside pairs at 12. Complete the triangle bringing in one more pair at pin 13, and leaving out one pair after pin 13 and the other pins on that side.

These triangles may be worked in half stitch as an attractive variation. Diamond shapes have six holes on each side and the pairs will come in diagonally from the triangles of cloth or half stitch.

Gimp threads   These surround and outline parts of the pattern. They are passed between the threads of the pair of bobbins that they must cross. In Torchon lace it is usual to have two twists on the pair of threads before and again after the gimp has passed between them. When taking a gimp thread from left to right it will pass under the first thread and over the second. When taking the gimp thread from right to left it will pass over the first thread and under the second. To introduce the gimp thread into this pattern put up a support pin at X and hang the gimp round it. Take it out through the pairs waiting to make the diamond. As soon as the top pin of the diamond is in position remove support pin X.

For the following pattern variations, refer to diagrams **32A** to **32F** and photographs **14A** to **14F**.

D 32

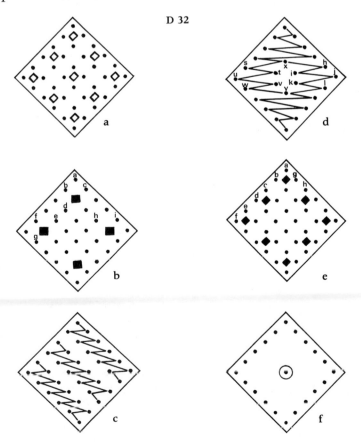

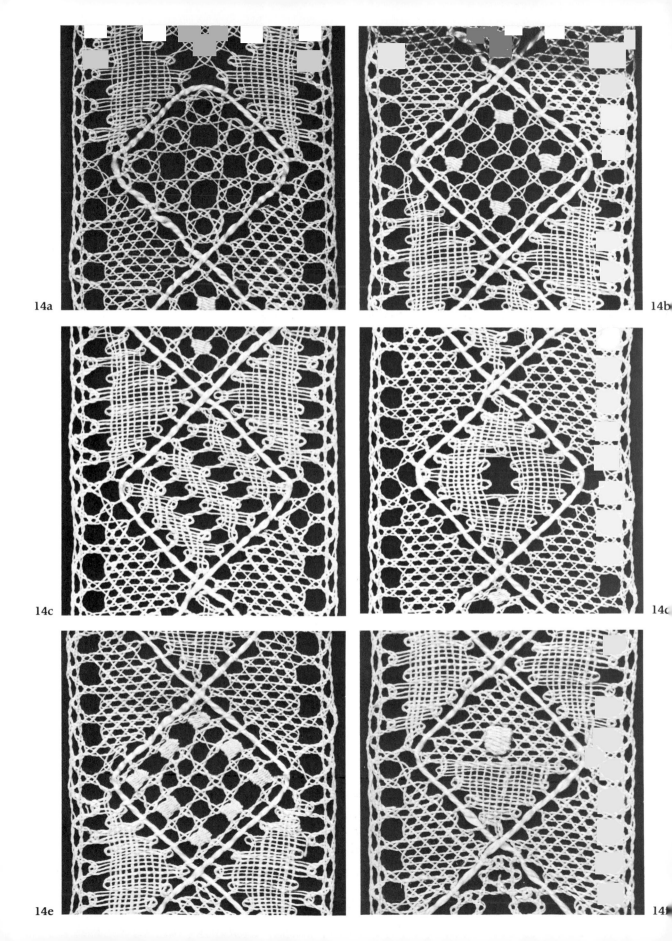

14a

14b

14c

14c

14e

14

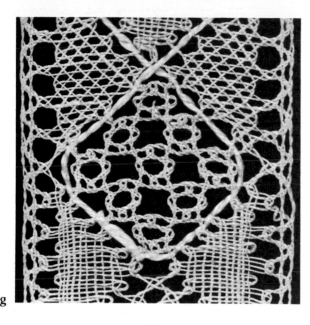

14g

14a *Opposite* Sampler filling: rose ground
14b Sampler filling: tallies in Torchon ground
14c Sampler filling: cloth stitch strips
14d Sampler filling: hole in a cloth stitch diamond
14e Sampler filling: tallies in Torchon ground using a different arrangement
14f Sampler filling: raised tally in a diamond made of cloth and half stitch
14g *Left* Sampler filling: rose ground using clothstitch and twist

Rose Ground

There are several variations of rose ground. In an earlier pattern one was described, using cloth stitch and twist between each rose ground unit. In the variation shown in diagram **32A** half stitch only is used between and on the outside of each unit. Refer back to diagram **23** on page 34 and a, b, g and h are half stitches.

Tallies, Square Leaves or Spots in Torchon Ground

Refer to diagram **32B**. From a work a complete row of Torchon ground in each direction. Take pairs hanging from b and c to make the tally. Twist each pair once more so that there are two twists on each pair.

Take the second bobbin of the four as weaver, and pass it over the third as if beginning a cloth stitch. Take it under the fourth bobbin and back over the top of it. Now pass it under the middle thread and over the left hand side thread. Continue weaving so to get back to the right hand side. To help the threads into shape it is essential to hold the weaver all the time, and, at the end of each to and fro weaving, the outside straight threads must be kept taut and the shape achieved by carefully pulling on the weaver. These tallies require much practice, they are easier to manage in thick thread.

At the end of the tally the two pairs are twisted twice each before continuing with the Torchon ground. It is important to work in the pair without the tally weaver before the other as any tension on that pair will destroy the shape of the tally. When pins d and e have been worked, the pair from e along with the pair hanging from f will make the next tally. After working pin g, two rows of ground from top right to lower left can be completed. Pairs hanging from h and i are ready for the tally, and by working ground pins as necessary the diamond can be finished.

Cloth Stitch Strips

This consists of three strips of cloth, the black line on the diagonal indicating the path of the weaver (diagram **32C**). One complete strip may be made before the next is started.

Hole in a Cloth Stitch Diamond

Usually these holes are marked with six pin holes (diagram **32D**). Begin by working a normal cloth diamond until there are only two holes remaining to be done on each side before the widest part. Work the weaver to the centre until the weaver and one passive pair are actually the centre pairs. Put up a pin at x and cover it. Temporarily these two pairs become weavers. The right hand pair weaving h, i, j, k and l, and the left hand pair weaving s, t, u, v and w, they both meet in the centre and are worked together in cloth stitch. Pin y is put up and covered with another cloth stitch. The left hand pair becomes a passive pair, and the right hand pair is the weaver which completes the diamond shape.

Tallies in Torchon Ground – A Different Arrangement

Work pins a to f (diagram **32E**) inclusive in half stitch, pin, half stitch. Twist all pairs once more as they are to be used for tallies. Make tallies with pairs from a and b, c and d, e and f, being sure to leave the weaver on the left lower side of the finished tally. Work the next diagonal row of ground from pin g from right to left, and this anchors the tallies firmly in position. The next diagonal row is worked normally as the first row, and the following row with the tallies as the second row.

Raised Tally

Added variety is introduced by using both cloth and half stitch in the same diamond (diagram **32F**). The raised tally may be made on either cloth or half stitch. Work to the end of the row on which it has been decided to make the tally, in this case the longest row. Take the two middle passive pairs and make a tally as previously described, at approximately twice the usual length (diagram **33**). Place a thick pin or in the case of very

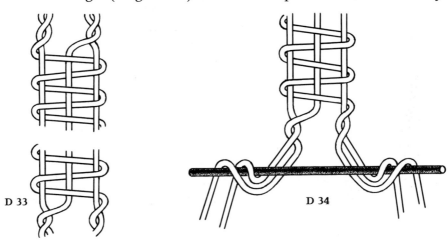

D 33   D 34

thick thread a fine knitting needle or cocktail stick on top of the tally. Refer to diagram **34**, and twist the ends of the threads over the needle as shown. Carefully ease the tally over the needle by pulling the threads that were twisted over the needle.

Rose Ground using Cloth Stitch and Twist

The last diamond is worked in rose ground but in this variety the stitches around and between the units are cloth stitch and twist and all the stitches before and after the pins are also worked in cloth stitch and twist.

To end off the sampler as it was begun   Work the end similar to the beginning until the very last pin-hole on one side has been reached. Then only the final row across the work has to be completed. Decide which pairs will come to each hole on the final row.

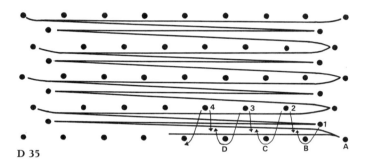

D 35

Ensure that the footside at pin A (diagram **35**) has been completed and the pin covered. Work in cloth stitch with the pair hanging from 1 and twist this passive pair three times. Put up pin B between these two pairs and cover with cloth stitch. The left hand pair of these two and the right hand of the two pairs hanging from 2 are now tied firmly together and thrown back across the work. The weaver now works through the other pair from 2 in cloth stitch, it is twisted three times and pin C is covered. The left hand of these two pairs and the right hand pair from 3 are tied together and discarded. Continue all the way across the lace.

At each end the pairs should be knotted together as tidily and neatly as possible. When the ends have been trimmed closely and the two pieces of cloth stitch folded up over the other two pieces, the knots are hidden inside. Neat sewing makes this a strong and satisfactory hem.

SIMPLE DECORATIONS

All pattern instructions, apart from the Torchon sampler, have been given starting on a diagonal row. This is the easiest way to understand the working of almost any pattern. However it is sometimes desirable to begin on a straight line. If the end is to be enclosed in a hem or seam or if the lace is purely decorative, a very simple method may be used.

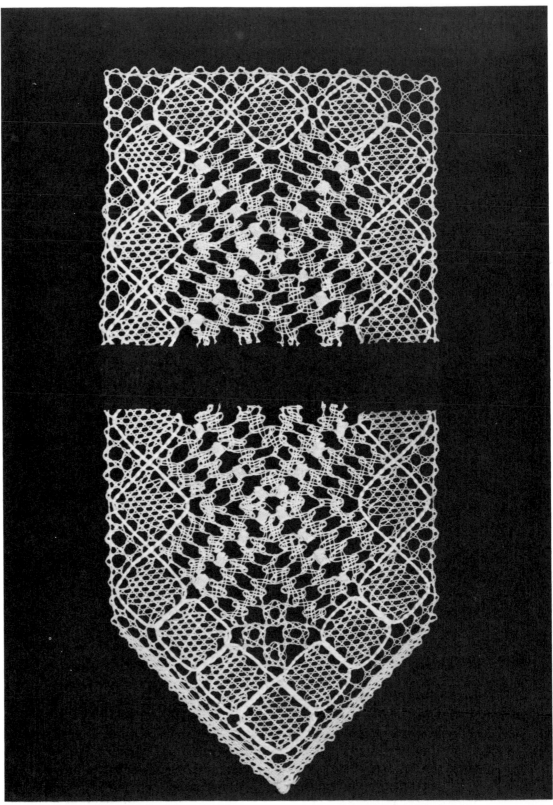

15   Decorative Strip A

Decorative Strip A

The next pattern may be mounted on ribbon for some form of decoration, or used as an insertion in a lampshade. See photograph **15**. Refer to diagram **36** to make a pricking and for the method of working. Note that one pattern repeat is indicated by a bracket.

Prepare 34 pairs of bobbins and hang two pairs on pins put up at A to Q inclusive. Start at one end and twist the bobbins in pairs, note that twists are on bobbins falling to one side of the pin and not on true pairs.

Take the right hand pair hanging from pin A, and work towards the right through all pairs in cloth stitch and twist. Put up pin 1 inside the weaver only, and do not cover the pin. Take the third pair from the right, and work cloth stitch and twist twice to the outside edge. Put up pin 2 inside one pair only, and cover the pin with cloth stitch and twist. Take the third pair from the left hand side and work out to the edge with cloth stitch and twist twice. Put up pin 3 inside one pair only, and cover with cloth stitch and twist.

Following the markings on the diagram the pattern may be worked. First fill in the ground stitches between the diamond shapes. Put a gimp in position to work the centre diamond, and work the complete diamond in half stitch. Take a second gimp pair, and put that across the pillow through the pairs hanging from the diamond. At either side these will cross the gimps from the top of the diamond, and be ready for use for the next diamond shapes. Complete the two corner diamond shapes on each side, crossing the gimp threads and running them together between the diamonds. The photograph shows clearly the way of working.

To complete the length to a point   Overlap the gimp threads as shown in

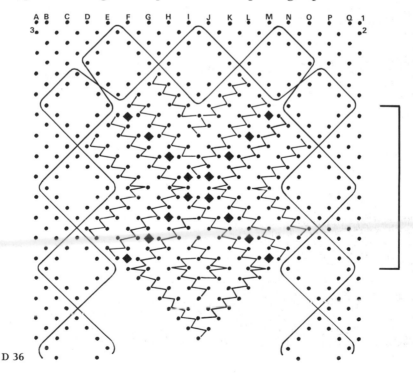

D 36

diagram **37**, and throw them back out of the way of working. Later they may be cut off. Twist the pairs as usual after the gimp, but this time enclosing a double thread. Work pin a normally, work pins b, c, d and so on as Torchon ground, i.e. half stitch, pin, half stitch.

Take the pair from b and work cloth stitch and twist to the edge through one pair, put up pin o, and cover the pin. Take the pair hanging at c, and work in cloth stitch and twist through two pairs to the outside edge, put up pin p, and work back through one pair in cloth stitch and twist, and the next pair in cloth stitch. Take the pair hanging at d, work in cloth stitch through two pairs, and through the edge pair in cloth stitch and twist. Put up pin q, work through the first pair in cloth stitch and twist, and through the next two pairs in cloth stitch. Take the pair from e, cloth stitch through three pairs, and then work cloth stitch and twist through the edge pair. Put up pin r, and cover with cloth stitch and twist. Work cloth stitch through the next two pairs, and throw out the third pair from the edge, i.e. the last pair worked through. Take the pair from f, and follow instructions for e, putting up pin s. Continue until all pairs except those from the bottom centre pin have been worked.

From the centre pin take a pair out each way to the edge, put up the pins and cover them. Ignore the outside pairs, and take the other pairs through each other (as half of a spider). Take the outside pair but one from each side, bring them together and knot firmly, allowing them to drop in the centre. Repeat this twice more. Take the outside edge pairs, cross them under the hanging pairs, and bring them to the top to tie firmly. These pairs, when trimmed tidily will form a tassle. Alternatively the hanging pairs may be thrown up over the lace and the edge pairs wound round them and tied again to anchor them back. The ends should be cut closely.

Decorative Strip B
This is worked from pricking **10** using 18 pairs of bobbins. See photograph **16**.

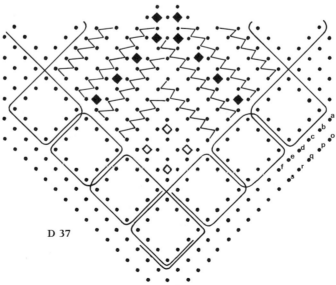

D 37

16   Decorative Strip B   Pricking 10

17   Bedfordshire laces

3 ❖ Bedfordshire or Beds-Maltese and Cluny Lace

The distinctive features of these laces are the plaits with picots, the leaves, and the trails of cloth or half stitch which move continually through the design. The name – Bedfordshire – indicates the type of lace, but it was made throughout the East Midland counties, and frequently it is called Beds-Maltese. Maltese lace usually has a Maltese cross in cloth stitch in the design if it has been made in Malta. Cluny lace is similar to Bedfordshire lace, the only distinguishing feature being a divided trail, achieved by twisting the weaver regularly to obtain a definite decorative effect. The name was adopted as lace of this type is in the Cluny Museum in Paris.

EXPLANATION OF TERMS USED

To cover the pin   Refer to page 23.

To hang pairs on a pin   Refer to page 23.

To hang pairs on a pin in order   Refer to page 23.

The footside   This is worked differently from Torchon in that there are more passive pairs – these may be either twisted or straight.

The plait, also known in some districts as the Leg   This is made using two pairs in continuous half stitch without pins.

The leaf, also known as the plait   This is the effect obtained by using two pairs of bobbins, and weaving one thread about the other three.

The trail   This is a continuous strip of cloth or half stitch which forms a prominent part of the pattern. It serves to take in or release pairs, plaits or leaves to facilitate the working of the rest of the design.

The crossing of four plaits or leaves, also known as the Windmill   This occurs when two plaits meet at a pin. There is an accepted method of placing the threads about the pin. See page 60.

The crossing of six plaits   This occurs when three plaits meet at a pin, see page 63.

The crossing of eight plaits   This occurs when four plaits meet at a pin, see page 211.

Ninepin   This is the name given to a traditional arrangement of plaits and picots on the headside.

The picot   This is the decorative loop found on the plait. In fine thread it is always worked with two threads to give it weight and maintain the loop when laundered. If thick thread is used a single-thread picot is adequate. The different picots are described now as it is important to select the correct method according to thread used.

Picot set to the left of the plait using fine thread   See diagrams **38A** and **38B**. Take the two left hand threads of the plait, and twist three times. Take a pin in the right hand and hold it – point to the left – over the extreme left thread. Bring the point under the thread towards the worker and over into the picot hole. Keep it loosely around the pin. Take the other thread and put it around the same pin, bringing it to the front and clockwise behind. Twist the two threads together three times more, and pull tightly together. The threads should run twisted together about the pin to form a sound double picot. If the threads remain as two separate loops when the pin is removed the picot is incorrect. This happens when threads are tightened separately before the final twists are added.

Picot set to the right of the thread using fine thread   See diagrams **39A** and **39B**. Twist the two right hand threads of the plait three times. Take a pin in the right hand and hold it – point towards the left – under the right hand

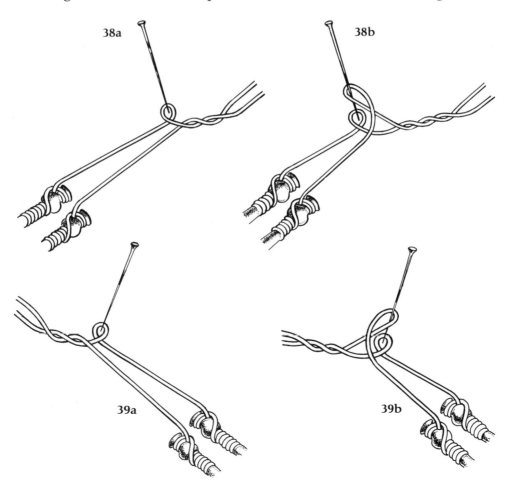

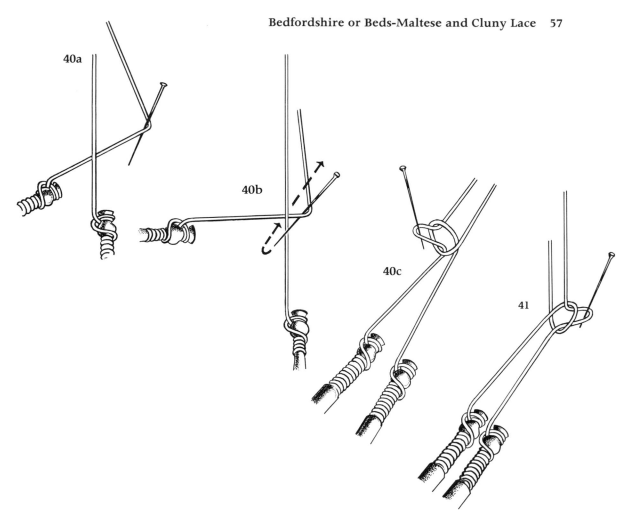

thread, bring the point over the thread towards the worker, and into the picot hole. Take the other thread and bring it in front and behind the pin in an anti-clockwise direction. Twist the pair three times and pull tightly together.

Picot set to the left of the plait using thick thread   See diagrams **40A**, **40B** and **40C**. Take the two left hand threads of the plait in the left hand and hold them taut. Take a pin in the right hand, put it under the right of these two threads, and pull the left thread across underneath it (**40A**) so that the threads are crossed. Bring the pin towards the worker over the crossed threads, then turn the point of the pin away taking it under the crossed threads and up between them (**40B**). Stick the pin into the picot hole to the left of the plait and ease the threads until a single picot thread appears about the pin (**40C**). It is important to manipulate the threads until a single tight picot appears on one side of the plait.

Picot set to the right of the plait using thick thread   See diagram **41**. A very satisfactory picot is achieved if instructions for a picot on the left are followed exactly, and the pin inclined to a hole on the right of the plait.

Picots on both sides of plaits   Work one picot and then make a half stitch before working the second picot. This avoids an ugly hole between picots.

Bedfordshire picot   Traditionally a single picot was made by twisting the thread about the pin as for the first part of a double picot. This method produces a picot which does not hold its shape very well and therefore the single picot described earlier is recommended.

Thread   This is a general guide only as the thickness and type of thread is dependent upon the result required. D.M.C. *Cordonnet special* works up firmly, and launders well, whereas D.M.C. *Retors D'Alsace* is softer, and no. 60 is particular suitable for fine Bedfordshire lace.

> D.M.C. *Cordonnet special* no. 150 suitable for pattern 11 (on a grid of 12 squares to 25mm). Suitable for pattern 12 (on a grid of 8 squares to 25mm). Suitable for almost all prickings in this section, except prickings 18, 19 to 22, 26, 34 and the finer of the prickings when they are given in duplicate.
>
> D.M.C. *Cordonnet special* no. 100 suitable for a closer lace, as this is a slightly thicker thread.
>
> Bocken's Swedish linen thread no.35 and no.50 suitable for pricking 26 (mat), and pricking 18 (edging).
>
> D.M.C. *Retors D'Alsace* no.40, no.50 and no.60 suitable for the fine old prickings 19 to 22 and 34.

PLAITED LACE No.1

Prepare pricking **11** and wind eight pairs of bobbins. Refer to diagram **42** and photograph **18**. Hang two pairs of bobbins on A1, and two pairs in order on B. Hang two pairs in order on C and two pairs on D.

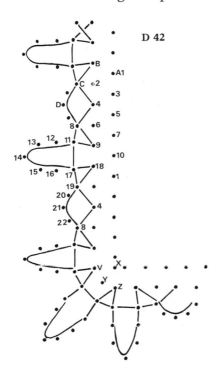

D 42

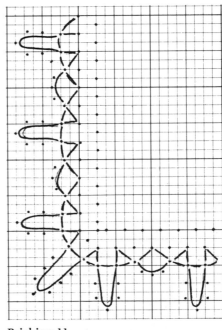

Pricking 11

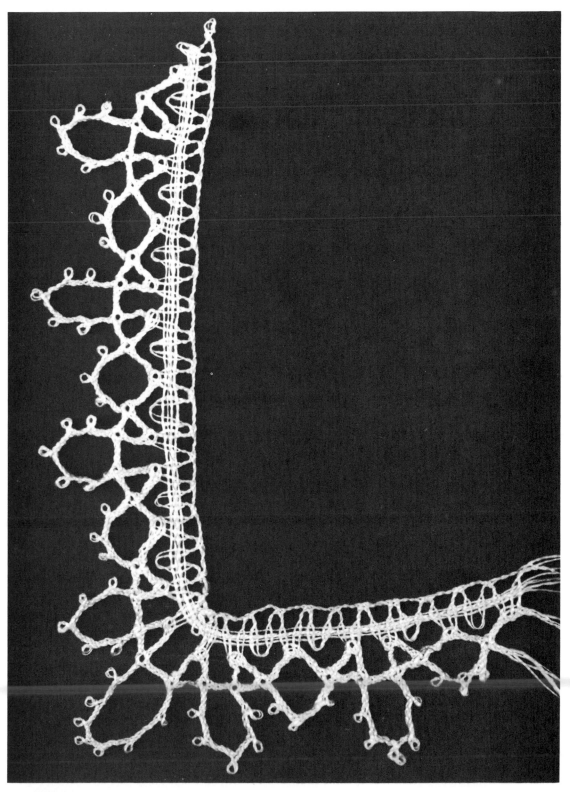

18   Plaited lace

To begin at the footside   Using the two pairs hanging at A1, twist the threads to the right of the pin three times, and work cloth stitch and twist to cover the pin. Give each pair one extra twist. In future that stitch will be referred to as *cloth stitch and two twists*. (Reference may be made to *cloth stitch and twist twice* – this instruction requires that cloth stitch and twist be worked through two pairs.) Discard the right-hand pair. Take the inner (left hand) pair, and work cloth stitch and twist twice through the two pairs hanging at B. Twist the weaver twice and put up pin 2 to the right of the weaver pair.

To work the footside   When instructions require that the next footside pin be worked, proceed as follows. Take the fourth pair from the outside edge, and work cloth stitch through two pairs towards the edge. Twist the weaver twice, and with the outside pair work cloth stitch and two twists. Put up the pin inside two pairs (in this case pin 3). Ignore the outer pair and with the left hand pair work cloth stitch through two pairs to the left.

To join in pairs for a plait   Using the same weaver work in cloth stitch through the two pairs hanging at C. Twist the weaver twice, and put up pin 4 to the right of the weaver. Work cloth stitch back through these two pairs, and then discard them to the left of the pillow for use later. Remove the support pins at C and B and ease the pairs down. Work the footside and pin 5.

Put up pin 6 as pin 2, and repeat the footside and pin 7. Remember to complete the sequence and leave the weaver as fourth pair from the outside edge.

The plait   Using the two pairs hanging from pin 4, plait as far as pin-hole 8, but do not put up the pin.

To plait   Use the four threads, make a half stitch, and repeat half stitches for the required length. It is not usual to count the number of stitches, but estimate by the appearance of the work. In order to achieve a close and flat plait pull the pairs of threads well apart between each half stitch to improve the tension and to keep the plait firm. See diagram 43.

The crossing of four plaits   The pairs at D (diagram 42) are introduced at pin 8. Normally they will be in the lace as a plait. However, it is neat and easy to join in the pairs at a crossing rather than have a short unattached plait at the beginning. Pairs from D and pairs from the plait from pin 4 will make the crossing.

D 43

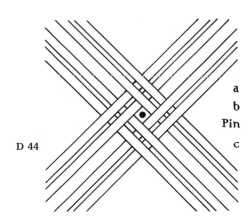

D 44

a
b
Pin
c

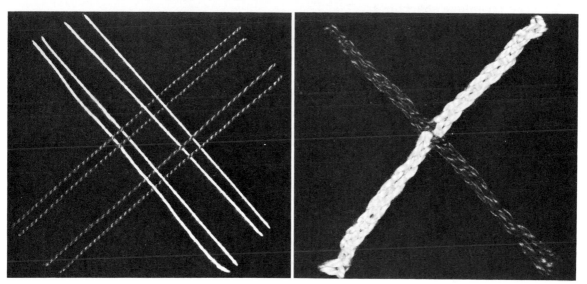

19a, 19b   Windmill

To work a four plait crossing   Use the two plaits and consider them as four pairs. Use each pair as a single bobbin is used in cloth stitch. Place the second over the third. At the same time place the fourth over the third and the second over the first. Put up the pin (in this case pin 8). Place the second over the third. The plaits have crossed each other. Refer to diagram **44** and photographs **19A** and **19B**.

To continue   Follow the black markings (diagram **42**) which indicate the position of the plaits. Plait from pin 8 as far as pin 9. Take the fourth pair from the right (weaver), and work cloth stitch through the two pairs of the plait. Put up pin 9 to the right of the weaver, and work back through the plait pairs. Work the footside and pin 10.

Plait the other two pairs at pin 8 and the pairs hanging from pin 9. Make a crossing at pin 11. Plait the right hand pairs ready for use at 17 and the left hand pairs as far as 12, where a picot is made to the left of the plait. Select the correct picot for the thread being used. Continue plaiting, making picots at 13, 14, 15 and 16. In order to keep the picot at 14 tight to the plait, it is necessary after that pin to keep the threads in a straight line from pin 13, and to turn the plait only when it is the correct length to work the picot at 15. Continue plaiting as far as 17 where a crossing of plaits is made using this plait and the plait from pin 11. Plait in both directions ready for use.

Work the fourth pair from the right (weaver) through the right hand plait from 17 in cloth stitch. Put up pin 18 and work in cloth stitch back through the plait pairs. Plait these pairs and with the plait from 17 make a crossing at 19. Use the left hand pairs to plait to 8, making picots at 20, 21 and 22. Take the right hand pairs and plait to 4. Work the footside pin 1.

It is now possible to put up pin 2 and follow the instructions through again.

The corner   Follow the markings on the pricking which indicate the plaits. The footside is worked normally to V – the same position as 18 – and the normal footside sequence is worked with the corner pin X. Pin Y is put up and the footside repeated using pin X for the second time. The weaver works through the plait which has made the corner ninepin, and pin Z – the same position as 9 – is put up.

To join lace   Follow instructions given for Torchon on page 18. When joining plaits, pull two of the threads through as loops, put the other two threads through the loops, and pull together closely. Knot the threads together in pairs, using one loop thread and one which passed through each time.

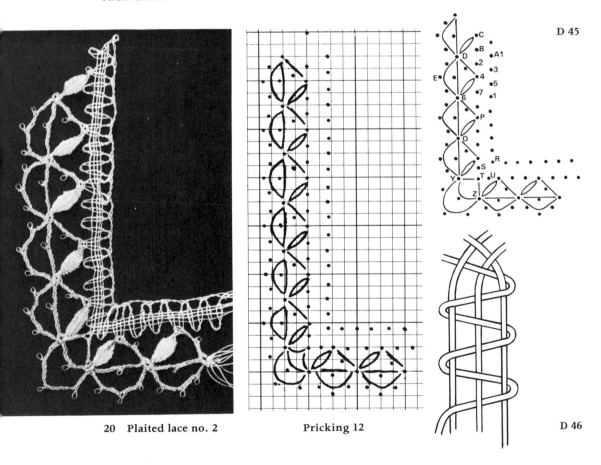

20   Plaited lace no. 2   Pricking 12   D 46

PLAITED LACE No.2

Prepare pricking **12** and ten pairs of bobbins. See diagram **45** and photograph **20**. Hang two pairs on each of pins A1, C, D and E, and two pairs in order on B. Work exactly as for the previous pattern as far as pin 5 with the footside completed and the weaver in position as fourth pair from the outside edge.

To make a leaf   This fills the space between 4 and 6 and is made using the pairs discarded after pin 4. Refer to diagram **46**. Take the two pairs, and work a cloth stitch being careful to pull it up very closely. Lengthen the thread which completed the stitch. Take it to the right under the outside thread, and back over it. Take it under the centre thread, over the left hand thread, back under it, and over the centre thread. Weaving in this manner is continued for the length required.

In order to achieve a neat edge to the leaf, the weaving thread must be kept evenly about the outside threads, which determine the shape of the leaf. The outside threads are held one in either hand, the right hand thread bobbin being kept between the third and fourth fingers so that the weaver bobbin can be held between the thumb and forefinger. The weaver should be manipulated until the thread fits snugly about the outside threads, which must be kept widely apart to assist in the shaping of the leaf. In the beginning it is necessary to pull the weaver thread fairly closely to achieve a pointed effect. At least three quarters of the leaf is worked before any adjustment is made to bring it to a point. The weaver thread is gradually tightened to obtain the correct effect. The leaf is completed with cloth stitch.

This is probably one of the most difficult techniques to manage well. It is easier to work in thick thread than fine thread, and practice is necessary to perfect the shape.

To continue the pattern   The pairs hanging at E would normally make a plait with picots on the headside, and the pairs hanging at D would also be plaited. However these pairs are brought directly into the pattern at the crossing at 6 as it is the beginning of the lace. Also to come in at pin 6 is the leaf from pin 4.

Six plait crossing   Six pairs from three plaits hang ready for use. Treat each pair as a single thread, keeping them together throughout the working. Spread the pairs well out on the pillow for easy identification. See photographs **21A** and **21B**.

Take the right centre pair over the next pair to the right. Take the left centre pair under the next pair to the left. Cross the new centre pairs right over left. Put up the pin between them. Take the pair to the right of

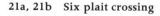

21a, 21b   Six plait crossing

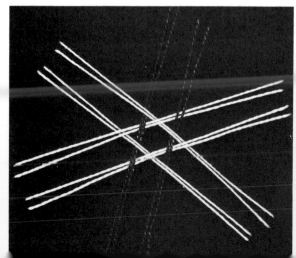
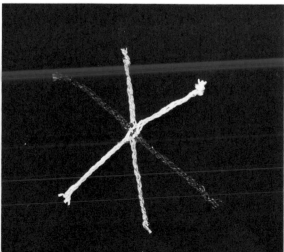

the pin out to the right over the next pair and under the outside pair. Take the pair to the left of the pin out to the left under the next pair and over the outside pair.

Find the new centre pairs, and take the right pair over the next pair to the right. Take the left centre pair under the next pair to the left. Cross the new centre pairs right over left. Take the right centre pair over the next pair to the right. Take the left centre pair under the next pair to the left. Remove support pins D and E. Pull up into position. The pairs are ready for use as plaits or leaves.

To continue the pattern   Plait the left hand pairs with picots as far as O. Plait the centre pairs with picot as far as O. Plait the right hand pairs with picot as far as P. Return to the footside and the weaver which should be fourth pair from the outside edge, put up pin 7, and work the complete footside sequence including pin 1. A pattern is complete.

The corner   A clear neat corner is achieved by changing the passive pairs on the footside. Study the photograph as the lace is worked.

Work the footside normally and put up pin S, weave back through two passive pairs, and leave the weaver hanging to become the new right hand passive pair after the corner. Plait the two right hand pairs from the crossing at Y to the corner at T, and put up pin T between them. Weave the right hand pair through the two passive pairs, and leave it hanging to become the new left passive pair after the corner. Take the old left hand passive pair, which is now lying to the right of pin T, and the remaining half of the plait, and plait them together to Z. Put pin U to the right of the old remaining right hand passive pair.

Turn the pillow. Take this pair which lies to the left of pin U and work the footside sequence using pin R for a second time. Note that the weaver passes through the two new passive pairs which fall from S and T.

Pattern reversal   This is necessary to achieve a symmetrical corner. A leaf is worked out from the footside to the corner at Y, and, to correspond, a leaf is worked from Z into the footside. After the corner has been turned, all leaves are worked into the footside and plaits worked out from it. At a centre point the leaf worked into the footside is worked out again as another leaf.

PLAITED LACE No.3

These laces can be designed quite easily, and several interpretations made from the same pricking. Wide lace can be made quickly and effectively using coarse thread. Prepare the pricking from diagram **47** and use photograph **22** for guidance. The lace is worked from pin A with two passive pairs. Two pairs are joined in at B, and released for a plait. Four plait crossings are made at O, P, Q, R and S, and plaits and leaves worked as indicated on the diagram.

In the corner the weaver is well twisted between pins, and works from Z through plaits in cloth stitch at U, V, W, X and Y, then back to Z.

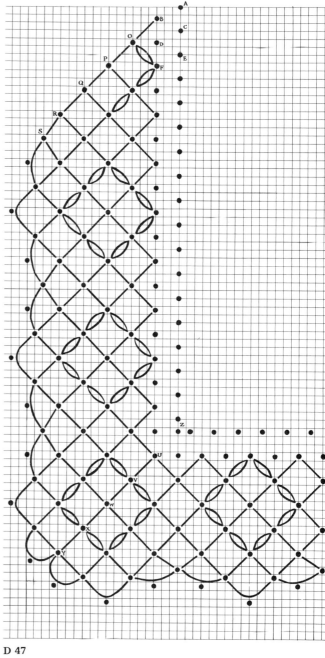

D 47

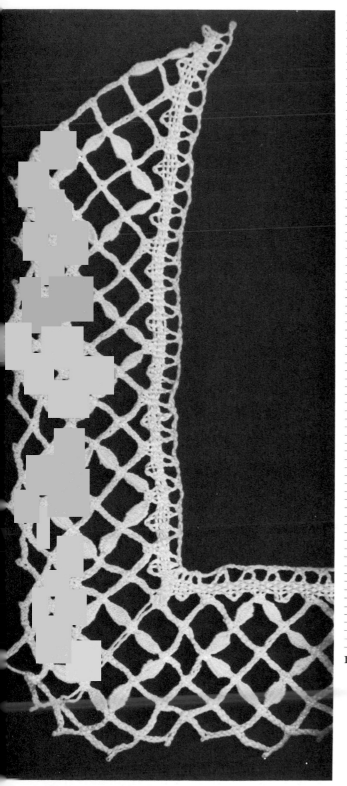

22   Plaited lace no. 3

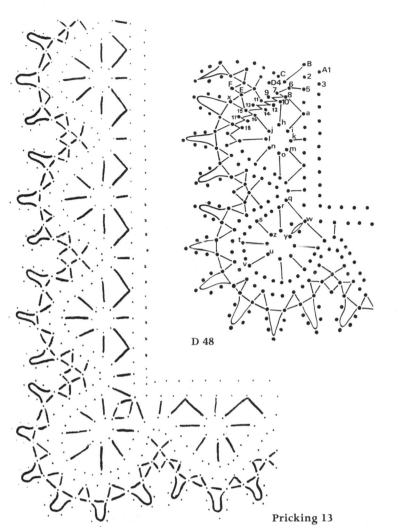

D 48

Pricking 13

23a Spider pattern

BEDFORDSHIRE SPIDER PATTERN

Prepare pricking **13** and 18 pairs of bobbins. Two pairs extra are required for the corner. See diagram **48** and photograph **23A**. Hang two pairs on A1, two pairs in order on B and nine pairs in order on C from right to left. Hang one pair on D and two pairs on each of E and F. Work exactly as for the previous pattern as far as pin 3 and complete the footside leaving the weaver as the fourth pair from the outside edge. Twist the weaver twice.

The trail   Use the pair on D4 as weaver, and work cloth stitch through the nine pairs on C. Twist the weaver twice.

Crossing weavers, often known as a 'kiss'   Take the weaver from the trail and the weaver from the footside, and put up pins 5 and 6 to support the threads. Work the weavers together in cloth stitch and two twists. The pair on the left works through the nine pairs of cloth stitch trail, and pin 7 is put up. The pair on the right is the fourth from the edge and works out to the footside edge. Note that the weavers have changed positions.

The weaver in the trail at pin 7 works across through all nine pairs, and pin 8 is put up to the left of the weaver. It works back to pin 9 and then through seven pairs only to pin 10. Thus two pairs are left out after pin 8 in readiness to make a plait to a. Remove pins at C and B and ease the pairs down.

Continue the trail to pin 11 and back through five pairs to pin 12. Thus two pairs are left out after pin 10. Continue the trail as far as pin 15, and weave through the two pairs hanging from E before putting up this pin. Work to the right through these two pairs, which will become the plait from 15 to x, and the five trail pairs. Put up pin 16. Continue to 17 and back through three pairs only to pin 18. Thus two pairs are left out for the plait after 16. Remove pin E.

The ninepin edge   Plait the pairs hanging at 15 as far as x and make a crossing with the pairs from F at x. Remove pin F.

The footside   Continue with the fourth pair from the edge which is the right hand pair of the 'kiss' as far as pin a where a plait from pin 8 has to be joined in.

In the plaited lace patterns a simple and satisfactory method is described, but the following method is neater and results in better tension.

To link a plait into cloth stitch   See diagram **49** and photograph **23b**. Using the weaver, work through both plait pairs in cloth stitch as usual. Put up the pin between the plait pairs (i.e., in this case, to the right of two

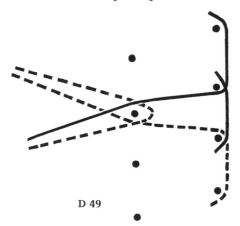

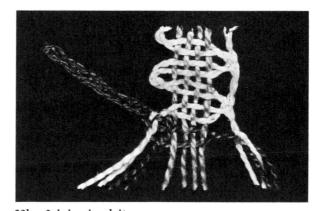

D 49

23b   Joining in plait

pairs) and cover the pin using the pair either side of it in cloth stitch. The weaver from the footside has become part of the new plait, and the left hand pair from the old plait has become the new weaver. This method can be used whenever plaits or leaves join and leave a trail at the same pin.

Work the footside and trail with ninepin as far as the centre of the half stitch circle.

Half stitch circle   Make plaits from 16, 10 and a. Put up pin h in the middle of the centre plait, and cover the pin with half stitch. Take the right hand pair as weaver and work to the right through one more pair (i.e. half the plait from a). Put up pin i and weave back through two pairs already part of the circle and through one more pair (i.e. half the plait from 16). Put up pin j. Weave across through the three circle pairs in half stitch and through the other pair from the plait from a in cloth stitch and twist. Put up pin k and work a 'kiss' crossing with the weaver from the footside. Work back through the first pair in cloth stitch and twist, and through the next three pairs in half stitch.

Work on through the other half of the plait from 16 in cloth stitch and twist. Put up pin 1 and work a 'kiss', crossing the weaver from the trail. Work back through the first pair in cloth stitch and twist, and through the next three pairs in half stitch. Put up pin m, and work back through three pairs to pin n. Work half stitch through two pairs and put up pin o and cover it with half stitch.

The trail   The ninepin plaits are worked in when necessary, and the plaits are brought back into the trail from the half stitch circle. To bring in plaits and retain them as part of the trail, take the weaver through the trail and on through the plait pairs. Put up the pin as usual, so that the weaver passes round the pin and continues with the two plait pairs as part of the trail. This becomes thicker as more pairs are brought in and care is needed to ensure good tension.

The corner   The trail and ninepin edge are worked normally. Pairs are left out for plaits at q, r and s. At t, it is necessary to add in two extra pairs – otherwise only one pair would remain in the trail.

To join in two pairs on the edge of a trail   Weave through the trail pairs to t, and through two more pairs which have been hung in order on a pin placed temporarily at z. Put up the pin at t, and weave back through these pairs and through the trail pairs. Remove pin z, and ease the pairs down. Continue the trail using the three passive pairs as far as v.

The footside   Work to w and join in the plait from q. The pair that should work back to the footside is left hanging ready for use later. The plait will be worked to the half stitch circle and back to the footside.

The half stitch circle   Begin using the plait from s as centre plait, and put up pin z. Work the circle making a 'kiss' between u and v. At y the plait from w is worked in and immediately released for return to w. Complete the circle.

The corner footside   The pin at w is removed, the pair hanging joins the plait to the footside, and the pin is replaced. The weaver works a normal footside but uses the corner pin a second time.

CROSSING TRAILS AND LEAF PATTERN

In this pattern the method for crossing trails is practised, and a different arrangement of passive threads in the footside is introduced. In Bedfordshire lace the footside is worked at the discretion of the worker, but thought must be given to achieve a balance of cloth, half stitch, plaits and leaves.

Prepare pricking **14** and **22** pairs of bobbins. See diagram **50** and photograph **24**. Hang two pairs on A1, three pairs in order on B, two pairs in order on C and two pairs on D. Hang one pair on E, and three pairs in

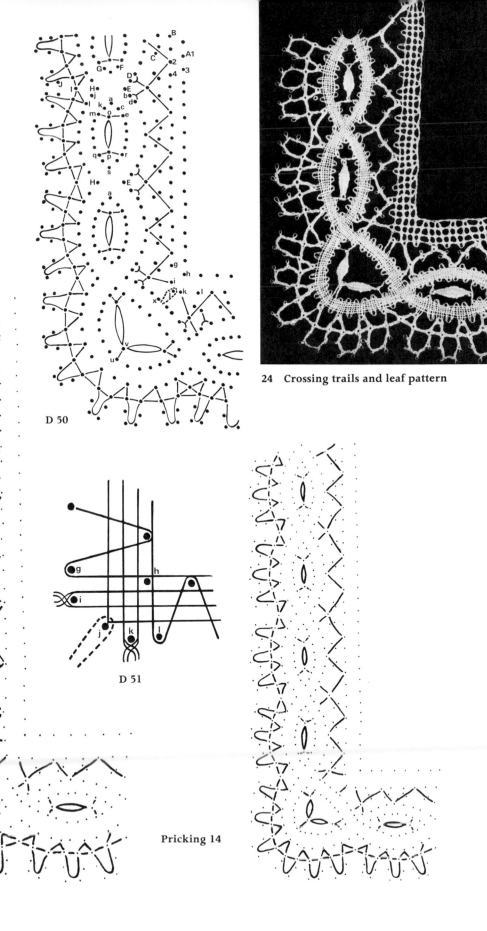

D 50

24 Crossing trails and leaf pattern

D 51

Pricking 14

order on F from right to left. Hang four pairs in order on G from left to right, and one pair on H. Hang two pairs in order on I, and two pairs on J.

To work the footside with twisted pairs   Twist the right hand pair three times, and cover pin A1 with cloth stitch and twist. Give the right hand pair an extra twist, and discard to the right. Take the other pair as weaver, and work cloth stitch and twist through the next three pairs hanging from B. These pairs will remain as twisted passive pairs. Weave through the two pairs hanging from C in cloth stitch. Twist the weaver twice and put up pin 2. Weave back to the right in cloth stitch through the two pairs, which are then left out for a plait. Continue weaving through four pairs to the right in cloth stitch and twist. Put up pin 3 inside two pairs, twist the outer pair once more, and discard to the right. Take the inner pair back through three passive pairs in cloth stitch and twist. Twist the weaver twice and put up pin 4. Continue the footside using this arrangement of pairs. Remove pins at B and C.

Plaits   Plait with picots the pairs from 2, remembering to make a half stitch in the plait between the picots. Using these pairs and pairs from D, make a four plait crossing, and then remove the pin at D. Make plaits, and work the footside to link in the plait on that side.

The trails   Using the pair at E as weaver, work cloth stitch to the left through the three pairs hanging at F. Using the pair at H as weaver, work cloth stitch to the right through four pairs hanging at G. The weavers are side by side; cloth stitch them together, put up pin a, and cover with another stitch. These pairs work out, one each way, as weavers for the cloth trails.

On the right side weave through the three trail pairs, and on through one more pair, i.e. half the plait. Put up pin b and weave back through four pairs, and put up pin c. Take care not to take in the weaver for the left hand side. Continue with this trail and bring in the other half of the plait at pin d. After pin e leave out the edge passive pair which will become part of the leaf.

On the left side take the weaver hanging from pin a, cloth stitch through the four pairs, and put up a pin at j. Continue weaving but before putting up pin 1 work through the two pairs hanging from I. After pin m leave out the edge passive pair to become the other half of the leaf. Remove support pins F, G and I.

The ninepin   Plait the pairs hanging from l and make a four plait crossing with the pairs hanging from J. Remove pin J.

The leaf   Using pairs from m and e, twist each pair twice, and work together in half stitch. Put up pin o, and cover with cloth stitch to begin the leaf. Complete the leaf to pin p, and cover with a half stitch. Twist pairs once more.

The crossing of trails   Continue each trail, linking in the plaits where necessary, and weaving in the pairs from the leaf at q and r. Cloth stitch the weavers together, and put up pin s. Cover the pin with cloth stitch, weave each back to pinholes H and E, and put up the pins. There are four passive trail pairs on the left, to the right of pin H, and three passive trail pairs on the right, to the left of pin E. When the crossing is completed the same arrangement of pairs must exist for the next pattern repeat. Therefore three pairs from the left side must be transferred to the right side, and all three right hand pairs must go to the left. The left hand pair next to pin H remains unused in that position, and is ignored during the crossing. The three pairs on the left are passed through the three pairs on the right in exactly the same way that the first half of the Torchon spider is worked. This is as follows:

Spread out the six pairs so that they can be easily counted. Take the third pair, and in cloth stitch work towards the right through the remaining three pairs. Still working towards the right, take the second pair through three pairs, and finally the first pair through three pairs. The work must lie flat – the three pairs have passed through in order. One pattern is now complete.

Take the weaver to the left of pin H, and work through four pairs – one pair that remained on that side and three that have crossed over. On the other side, the weaver to the right of pin E works to the left through three pairs that have crossed over. Cloth stitch the weavers together, and put up pin a and cover.

The corner   Trails can be seen in the photograph, and the working is straightforward. At u, the weaver is twisted five times, then worked through the leaf pairs, and a pin put up at v. The weaver works back through the leaf pairs, it is twisted five times, and worked back across the trail.

The footside   Study the photograph and diagram **51** in which each pair is indicated by a single line. Cloth stitch and twist is used throughout. The lettering is the same as in diagram **50**.

Work as far as pin h, and put the pin as usual inside two pairs. Leave the threads in this position – do not cover the pin. Plait to pin i and put up the pin in the centre of the plait. Take the right hand pair of the plait and work through the next three pairs of the footside. Take the left hand pair of the plait, and work through the same three passive pairs. The weaver from the inner trail at x is twisted three times and works through the next pair to the right (i.e. the left hand passive pair). Pin j is put up, covered and the weaver returns to the trail. The pair hanging at pin j remains to the left of the three passive pairs after the corner has been turned. Work it through the next two pairs to the right. The three new passive pairs are now complete, one hanging from j and two from i. Before turning the pillow take the two remaining passive pairs on this side and put up pin k between them. Plait ready for use after the corner has been turned.

Turn the pillow. Take the second pair from the right which is the footside weaver at h and work through these three pairs to the left in cloth stitch and twist. Put up pin l and continue.

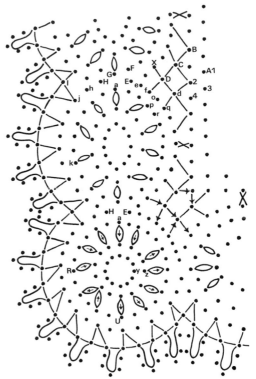

Pricking 15

D 52

OPEN CENTRED FLOWERED PATTERN

In this pattern one method of making a complete cloth ring is given. Also, a neat way of passing plait pairs straight through a trail to form another plait or leaf is shown. Refer to diagram **52** and photograph **25a**.

Prepare pricking **15** and 29 pairs of bobbins. Four pairs extra will be required for the corner. Hang two pairs on A1, four pairs in order on B, and two pairs in order on C. Hang two pairs on D, and one pair on E. Hang three pairs in order on F, and ten pairs in order on G. Hang one pair on H, and two pairs on I. Later, two pairs will be hung on X.

25a   Open Centred Flowered pattern

To work the footside   Twist the right hand two bobbins three times, and cover the pin with cloth stitch and two twists. Use the left hand pair, work cloth stitch through the next two pairs, twist the weaver once, and weave in cloth stitch through the other two pairs from B. These will remain as four passive pairs with a centre twist throughout the pattern. Continue to weave through the pairs from C in cloth stitch, twist the weaver twice and put up pin 2. Weave back to the right through the pairs from C – these will become a plait, and then work the footside and pin 3. Remove pins B and C.

Plaits   Plait pairs from 2, and make a four plait crossing with the pairs from D at pin d. Remove pin D, and plait both ways ready for use.

The pattern consists of trails which cross creating the effect of circles and leaves about an open ring. Each part will be considered separately.

The trail   The weaver from E works to the left through the three pairs from F in cloth stitch, and the weaver from H works to the right through the ten pairs from G in cloth stitch. Work the weavers together in cloth stitch, put up pin a, cover with cloth stitch, and work each weaver back to its own side putting in pins at h and e.

The number of pairs in each trail can be explained as follows: on the left – one pair for the centre leaf, four pairs for the two leaves entering the ring, three pairs to remain in the trail and two pairs to begin the ninepin edge. Normally there will be eight pairs on the left for the crossing, the ninepin pairs are only introduced here for convenience at the beginning of a new pattern. On the right – one pair for the centre leaf and two pairs for the trail.

The left hand trail   Take the weaver which is to the left of pin h, and work the trail, leaving out one pair immediately after pin a for the centre leaf and two pairs after j for the ninepin. Two pairs must be left out for each leaf, and the trail may be worked as far as k. In this trail pairs are left out in the same way as in the Bedfordshire spider pattern.

The right hand trail   Take the weaver which is round pin e, and work the trail, leaving out one pair after pin a for the centre leaf. Hang two pairs in order on pin X, and work them into the trail at f. These become part of the trail. It can be seen that a plait comes into the trail at q, and a leaf leaves the trail at p. This can be worked simply by bringing in and dropping out pairs as previously described, but there is a neater, less bulky way when the arrangement is such that the pairs are left out on the pin immediately before the others are brought in.

Working plaits through trails   Refer to diagram 53. The letters correspond with those on diagram 52. Each line represents one thread. The weaver round pin o works through the passive trail pairs to pin p, and is left hanging here where it will become part of the leaf and lose its weaving function. A plait is worked to q, and pin q put up in position in the centre of the plait. Take the left hand pair of the plait, work it through the passive trail pairs, and leave it hanging. There is a pair on either side of

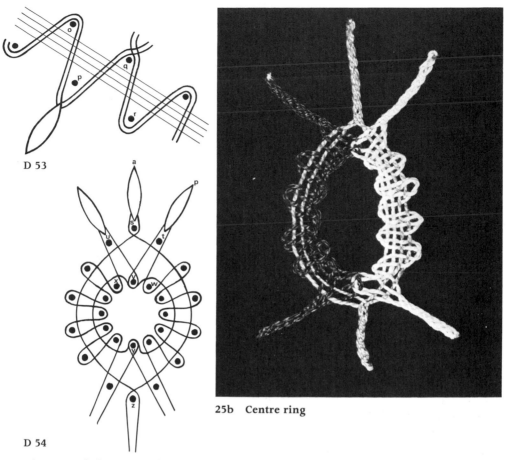

D 53

D 54

25b   Centre ring

pin p and these work the leaf. The other half of the plait to the right of pin q becomes the new weaver, and works to pin r, and so on. Note that the weaver has changed, but the passives run uninterrupted. The same method is used to make the next leaf, and bring in the plait. The trail is worked as far as the 'kiss'.

The ring   In preparation, work the five leaves. Refer to diagram **54** and photograph **25b**. Pin s is put in the middle of the leaf from a, and covered with a cloth stitch. The pairs become passives on the outer edge of the ring, one pair travelling in each direction. The leaf from p has pin t put up in the middle, but it is not covered. Similarly, the leaf from the other side has pin u put up, but not covered. The pair to the right of pin u works one cloth stitch to the right through the pair hanging from s. The pair to the left of pin t works similarly to the left through one pair hanging from s. These pairs are worked together in cloth stitch. Pin v is put up and covered with another cloth stitch. These pairs form the inner passives in the ring, one travelling in each direction.

The left hand pair at u becomes a weaver working through the two passive pairs to x. It continues round the ring weaving to and fro in cloth stitch. The right hand pair from t becomes a weaver working to w, and so on. Note that leaves enter and leave the ring in the normal manner, the pairs becoming very temporarily part of the cloth ring.

To complete the ring, weave to the last pin holes on the outer edge on each side, put up pins and leave the weavers hanging. Take the inner passive pairs from each side, work them together as a cloth stitch, and put up pin y and cover with cloth stitch. Work the right hand pair to the right through the outer passive pair, and it falls alongside the pin and weaver to work the leaf. Take the left hand pair from y, and work out through the passive pair on that side to make a leaf. The outer passives are worked together, pin z is put up, covered, and these pairs make the centre leaf.

The trail   To continue the trail, the leaves must be worked, and the left hand trail can be worked as far as the bottom centre pin. On the right side the weaver will be left hanging at the pin where the plait is indicated. A pin is put up in the centre of the leaf where it enters the plait, the right hand pair passes straight through to become the other half of the plait, and the left hand pair becomes the new weaver. At the bottom centre, pin the weaver from each trail, working to the centre, each passing through one leaf pair. They work together in cloth stitch, a pin is put up, covered, and the weavers worked back to H and E.

The crossing of trails   There are three pairs in the right hand trail, and eight pairs in the left hand trail. Put the five left hand pairs of the left trail to the side, and cross the other pairs through each other. Take the weaver at H through eight pairs, and the weaver at E through three pairs. Work them together in cloth stitch, put up pin a, and cover.

The corner   Follow the directional arrows on the leaves in the diagram and note the following points:

1   Three leaves are brought in as usual to begin the ring.

2   The right hand trail is short, and the left hand trail works the complete curve of the corner. Extra pairs are joined in for leaves at R and knotted out after U.

3   The ring will be completed at y and z.

4   The left side of the ring becomes very thick with passive pairs from the extra leaves but these are taken out after the half-way mark.

5   The corner footside requires a neat arrangement of threads, and an extra pin-hole c should be made, see diagram 55. The footside is worked

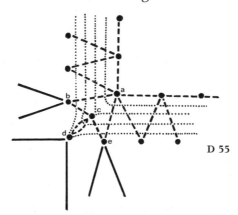

D 55

normally from corner pin a to b, where a plait is linked in. The weaver works back through two pairs only, is twisted once, and works a cloth stitch with the next passive pair. Pin c is put up and covered. The left pair works back to pin d where another plait is linked in. Work back through the two passive pairs to pin c, remove this pin and work the weaver and the pair at the pin with cloth stitch, replace the pin, and cover it. Turn the pillow for the next side. Take the left hand pair from pin c out to the left to e, where another plait is linked in. Work across to pin a, through all four passive pairs with a centre twist, remove pin a, work the normal footside and use the pin-hole a second time.

DIAMOND AND DAISY PATTERN

An attractive feature of this pattern is the scallop edging which is far easier to launder than ninepin – see photograph **26a**. Other new techniques include the leaf lying over half stitch, and a different footside – sometimes known as kat stitch foot, as the arrangement of threads is similar to that used in kat stitch in Bucks Point.

Practising the kat stitch foot   Before attempting the pattern it is advisable to take four pairs of bobbins and practise this footside. The two lines of holes on the pricking for the Diamond and Daisy pattern may be used.

26a Diamond and daisy pattern

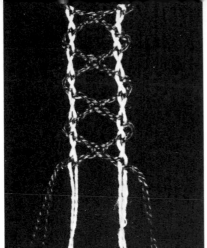
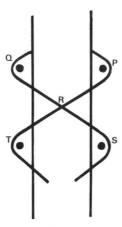

26b   Kat stitch foot   D 56

Refer to diagram **56** and photograph **26b**, and put two pairs of bobbins on each of pins at P and Q. Twist the outer threads, and work cloth stitch and twist to cover each pin. In some way mark the outer pairs – four rubber bands, one twisted around the shank of each bobbin will identify them temporarily. These are the passive pairs, and remain straight throughout. The inner two pairs are the weavers, and they are worked together in cloth stitch and twist at R, *no* pin is put in, and the weavers only cross through each other.

   The left hand weaver works through the next pair to the left, pin T is put up, the weaver is twisted once more, and the pin is covered with cloth and twist. The right hand weaver works to the right, through the passive pair to the right of it, pin S is put up, the weaver is given one extra twist, and the pin covered with cloth and twist. The weavers now hang side by side in the middle again, ready to repeat the sequence of stitches and pins. This will begin with the cloth stitch and twist at R, which crosses the weavers without a pin.

   When this arrangement is used in a pattern, the right hand side outside edge is worked as described above, but the left hand side is joined into the lace. The join is made by taking the weaver immediately after it has worked through the passive pair, and continuing on through any pairs to be linked in. The pin is put up, the weaver brought back through the pairs joined in, and then through the passive pair to the normal position for crossing the weavers. There is not necessarily a link at every pin.

The pattern   Prepare pricking **16** and 18 pairs of bobbins. Two pairs extra will be required for the corner. Refer to diagram **57**. Hang two pairs on A, and two pairs in order on B to I inclusive.

The half stitch diamond and raised leaf   It is usual to work the leaf underneath the half stitch so that the wrong side of the lace is facing the worker. Take the left hand pair from E and the right hand pair from F, and make a half stitch. Put up pin 1 and cover with a half stitch. The right hand pair becomes the weaver. Remember that in reality only one thread travels across the work, but the pair is known as the weaver pair, and the pin at

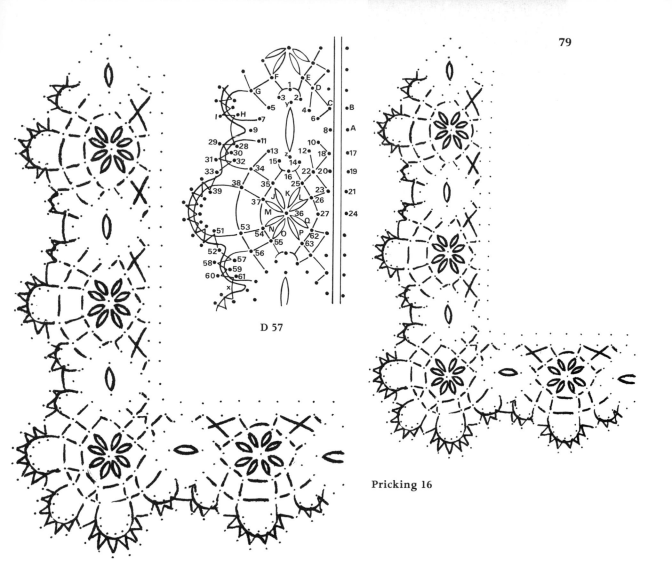

D 57

Pricking 16

the end of a row will still go inside two threads. Weave in half stitch through one pair to the right (the other pair from E), and put up pin 2. Weave back to the left, bringing in the other pair from F, and put up pin 3. Hold the weaver firmly, and remove support pins E and F.

Continue weaving, and bring in both pairs from D at pin 4, and both pairs from G at pin 5. Find the two centre pairs in the half stitch diamond, put up pin y between them, cover with a cloth stitch, and make a leaf as far as z. Place a cloth across these threads and bobbins and ignore them. The cloth will enable the worker to work over them fairly easily.

Take the pair either side of the pin at y, and work one half stitch. This keeps the half stitch patch close and neat under the leaf. Find the weaver at pin 5, and continue to weave bringing in two pairs from C at 6, H at 7, B at 8, and I at 9. Continue, leaving out two pairs after pins 8, 9, 10 and 11. At pin 12 stop weaving in order to put the leaf threads back into position in the centre of the half stitch.

From pin 12 weave to the left through three pairs of half stitch, through the two leaf pairs, and through two pairs of half stitch. Put up pin 13, and complete the diamond, leaving out two pairs after pins 12 and 13, and one pair after pins 14 and 15. There are two pairs at pin 16 which must be covered with half stitch. As pattern repeats are worked, only one pair enters and leaves at pins 8 and 9, but at the beginning of a strip of lace it is convenient to join in pairs in this manner.

The footside   Work the two pairs at pin A, and the two pairs hanging from pin 8 in cloth stitch and twist. Of these four pairs, the middle pairs are weavers and the outside pairs are the passive pairs. The weavers cross in cloth stitch and twist (equivalent to R on the practice strip). The right hand pairs work pin 17, and the left hand weaver passes through the passive pair and through the plait from pin 10. Put up pin 18, and take the weaver back to the right through the plait pairs and through the passive pair. Work pins 19, 20 and 21. Pairs are plaited from 18 and 12, and a crossing made at 22. Work pin 23.

Plaits   Plaits from pins 10 and 12 have already been used. Plait the pairs from 14/16 and 15/16 together, also the pairs from 13. Work four plait crossings at 25 and 26, and plait the right hand pairs from 26 to be linked in with the footside weaver at 27.

The heading   Two pairs hanging from pin 9 become weaver and outside passive pair for the scallop, and retain these functions throughout the pattern. The passive pair is twisted and forms the edge curve. It enters and leaves the point of the diamond at pin 9. The weaver does not enter the diamond.

The scallop   This is worked as follows: * Use the outside left hand pair as weaver, and work to the right, through the passive in cloth stitch and twist, through the next two pairs in cloth stitch, put up pin 28, and twist the weaver twice. Work to the left through two pairs in cloth stitch, twist the weaver once, and work cloth stitch and twist with the outside pair. Put up pin 29, and twist the weaver once more **.

Work from * to ** pins 30 and 31. Work from * to ** pins 32 and 33.
Plait the four threads hanging from the cloth at pin 32 and make a crossing at 34 with the plait from 13. At 35 make a crossing with plaits from 34 and 15/16.

The flower centre   Makes leaves J, K and L from 35, 25 and 26. Work a six plait crossing into pin 36. The left hand pairs are used to make leaf M but the other four pairs must *not* be used at this stage. Leaf M and plait from 35 make a crossing at 37. The left hand plait from 37 and the plait from 34 cross at 38. Plait the left hand pairs as far as 39, but do not put up a pin.

The scallop weaver is on the far left, and works as in the previous scallop, using the twisted pair at 33 and the pairs from the plait as passives. Work * to ** as far as 52. The pairs from 51 are plaited to make a crossing at 53 with the plait from 38. Plaits from 37 and 53 make a crossing at 54. The right hand pairs at 54 make leaf N back towards the flower centre.

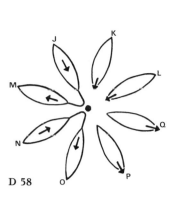

D 58

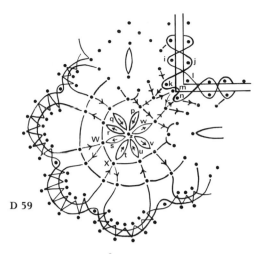

D 59

Remove pin 36. The two leaf pairs and the four pairs left hanging at 36 make a six plait crossing as tightly as possible, and pin 36 is returned to position at the appropriate stage of the crossing working. Work three leaves O, P and Q out from the crossing.

Refer to diagram **58** for a summary of the flower centre working. Make leaves J, K and L, and a six plait crossing. Take the left hand pairs to make leaf M which is used in the scallop, and returns as leaf N. Remove the pin, and repeat the six plait crossing using leaf N and the four hanging pairs. Make leaves O, P and Q.

The left hand leaf and the plait from 54 cross at 55, and plaits from 53 and 55 cross at 56. At 52 the left hand pair is weaver and the third scallop can be worked in the same manner as the others. Note that the weaver returns to the outside edge at the end of the scallop at x, but there is no pin. The plait from 27 and the right hand leaf Q cross at 62, and a plait from 62 and the middle leaf P cross at 63.

The corner   Refer to diagram **59**, and note the following points:

1   On the footside the weavers from j and i cross normally. Pin k is worked linking in the plait, and the weaver returns through its passive pair. Pin 1 is worked, and both pairs remain at the corner until the pillow has been turned. The inner corner pin m is worked using the left hand *passive* to link in the plait, work the plait out from the corner, and leave the passive hanging freely again to the right of the plait. Pin n cannot be worked until the corner is complete. When leaf w has been worked, and the plait worked to n, take the weaver from k – this should hang as third pair from the outside edge. Work to the left through the passive in cloth stitch and twist, link in the plait at pin n, and take the weaver back through plait and passive to cross with the weaver from the corner at l.

2   The flower requires the addition of two pairs extra. Work leaves p and q, use these pairs together with two pairs extra supported on a pin to the left of the centre, and work a six plait crossing. Remove the support pin, and ease the newly introduced pairs to the centre. Leave the right hand two pairs hanging, and make leaves r and s. Take leaf r

out and into the scallop, and back to W, where a six plait crossing is made using these plaited pairs, the centre plait and leaf s. Take the left hand pairs, plait them into the scallop, and back to X. Use the other four pairs to make a thick plait to X, and then make a six plait crossing using the same pairs as at W. The left hand pairs make another scallop, and the right hand pairs make leaf t. When the scallop is complete, make leaf u. To complete the centre there are six pairs available, two from u, two from t, and two hanging in the middle at Z. Remove pin Z, and make the crossing replacing the pin at the correct stage in the working. Turn the pillow. Use the left hand pairs to make leaf v and the right hand pairs to make leaf w. The two centre pairs are knotted together and discarded.

27   Butterfly edging

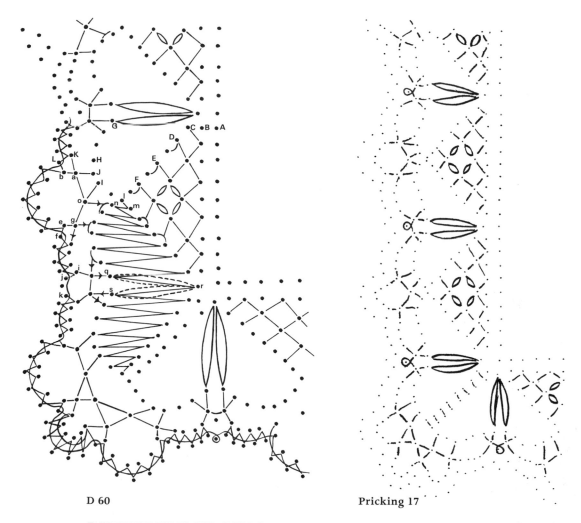

D 60   Pricking 17

BUTTERFLY EDGING

The leaves which make the body of the butterfly are worked underneath the half stitch. Photograph **27** shows the right side of the lace, but a flat edged mirror held vertically to one side of the lace will show the pattern reversed and correspond with the working diagram **60**.

Prepare pricking **17** and 24 pairs of bobbins. Also required is one gimp thread pair to outline the shape. Hang two pairs on each of A and B, and two pairs in order on C, D, E and F. Hang four pairs in order on G, one gimp pair on H, and two pairs on I, J, K and L.

The footside   Work as in the previous pattern as far as the base of the butterfly body. The two pairs from C are linked to the footside, and then plaited across the lace. The plait works crossing with pairs from D, E and F. Remove pins at D, E and F. Work leaves and plaits for the footside, and in readiness for the working of the half stitch. Pairs at K and J work a crossing at a. Remove pins K and J, and plait to b and o. At o, a crossing is made using pairs from I and the plait.

The scallop heading   Cover pin L with cloth stitch and twist, and, using the right hand pair as weaver, work through the two plait pairs in cloth stitch. Put up pin b. Complete this scallop to pin f. The pairs at e will plait to make a crossing at g with the plait from o. The next scallop can be completed, use the plait pairs from g for the cloth stitch, and work to j. The pairs from i are plaited to a crossing with the pairs from the half stitch.

The half stitch   Put the right hand gimp through the pairs hanging at G, and then through the pairs of the four plaits waiting to come into the half stitch on that side. Twist each pair twice after the gimp. Take the left hand gimp thread through the pairs of the plaits from o and g, and twist the pairs twice to enclose the gimp. Take the centre pairs from G, and make a half stitch. Put up pin l, and cover with half stitch. Using the right pair work through the next pair to the right which also hangs from G, put up pin m and weave back through the three pairs in half stitch, through the other pair from G, and through half the plait from o. Put up pin n, and continue the half stitch bringing in pairs and plaits as indicated, work to q.

At q, work the weaver through one pair of the plait only, using cloth stitch and twist, put up pin q, and cover. Work these four threads as a leaf to extend as far as r. As the leaf lies under the half stitch it is advisable to cover the threads and bobbins with a cloth to facilitate the weaving across over the threads. Take the other half of the plait which hangs to the left of q as weaver, and weave to r. The footside weaver works through the leaf pairs in cloth stitch, and then works with the weaver in the half stitch. Pin r is put up, and covered in half stitch.

The new footside weaver works back through the leaf pairs, and through the passive pair. The other weaver and the pair to the right of it work a leaf back to s. Cover until the half stitch has been worked from r to s. Use the pair to the right of pin r (i.e. the remaining leaf pair from the first leaf) as weaver, work across through the half stitch pairs, and then through the leaf pairs. Put up pin s to the right of all three pairs. The two left hand pairs are twisted, the gimp passed through, and then they are plaited out. The third pair, immediately to the left of the pin becomes the new weaver, and weaves back. When the half stitch wing is complete, it is enclosed with the gimp which crosses at the bottom of the half stitch before the next pattern repeat.

SUNFLOWER PATTERN

At first sight this may appear complicated – see photograph **28a** – but there is nothing new in it. More pairs are required, but the pattern is regular and uses those techniques already practised in previous patterns. A good understanding of the basic principles of Bedfordshire lace, an aptitude to make lace using a photograph or the actual lace, and willingness to experiment will lead to success. Working diagram **61** is given together with a pattern analysis to assist the worker. Prepare pricking **18**

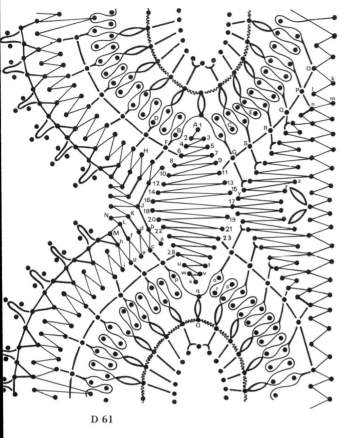

D 61

28a   Sunflower pattern

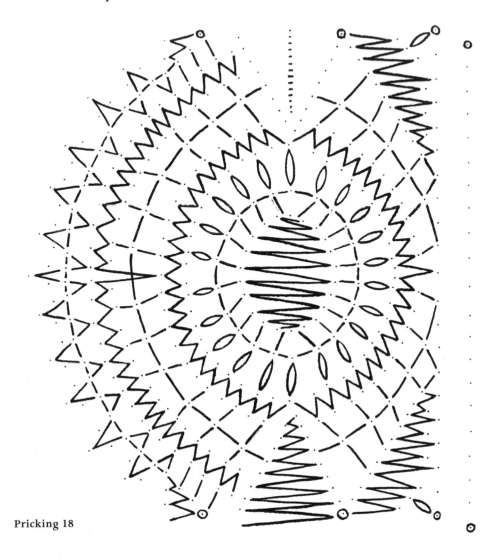

Pricking 18

and pairs of bobbins. It is unnecessary to count the exact number of pairs as they will be used as required to set in the pattern.

Analysis   The diamond is a very definite part of the design, and a sensible place to begin. It is worked in cloth stitch with a twist on the weaver. Concentrate on getting the correct number of pairs on the support pins and into the diamond. Hang two pairs on A1, and cover with cloth stitch. One of these will become the weaver. Remember that pairs are hung on pins *in order* in readiness for bringing in as separate pairs. The position of the support pins is at the discretion of the worker, and suggestions are given here to facilitate explanation.

Hang two pairs at B to bring in at 2, two pairs at C to bring in at 3, one pair at D to bring in at 4, one pair at E to bring in at 5. No pairs are brought in at 7, 8 or 9. Hang two pairs on each of F and G for use at 8 and 11.

On the left side of the diamond, pairs come in from the trail as follows: hang up nine pairs at H, and bring in three pairs at 10, 12 and 14. At 17, the weaver will link with the weaver from the half stitch triangle, and the diamond cannot be completed until the triangle is worked to this point. From this position the diamond is gradually reduced to two pairs about pin x. Use photograph **28b** as a guide.

The heading This is started after the small cloth triangle as it is easy to see how the pairs are joined into the trail. Nine pairs should hang from pins 18, 20 and 22. Take the left hand pair as weaver, and work in cloth

28b Sunflower pattern enlarged

stitch through the eight pairs to pin a, then work back. Four plaits join the trail from the small triangle at the next four pins on that side. Hang up two pairs on each of J, K, L and M, and bring them in at b, d, f and h. Remember to leave out two pairs for plaits after c, g and h, and so on. The plait from h begins the ninepin, and works a crossing with two pairs hung up at N. Refer to the working of the half stitch triangles in the Torchon sampler on page 43 and diagram 31.

The footside   This is unusual in that the footside pin has been placed inside one pin only at the edge; the worker may introduce an extra pair and work the normal footside if preferred. Hang two pairs of bobbins round pin k, and cover with cloth stitch and twist. The right hand pair is the outside passive pair, and the other pair is weaver. Three more passive pairs are required, and should be hung on a pin at O. Weave through the next two pairs in cloth stitch, twist the weaver once, and weave through the last pair in cloth stitch and twist. Put up pin l, and work on to pins m and n where a plait is linked in using pairs from P. Weave back to the footside.

The half stitch triangle is made using a plait from n, and four plaits coming in on the left. Hang pairs for these plaits on Q, R, S and G, two pairs on each pin. On the left of the triangle the plaits are split so that one pair is brought in at each pin. This makes a neater edge. Begin the triangle with the pairs from n, put up the pin and cover, then take the right hand pair as weaver, and immediately work it with the footside weaver in cloth and twist. Put up the pin and continue to weave. On the left pairs are brought in at all pins other than y. On the right side the weavers cross at alternate holes, and, at the holes marked z, pairs are left out for a leaf. These pairs return to the triangle later.

The centre   This should be tackled methodically, and reference made to the open centred flower pattern on page 74. Work the trail which is marked a, b, c as far as the centre. Work the plait from 28 and cross the plaits from the trail so that they come into the divided ring. Work a plait from 23, and cross the plaits from the half stitch triangle through it so that they are available for the divided trail. At the bottom of the diamond, single pairs from u and t, two pairs each from v and w, and single pairs from x form the passives for the ring. The working is the same as for the footside in this pattern, with twisted pairs either side of cloth. Pins o and p are placed in the centre of the plaits on either side, the pairs nearer the centre work through the passive pairs, meet with cloth stitch and twist at pin q, and make a leaf to Q. The other pairs become weavers on either side of the ring. Plaits are worked through, and pairs for leaves left out as far as the half-way mark. Work the five leaves on each side. The pairs at Q are well twisted, and work each way through the leaves in cloth stitch. Pins support these stitches. The plaits work the circle in half stitch, and the pairs left out are plaited, worked through the twisted pair, and through the divided ring.

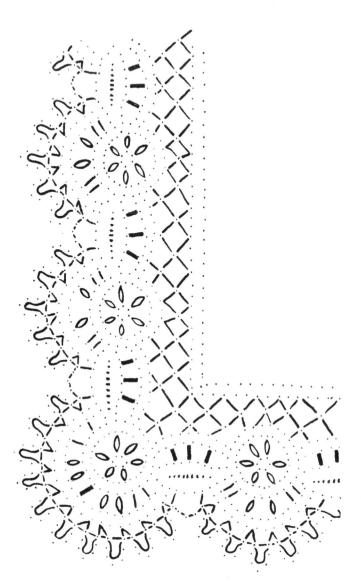

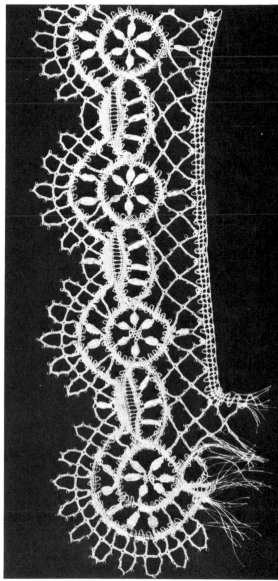

Pricking 19   29 Old Bedfordshire pattern

In order to work this pattern, frequent reference must be made to the photograph. Other patterns may be analysed similarly. It is essential to add pairs as required, rather than to adopt a prefixed idea of the number to be worked in. Regular patterns are fairly easy, but some of the old patterns may have slightly different positioning of the holes in each repeat. The finished result will look even but the working is more difficult, and the worker will require initiative to use the pairs to best advantage. Photograph **29** and pricking **19** will be an excellent exercise for those workers who wish to attempt to make a lace from an old pattern.

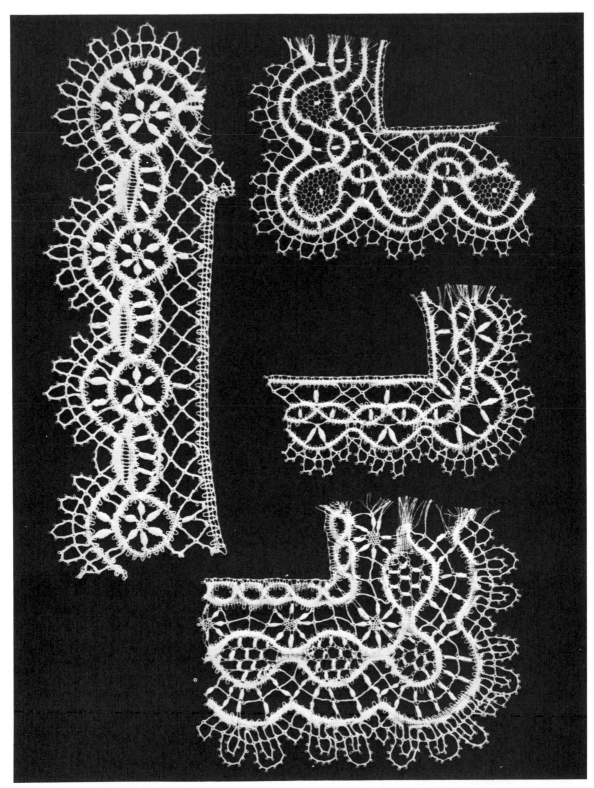

30   Old Bedfordshire patterns

OLD BEDFORDSHIRE PATTERNS

All patterns worked so far with the exception of photograph **29** are accurate. There are the correct number of holes to weave regular trails, cloth or half stitch solid blocks, and an even footside. Each repeat is identical with the previous one. Old patterns may have been misused and extra holes made, or with years of use the holes may be enlarged and out of line. Where attention has been given to design, the holes may have been put in position to create the curve required rather than with thought to the way of working. Slight variation in the design is acceptable as it adds to the charm of the hand created article. It is not good to attempt to 'true' every pattern, but it is necessary to improve upon those that are badly out of line.

To 'true' an old pattern   Take a rubbing of the pattern, choose a repeat pattern that looks to be accurate, and draw two lines across the strip to isolate it. Using the holes as a guide, draw in the curves accurately and any other important pattern features. Draw a series of curves on the heading in order to space the ninepin, and lightly draw in the position of the plaits. Mark in other plaits and leaves. Use another colour to mark in the weavers in the trails, footside and cloth or half stitch. The pin-hole on one side of a trail, block, or footside should fall actually on the repeat line, as this facilitates the making of a series of repeats into a strip for working. Care must be taken to ensure that the plaits and leaves enter and leave the trails regularly, and that the direction of these is acceptable. The holes on the footside should be equidistant.

Place this adjusted rubbing over three sheets of paper, and prick in the holes from the weaver lines. Prick in the other features and the crossings. Other than ninepin do not prick in holes for picots as these can be added later by 'eye'.

Cut along the repeat lines of two of the prickings, and place them carefully in position, one on either side of the third. Mark in plaits, leaves and weavers on the complete strip. If satisfactory, fasten them firmly together, and make a pricking on card.

An alternative method of adjusting a pattern is to measure it up, select a suitable graph paper and work a repeat out accurately. The fine grid helps to achieve even curves and an even footside. Sometimes a short length of the pattern may be better than the rest and repeats of this can be used.

To 'read' a pattern   Frequently workers are concerned that they cannot picture the finished lace from a pricking. It is important to study each pricking with its photograph and finished lace to achieve some understanding. The following points will help to interpret the ink markings on prickings:

1   Plaits are marked with straight lines, usually there are picot holes to the side. Occasionally the picot hole is surrounded by a small ring to indicate on which side the picot falls.

2   The leaf shape denotes the leaf.

3   A short single line between the trail and the footside, or between two trails indicates that the weavers meet and cross. The usual form of crossing of weavers is a 'kiss'. A slightly thicker line indicates that the weavers make a tally. This is frequently found in the heading – leaves are worked in to the centre, back out again, and when the number is uneven a tally is worked at the centre. An example of this is on page 96.

4   A small cross in the middle of a block indicates that it is worked in half stitch. Trails are marked with an occasional cross when the working is in half stitch.

5   A circle about a hole in the centre of a block or floral shape denotes a raised tally. This can be seen in the Torchon sampler on page 43.

6   A thick line around any shape indicates the presence of a gimp thread. Half stitch benefits from being enclosed with a gimp, as alone it has untidy edges.

7   Thick lines are sometimes drawn through a trail in order to indicate its position and importance.

8   Patterns with point fillings may have additional markings, but these can be found in the chapter on Bucks Point lace.

PATTERN INTERPRETATION

With use and age the ink markings on a pattern may become faint and indiscernible, and the worker has to decide on the design and its execution. Pricking 20 may be used to illustrate this point. Make the pricking and study it before marking it in.

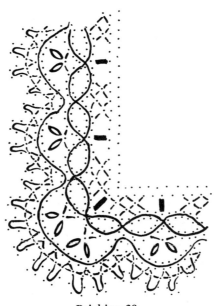

Pricking 20

Take a rubbing and use this to work on. Study the reverse side of the pricking as it is usually easier to recognize the prominent features from here.

1   Mark with a continuous line any obvious trail. Do not continue where parallel rows of holes are not clearly visible.
2   Are there any circles or regular shapes? The ovals with double rows of holes around them indicate crossing trails. Mark these with continuous lines.
3   The footside is obvious, and the holes between the footside and the rest of the design must be for plait crossings.
4   Plaits, in most patterns, touch the footside, and return to the design, but in this pattern may distract the eye from the trails. Also there is a large area without crossing holes. A suggested arrangement is shown. The plait pairs become part of the footside and are carried there until required as plaits again. This added weight will compensate for the large space, and the weaver at the footside and the weaver at the trail crossing will work a tally.
5   The oval spaces in the centre of the crossing trails are large and ugly, and a tally is worked using the weavers from each side.
6   The ninepin is clear and straightforward.
7   The arrangement and number of holes at the meeting of the three trails is confusing, and time is well spent elucidating the purpose of each hole. The whole design depends on the line and strength of each trail. The large working diagram **62** clarifies the method used. In each head there are three pin-holes common to both trails, and at these the weavers meet. To keep the headside trail independent of the others, the headside weaver is twisted before the weavers are worked together in cloth stitch and twist. The pins are covered and the weavers return to their own trails.
8   The position of pin-hole d indicates the need for two large leaves linked to the inner trails with plaits.

When all the features and their possible interpretations have been considered, a pricking can be made. If any minor hole alteration is needed it will be necessary to follow the procedure for 'true-ing' a pattern and a new copy made. When a pattern is unknown and adapted according to the worker's ideas, it is usual to work a sample piece in order to find any pitfalls, assess the ease of working, the attractiveness of the design, and to find out the thickness of thread required. It is important to work three repeats to achieve a satisfactory impression.
The pattern   Prepare pricking **20** and carefully add the ink markings. It is worthwhile to spend some time marking a pricking satisfactorily as the markings are the only guide lines to success. Refer to diagram **62**, although this can only serve as a general guide as the number and position of holes will vary from repeat to repeat. If necessary, a hole in the trail may be

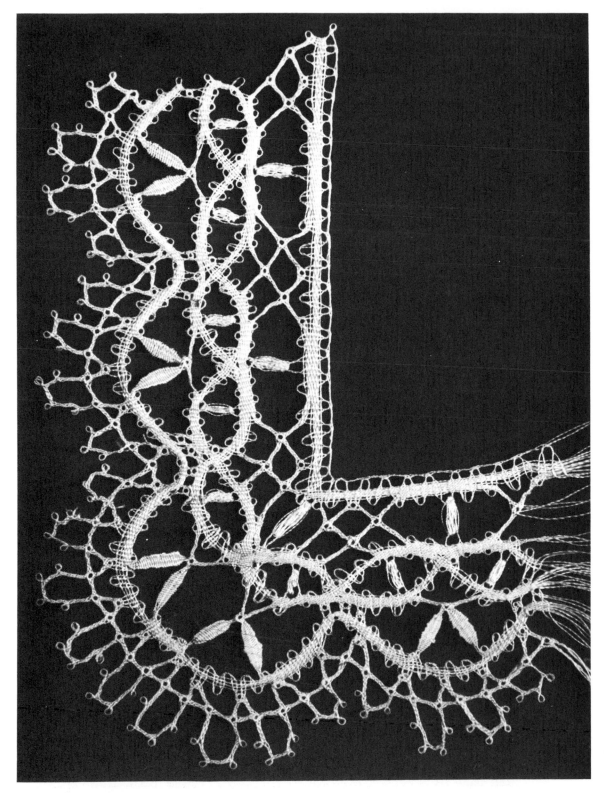

31   Oval trails

used twice for even working. Photograph **31** should be studied closely. The weavers are marked in on the working diagram to simplify the working, and the method of starting can be seen from the photograph.

Crossing of trails at A   The weavers are left at a and b. The tally is worked with the weaver from b and the footside weaver. When a sufficient length of tally has been made, allow the thread that has woven to and fro to be to the left of the other three threads. Twist this thread with the left of the three, and twist the right and centre threads together. Work the footside at once so that the tally is locked into position. Only then is it safe to weave into the trail using the thread which had formed the tally. In the actual crossing only two pairs are woven from right to left for the trail, and the

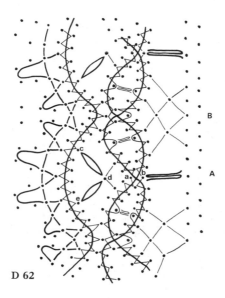

D 62

other pairs are retained on the right hand side to be included in the right hand trail so that they are available for the plaits to the footside later.

Crossing of trails at B   The crossing of trails and linking in with the head-side trail must be considered at the same time. The headside trail weaver works with the weaver of the crossing trails at the point of crossing. It also links with these trails at the pin before and after. Each time it is linked with cloth stitch and twist before and after the pin, and the weaver must be twisted when working out of cloth stitch. After crossing, four pairs will be required on the left hand side, i.e. two for the trail and two for the plait. On the right hand side only two pairs for the trail are required, therefore two pairs from the right cross with two pairs from the left. The other two pairs on the left remain there to become part of the new trail on that side.

The leaves   Two pairs are left out after pin c to make a leaf. After the four plait crossing a leaf is made back to e, and becomes part of the trail again.

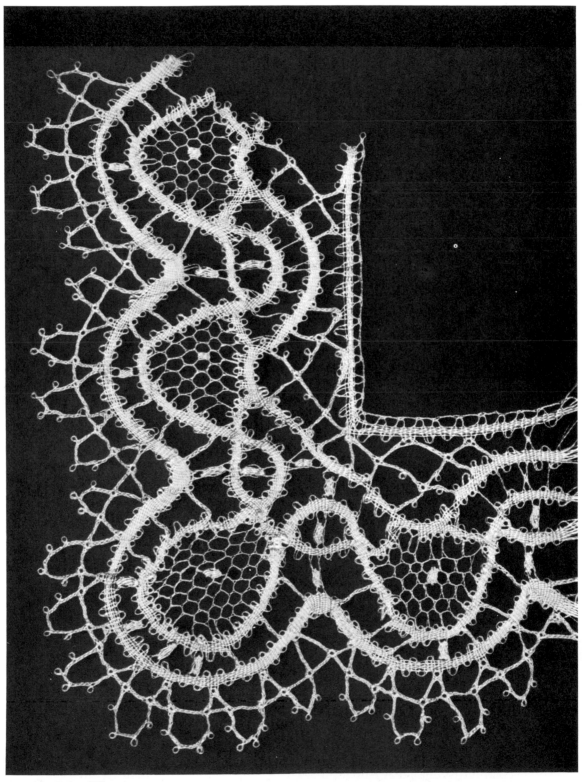

32 Point filling

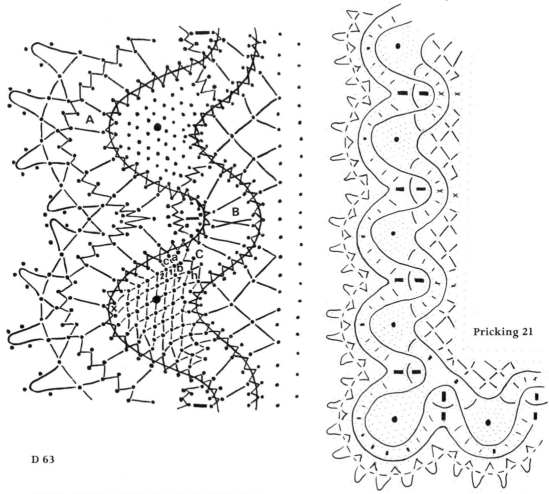

Pricking 21

D 63

OLD BEDS PATTERN WITH POINT FILLING

Working diagram **63** and pricking **21** are given, but can only act as a general guide, as this is an old pattern with irregularities. When the lace is observed at a distance (photograph **32**), it is the double trails which are the predominant feature, and their continuity must be preserved by keeping the same weaver and at least half of the passive pairs. On the large curve of the head area A, plaits will pass from the outer to the inner trail, being dropped as single pairs from the inner trail to the net. On the curve in the footside area B, the pairs need to be kept in the lower larger curve, and only twisted pairs link the trails. The pairs and plaits move symmetrically either side of the centre point. The small joining trails take an end passive pair from the main trail as weaver, and work through other released passives to the first pin of the small trail.

The point filling Study the working of the Bucks ground on page 134. It is easier to work if the headside trails are worked to the half-way mark and the small trail C is complete. Pairs left hanging from a and b should be twisted three times each, and a point ground stitch made. The point ground stitch consists of a half stitch with two twists extra on each pair.

Pin 1 is put up between the pairs and the stitch is *not* covered. Discard the right hand pair, take the left hand pair and the pair from c which must be twisted three times, make another point ground stitch, and put up pin 2 between the pairs. Complete the diagonal row discarding pairs on the right, and bringing in new pairs from the left. To begin the next row take the pair from h, which must be twisted three times, and the pair to the right of pin 1 to make the stitch at pin 7. Complete the row. Working the trail to release and take in pairs as necessary, work the whole filling. In

Pricking 22

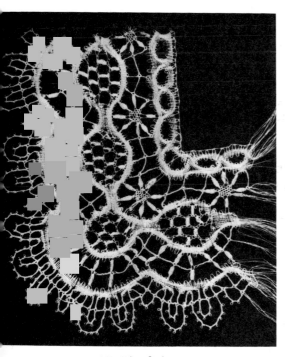

33   Pin chain pattern

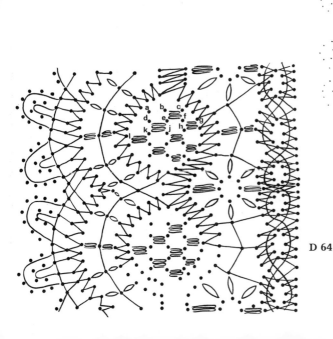

D 64

the centre of the point ground is a tally. Instructions for this are on page 143.

OLD BEDS PATTERN WITH PIN CHAIN AND TALLIES FILLING

This old pattern was originally used as an edging in which ribbon could be threaded through holes in the footside. A corner has been added for the use of the twentieth century lace maker, and the holes retained as a decoration in the pattern given here.

Make pricking **22** being very careful to include all the ink markings. Study photograph **33** and diagram **64**. Approximately 60 pairs of bobbins are required. The diagram can only be a general guide but is much easier to see than a fine pricking.

The plaited heading   This is a double ninepin, and the method of working can be followed from the diagram and photograph.

The headside trail   This will vary in thickness as pairs will be carried when not required as plaits in the ninepin. Two leaves pass from the headside trail into the left centre trail and then out again. In the middle, tallies are worked using half of the plait and the weavers from either side.

The footside   This is worked with crossing trails, the weavers being shown in the large diagram.

The centre filling   This is a Bucks Point pin chain filling and can be studied on page 184. Two pairs are required at pins a, b and c, and these must be released from the trails above the pin-holes mentioned. Two pairs for pin a work a honeycomb stitch, pin a is put up, and a second honeycomb stitch worked. A honeycomb stitch is a half stitch with one extra twist on each pair. Note that in this filling the pins are covered.

Work similarly and quite independently at pins b and c. The pairs at pin a work in pin chain to pin d, pin d is put up between the pairs, and covered with a honeycomb stitch. The left hand pair from c and the right hand pair from b work a tally as far as the next pin-holes. The left hand pair from b, and the left hand pair from the tally work honeycomb stitch. Pin e is put up and covered.

Similarly the right hand pair from c, and the right hand pair from the tally make a honeycomb stitch, and pin f is put up and covered. Remember to twist the tally pairs before taking them back into the pin chain, and to use the pair *without* the weaving thread first. This helps to achieve a good tally.

The trail weaver at g and the right hand pair from f make another tally. The right hand pair returns to the trail as weaver, and the left hand pair works with the other pair from f into h. Pairs from d and e make a tally, and are worked back into the pin chain at j and k. The pair from k and the trail weaver at l make a tally, the weaver returning to the trail, and the other pair into the pin chain. All the weavers are on the large diagram to facilitate working.

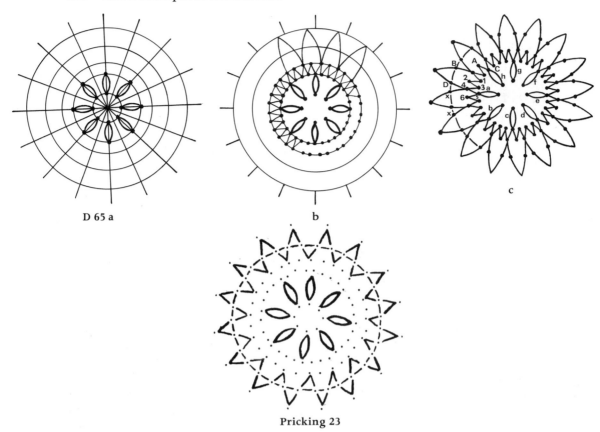

D 65 a

b

c

Pricking 23

MEDALLIONS

These are useful to mount under glass paperweights, in the base of small dishes, or for decorative mounting or insertion. The simple designs are most effective, and the worker may design original motifs very easily. There are several ways of working a circular motif, but many designs can be made by starting on a line radiating from the centre and working in a circular direction to finish on the same line. This is straightforward, easy to understand, and requires comparatively few bobbins.

To plan a circular motif   A very simple example is described here – see diagram **65A**. Decide on the diameter, and draw a circle, inside which all holes must fall. Mark in the radiating lines according to the design envisaged. Eight is a good number to begin a simple pattern. Draw in concentric circles to suit the design planned. Mark in eight leaves around a centre circle. Add radiating lines between those already in use. By 'eye' put three dots between each leaf, and these and the points of the leaves represent pin holes. Refer to diagram **65B** and mark in the path of a weaver in a circular trail. Add the ninepin edging. Diagram **65C** shows the motif almost complete.

To work the motif   Prepare pricking **23** and 15 pairs of bobbins. Refer to working diagram **65C** and photograph **34**. Hang two pairs of bobbins on A and one pair on pin 1 as a weaver. Weave in cloth stitch to the left

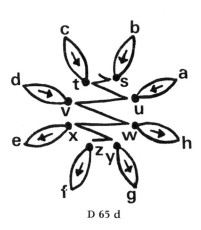

D 65 d

34   Simple medallion

through the pairs on A, and put up pin 2 to the right of the weaver. Weave back to pin 3, and remove support pin A. Hang two pairs on B. Take the weaver at pin 3, and weave to the left through the trail pairs, and through the pairs on B. Put up pin 4 to the right of the weaver. Weave back through the two pairs from B, which will be released for the ninepin, through the two trail pairs, and through two pairs hung on a pin at C. Put up pin 5. Weave to the left through the pairs from C, these being left out to make a leaf in the centre, and through the trail pairs. Put up pin 6. Remove support pins B and C.

Plait the pairs left out at pin 4 for the ninepin, and work a four plait crossing with pairs hung on at D into pin x. Continue the trail and ninepin introducing fresh pairs for leaves b, c and d in the same way that pairs were introduced at pin 5 for leaf a.

Work each leaf and complete it with a cloth stitch. Do not put up the pins yet. In order to retain the shape of the leaf the weaver should be supported. At the end of each leaf take the weaver, and place it back over the work so that the weight of the bobbin is falling in the opposite direction from the other three threads.

The centre will be worked referring to diagram **65D**. Take the right hand pair of leaf c, weave in half stitch to the right through the two pairs of leaf b, and put up pin s to the left of the weaver. Weave back through these two pairs and through the other half of leaf c, and put up pin t to the right of the weaver. Weave back through these three pairs and the two pairs from leaf a, and put up pin u. Weave through the five pairs and the two from leaf d, and put up pin v. Weave through all seven pairs, and put up pin w, and back through the seven again to put up pin x. Weave through five pairs to y – two pairs are left out for the leaf at w. Weave through three pairs to z – two pairs are left out for the leaf at x. Cover pin z with half stitch, and these two pairs make the leaf from z. The other two pairs make the leaf from y. Make the four leaves.

Push the pins in the completed half of the medallion right into the pillow, and slide a piece of clear plastic over the pin heads. The cover cloths will hold it in position.

Work the second half of the medallion. To bring a leaf into the trail, weave it in, using the trail weaver, put up the pin and weave back through it. Knot the pairs together, and lay the threads back across the work away from the working area. They will be cut off later. Complete the trail and ninepin, and end off neatly as described on page 62.

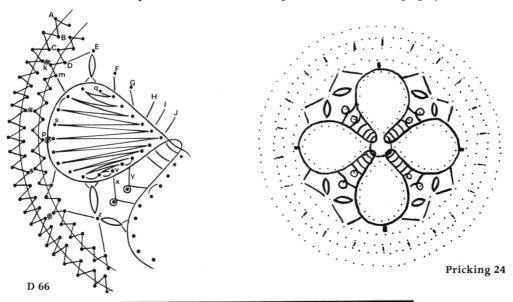

D 66

Pricking 24

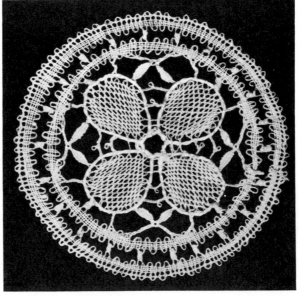

35   Four petal medallion

Four Petal Medallion

Prepare pricking **24**, and wind 18 pairs of bobbins. Refer to diagram **66** and photograph **35**. Hang three pairs of bobbins in order on A, and one pair on B – this pair will be the weaver. Weave a trail with two straight pairs in cloth stitch, and a cloth stitch and twist pair on the outside edge. If necessary refer back to the original Torchon Fan pattern on page 26. Work as far as tally k.

Hang four pairs on C, and one pair on D – this pair will be the weaver. Weave through the four pairs in cloth to tally at k. Put up the pins, make the tally, and continue the trails. In the inner trail, two pairs are left out after pin m for a plait, and there are two passive pairs left in the trail. Support pins A and C can be removed. Work trails with the tally as far as p.

The half stitch petal is outlined with a gimp thread. Place a gimp pair on a pin at q, hang up two pairs on E, two pairs on F and five pairs on G. Take the right hand gimp thread through all these pairs to the right. Take the left hand gimp thread through the plait from m. Twist all pairs twice after the gimp. Take one pair from E and one pair from F and work a half stitch. Put up pin q and cover with half stitch. Continue to weave as indicated in the diagram. Plaits should be brought in one pair at each pin, as this gives a neater line to the petal.

If no pairs enter or leave the half stitch work as follows: take the weaver through all the pairs and put up the pin (e.g. at pin s), and twist the weaver threads twice as usual. Pass the gimp thread between the threads, and twist them twice more. Now take the gimp back through towards the left, and twist the weaver threads again. Continue with the half stitch. This anchors the gimp, but care should be taken to see that the gimp is not pulled out of line. See diagram **67**. Note that single pairs enter and leave the petal at the three innermost holes.

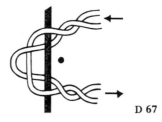

D 67

When the petal has been completed, and the last stitch covered with a half stitch, all the pairs left out must be twisted and the left side gimp brought all the way round the petal to the centre at j. Twist the gimp threads together several times, work picots and plaits at x and y, and leaves and plaits with a four plait crossing at z. Bring the gimp through to begin the next petal. The three remaining petals are worked in the same way, pins being pushed down into the pillow to facilitate the working of the last leaf. Ends are knotted in as described for previous patterns, and trimmed closely. The right side of the medallion is underneath.

36 Leaf medallion

37 Torchon mat

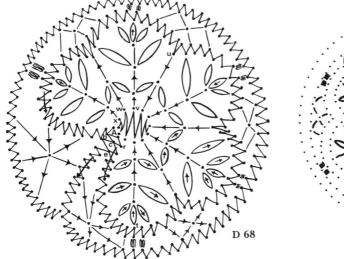

D 68

Pricking 25

Leaf Medallion

This is more difficult than the two previous patterns but the same principles are adopted. Instruction diagram **68** shows the method of working, but photograph **36** appears reversed as the medallion is worked from the wrong side. A mirror to the side of the photograph will show the lace as it is worked on pillow. Prepare pricking **25** and bobbins.

Hang two pairs of bobbins on A, and work in cloth stitch and twist to cover the pin. These are trail weavers. For the trail to the left of pin A, hang up three pairs in order on a pin behind the trail, weave to pin b, and back to pin c. Remove the support pin. For the trail to the right of pin A, hang up two pairs in order on a support pin, and weave from A through these pairs to r. Weave back, and work both weavers together at c, and again at e. Continue the trails independently, leaving out pairs for leaves and plaits as indicated. Work as far as pin u, and take the plaits through to the half stitch circle. Note that the plaits and leaves which travel to the centre from the edge trail are fresh pairs joined in, but the other leaves work round the design, entering and leaving the trail regularly. The six plaits are used to weave the half stitch circle, and when it is complete, plaits are made from v, w and x, and work out as indicated, returning to the outer trail where they are discarded.

The inner, scallopped trail is worked back to the centre, and the weaver hooked into the original trail at b and the next pin on that side. The pairs are tied, and cut off, leaving several inches which can be cut closely later. The pairs hanging from the half stitch circle must be tied firmly and cut off. The outer trail is completed and sewn to the outer edge. All threads should be secure before the pins are removed.

Circular Mat

This is a mixture of Beds and Torchon laces. See photograph **37** and pricking **26**.

Pricking 26

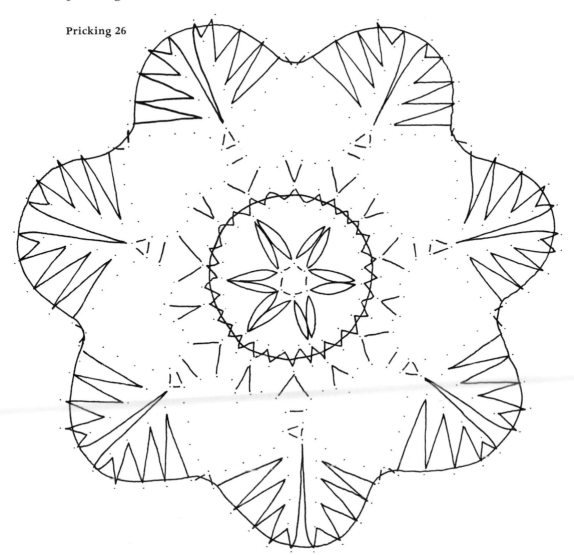

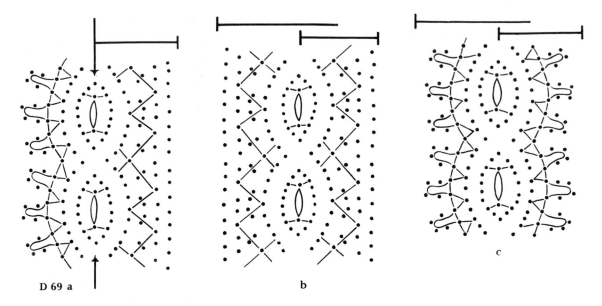

D 69 a   b   c

INSERTIONS AND DECORATIONS

Many patterns can be adapted easily to make an insertion or a decoration with two interesting headsides. The uses are many. Insertions may be used to complement the edgings on table or bed linen; they add interest to lampshades; or may be used as dress decoration. Fancy braids may be mounted on velvet as chokers, on ribbon for bookmarks, or on dress as an original adornment. Mounted under glass this lace makes attractive door plates and decorative plaques.

Crossing Trails and Leaf Pattern Insertion

To make an insertion from an edging refer to the lace on page 69, photograph **24**. Use a straight-sided mirror on the centre line of the lace to assess the appearance of the finished insertion. Refer to diagrams **69A** and **69B**.

Place two pieces of paper under the pricking and prick from the footside to the centre line and include the centre pin holes. Place one piece of pricked paper on a pricking board, cut the other piece of paper close to the centre holes. Overlap the papers to match the centre holes exactly, place pins in to set the position. Fasten the papers together with sellotape, remove the pins and make a pricking on card.

The method of working the insertion is the same as for the edging. See photograph **38** and pricking **27**.

Crossing Trails and Leaf Pattern Decoration

To make a length with two headings, the same method is used, but the pattern is pricked from the headside to the centre line. Refer to diagrams **69A** and **69C**. Usually it is desirable to have an attractive beginning and ending and this has to be designed by the worker. The trail requires re-shaping and the ninepin placed evenly either side of the centre. Turned upside down it can be used at the other end. Refer to diagram **70**.

Working instructions refer to photograph **39**, pricking **28**, and diagram **70**. When instructions state that pairs are to be laid across the pillow,

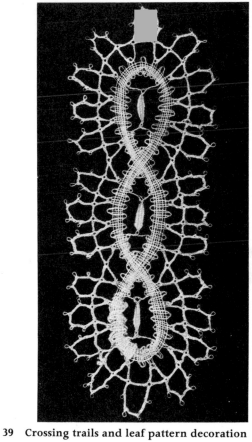

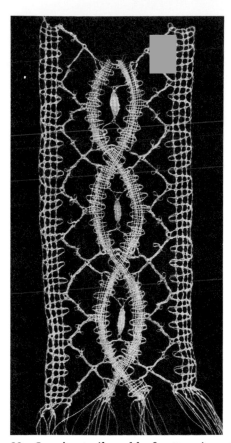

38 Crossing trails and leaf pattern insertion

39 Crossing trails and leaf pattern decoration

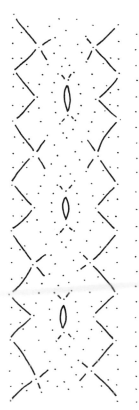

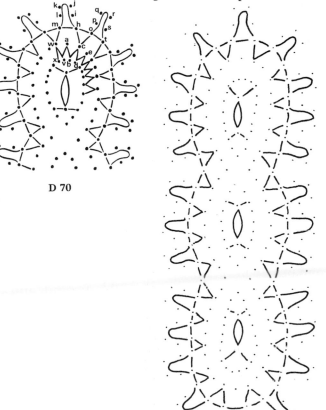

D 70

Pricking 27

Pricking 28

proceed as follows: take a pair of bobbins and lay the thread across the pillow with a bobbin falling to either side. When instructions state that pairs are to be placed vertically over a pin-hole the following is required: take a pair of bobbins and place the thread the length of the pillow with one bobbin falling into the working area, and the other lying over the back of the pillow. It is not easy to begin with threads so arranged as they are in no way kept in place, but they can be tightened as work proceeds. It is usual to turn the pillow to work threads lying to the back.

To begin, study photograph **39**, and notice that there are four pairs, i.e. eight threads, in each trail. Lay two pairs across the pillow, and put up pin a in front of them. These two pairs will become the weavers eventually weaving to b or v. Now lay eight pairs across the pillow below the pin. These will become the passive threads in the trail and give a continuous trail around the top, eight threads travelling to the right, and eight to the

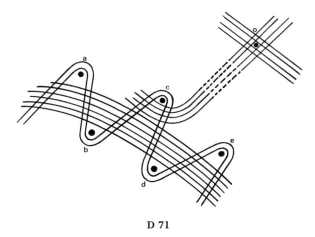

D 71

left. Take the two threads which lie furthest back on the right and work four cloth stitches towards the left through the eight threads on the right of the pillow. Put up pin b to the right of the weaver, and work back to the right through the same four pairs. Slide these pairs towards the centre working area on the pillow so that four pairs may be placed vertically over pin-hole c.

Continue to the right with the same weaver through the two pairs, i.e. four threads, and put up pin c to the left of the weaver. Weave to the left through six pairs and put up pin d. Weave to the right through four pairs and put up pin e. Note that the vertically placed pairs are linked in at pin c, they now hang freely to begin the ninepin, and will work in both directions. This is a useful method to use for a neat beginning, especially on a collar. Refer to diagram **71**.

To join in the plait which crosses the ninepin picot plait, work as follows: take the pairs released from c, and plait to o. Place four pairs vertically on the right hand side of the pillow, and use the four threads hanging into the working area as two pairs and work a four plait crossing with the pairs plaited from c. The plait from c through o will continue the ninepin with picots at p, q, r and s. Take the two pairs from o and plait to make a four plait crossing at t.

Turn the pillow round so that the back is nearest to the worker. Plait the pairs hanging at o and c to make a four plait crossing at h. Plait the left pairs with picots at i, j, k and l, and make a four plait crossing at m.

Turn the pillow to the normal position. Ease the threads towards the working area. Take the two threads behind (to the left of) a, and weave to the right through four pairs. Put up pin v, and work to the left through these four trail pairs and through the two pairs of the plait from m. Put up pin w, and continue to x. Single pairs are left out from each trail for the centre leaf. The general method of working is exactly the same as for the edging on the headside.

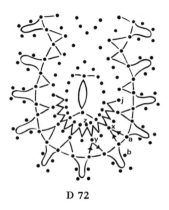

D 72

To complete the work neatly: refer to diagram 72. On the right, work the trail as far as z, bringing in the plait from the ninepin at pin x. Lay the threads back over the work and continue. Do not release the threads for more plaiting. Ignore the plait at y. At z tie each pair of trail threads together, and cut off. Press all the pins into the pillow. On the left side, the trail is worked as far as j. Continue working over the fringe from the other trail, and then raise each pin for use as it is required. This trail is quite separate from the one underneath, and there are no connections at all. At pin y, bring in and release the plait as usual. At pin x, bring in the plait and lay the threads back over the work. It is not released for more plaiting. At j, tie the trail pairs together, and cut off. The plaited edging is worked from b to a and sewn in neatly. Check that all ends are secure, cut off any bobbins, and remove the pins. Trim the trail ends closely, fold in and sew the trails together, tuck the ends of the plaits between the trails. This method of completing a continuous trail is useful on the neck edge of a collar.

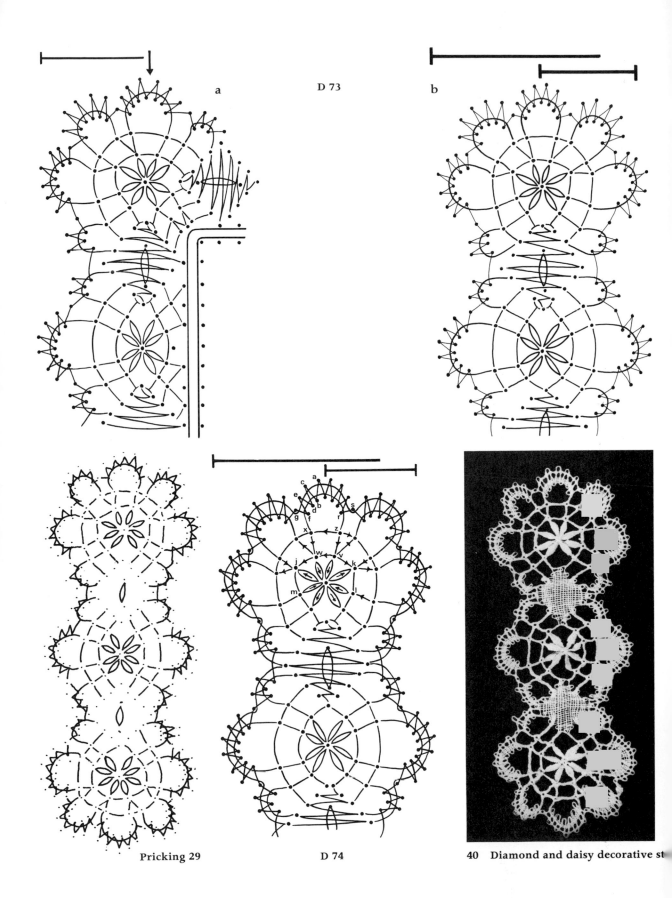

a

D 73

b

Pricking 29

D 74

40   Diamond and daisy decorative st

Diamond and Daisy Decorative Strip

The edging is given in photograph **26** on page 77. The pattern is made in the same way as the previous one, but the corner has been adapted to form attractive ends. Refer to diagrams **73A** and **73B** for the method of achieving the pricking, and to diagram **74** for the beginning. Prepare the pricking **29** and study photograph **40**.

To begin, place two pairs of bobbins across the pillow, and put up pin a below the threads. These pairs will become the scallop weavers. Lay six pairs across the pillow below the pin. These will be the passive threads in the scallop edging. Take the extreme left hand two bobbins and weave to the front through three pairs – the first pair in cloth stitch and twist, and the other two pairs in cloth stitch. Put up pin b to the left of the weaver, and weave back to c – through two pairs in cloth stitch, and, having twisted the weaver once, through the last pair in cloth stitch and twist. Put up pin c to the right of the weaver, and continue until pin g is covered with cloth stitch and twist. Take the extreme right hand pair, and weave to the left through three pairs for the other side of the scallop, complete this side as far as s.

The pairs from f and r plait into the pattern. Lay four pairs diagonally across the pillow to make a four plait crossing at z – this method was described in the previous pattern. Plait to the left to another four plait crossing at x, also plait as far as v. Again lay four pairs diagonally to make a four plait crossing at v, make the three plaits, but temporarily ignore the leaf as there are no available pairs to work it. With the right hand plait from x, and the left hand plait from v, make a four plait crossing at w. Plait both sets of pairs, but ignore the leaf as there are no available pairs to work it. Continue working as far as j and k.

Two pairs must be joined in as follows: remove pin v and pass a crochet hook through the hole to pull through two threads from fresh pairs. Pass one end of each pair through the loop, and pull up tightly. Replace the pin. Add two pairs at w in the same way, and make leaves to the centre hole. Work a four plait crossing, and make leaves to j and k. At j and k, work six plait crossings, and on each side take out one plait to make the scallop. The remaining eight threads are plaited together as far as l and m, then four are discarded.

Alternatively the leaves may be knotted out at j and k. The leaves from m and l are hooked into the centre crossing, and then more leaves are made to complete the eight leaf centre. The pattern can be worked in the same way as the heading of the strip pattern.

To complete the pattern refer to diagram **75**. Work leaves a and b together in a four plait crossing in the centre, and make leaves c and d. Work as far as J and S. On the right hand side at J, make the usual four plait crossing, and make leaf e with the left hand pairs. On the left side work similarly, making leaf f with the two right hand pairs. Remove the centre pin and link these leaves into the centre. Replace the pin and make

D 75

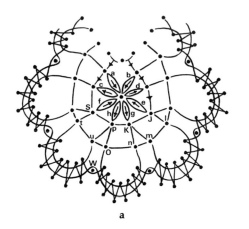

a

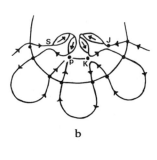

b

leaves g and h. On the right hand side at the end of leaf g, put up pin K, and cover with cloth stitch and twist. Using the *same threads*, plait as far as J. Remove the pin at J, and make a four plait crossing with the pairs hanging at J. Replace the pin. Knot and discard the right hand pairs.

Plait the left hand pairs for use in the scallop. At the end of the scallop, work the crossing at m, and plait to K. Hook the plait into K, and plait back to n for the next scallop. Work round to O, and then to p. On the left hand side put up pin p at the end of leaf h (there is no crossing), and plait to S. Remove pin S, work a four plait crossing and replace the pin. The left hand pairs are knotted out, and the right hand pairs continue through t and round the scallop to u and p. Join the plaits from u and O into pin p, and plait the eight threads to pin K. Knot firmly and cut off. The weavers and outside pairs of the scallops must be knotted and over-sewn at W. The plaits from u and n must be worked to O and knotted off.

To assist the worker, capital letters have been used to indicate the points where threads are knotted out. Make a tracing in colour of diagram **75A** and place it over diagram **75**. The path of the plaits will be seen clearly.

COLLARS

A collar should suit and fit a particular garment. Many of the attractive old collar patterns require alteration for modern use. Either the style is not in keeping with present day fashion, or the collar does not fit the neck of the dress. Almost all collars from the Victorian period need enlarging, and this is rarely an easy exercise. Today, most dresses have a centre back zip fastener, and collars made in two pieces are needed. These are infrequently found among old patterns unless intended for a dress with a deep V neckline. Many hours of work are spent in making a lace collar and surely it is worth the time to plan a collar that will fit and enhance the dress for which it is intended. A method of making a collar pattern using a straight edging is described here.

41   Collar no. 1

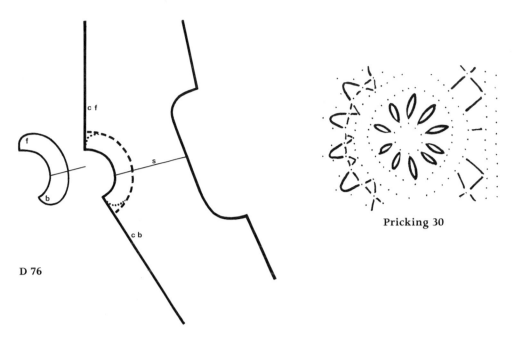

Pricking 30

D 76

Collar No.1

Making the collar pattern Use the commercial pattern or the actual garment to obtain the shape and neck edge required. If using the pattern, trim the seam allowance from the neck edge, and fasten the front and back pieces together, matching the shoulder seam line. Place over a sheet of paper and mark in the neck curve, the centre front and centre back lines, and the line of the shoulder seam. Cut out the shape and use it to make the collar pattern (diagram **76**). Measure an even distance from the neck edge for the collar width, and mark in a slight curve at back and front. Cut out the collar pattern.

Choose a simple edging (pricking **30**). Select one repeat that is accurate, and prick this through eight pieces of paper, putting the markings on each piece. Draw an outline of the collar on a sheet of paper, and indicate the front and back. Place the pattern repeats over the collar outline. Over-lapping will be necessary near the footside and the arrangement of plaits will require adjustment. Similarly, the ninepin edge will need attention. If the collar outline is pinned over a pricking board it will be easy to move the repeats, temporarily fixing them with pins. Refer to diagram **77A**. The centre back and front require adaptation and some redesigning. The holes in the neck edge will be put in by 'eye' and the crossing of trails will need attention. It is a good idea to mark in the weaver to ensure accuracy. See diagram **77B**.

Sometimes a slightly smaller collar is wanted, and a second row of passive threads can be introduced to reduce the curve and give a smaller neckline. Collar pattern pricking **32** has this arrangement of threads. It has the advantage of affording a little movement when fitted to a dress. *To work the collar* Prepare pricking **31** and bobbins. See photograph **42A**, and refer to diagram **78**. Detailed diagram **79**, used in conjunction with the large diagram, will explain the method of starting more clearly.

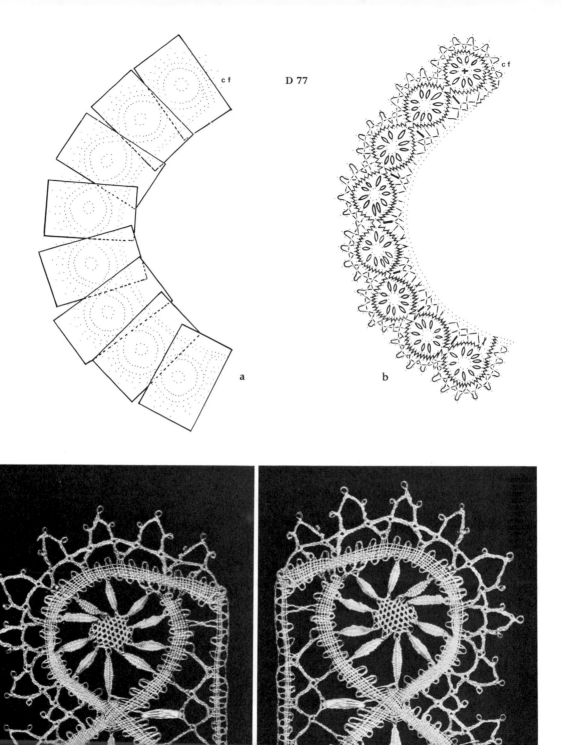

c f

a

b

42a   Beginning collar no. 1

42b   Beginning other side of collar no. 1

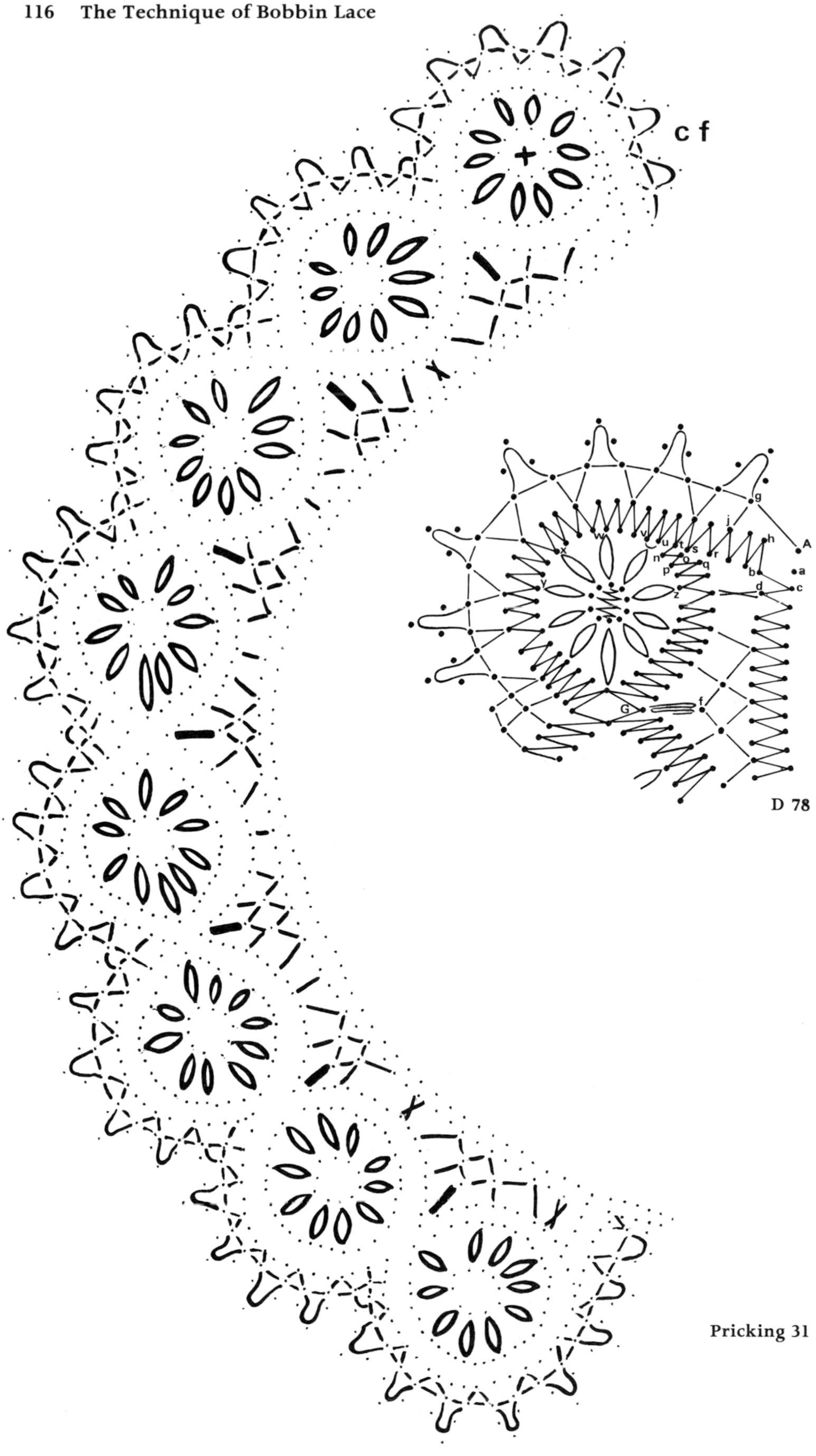

c f

D 78

Pricking 31

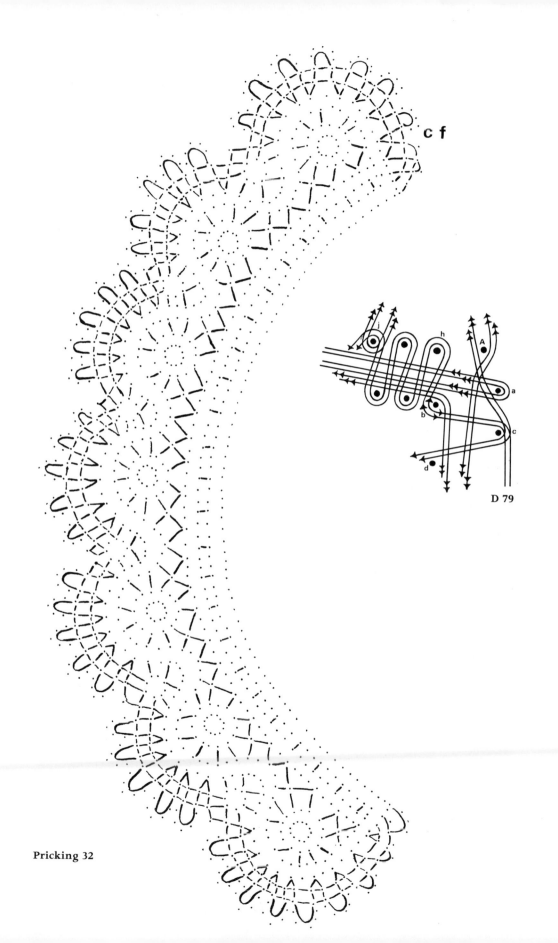

c f

D 79

Pricking 32

Put up pin A and lay two pairs of bobbins vertically either side of the pin. Enclose the pin with cloth stitch and twist. To do this, work a cloth stitch and twist with the four hanging threads, and then turn the pillow to make a similar stitch behind the pin. Put up pin a to the right of the threads already on the pillow, and hang two pairs on pin a. Using the left hand pair from a, weave in cloth stitch through the two hanging pairs to the left. Take the right hand pair from a, and weave to the left through the same two pairs. The two pairs from a will be passive pairs round the head-side trail. The pairs hanging become part of the footside, the left hand pair as a passive, and the right hand pair as one of the footside weavers.

Allow the horizontal pairs from a to lie across the pillow, and, ignoring them, place pin b below them. Put two pairs vertically either side of pin b, and enclose pin b with cloth stitch in front and behind, as at pin A. Of the four threads hanging to the front of the pillow, the left hand pair becomes a passive pair in the footside, and the right hand pair becomes the other footside weaver. Weave on to the right through one more pair, twist the weaver twice, and work cloth stitch and twist with the outside edge pair. Put up pin c, ignore the outer pair and weave back through two passive pairs to pin d. Later a 'kiss' will be made using the footside and trail weavers.

Turn the pillow a little to the right so that the headside trail may be worked more easily. Plait the two pairs from A for the ninepin. A cloth stitch encloses pin b. The right hand pair will be the trail passive, and the left hand pair, the trail weaver. Take this pair, and weave to the left through two more pairs (i.e. the pairs from a), and put up pin h. Weave back to the right through three passive pairs and continue the cloth trail joining in two pairs for the ninepin plait at j. Work the ninepin as required. At the first crossing of plaits, which is at g, use the pairs joined in at j, and the plait from A. Work the curved headside trail joining in one pair at each of pins r, s, t and u; these are left out immediately for the curved right side trail. Join in two pairs at pins v, w, x and y, and leave out immediately.

Return the pillow to the normal working position and use these pairs as follows. Begin the curved right trail by twisting pairs from r, s, t, u and v twice each. Take the left pair from v, and weave to the right through two pairs (i.e. the other pair from v and one pair from u), it will be the left hand passive in this trail. The pair from t becomes the trail weaver, and weaves in cloth stitch through one pair to the left, and pin n is put up. The same weaver works to the right through the one passive pair, and through the pair from s. Pin o is put up, and the weaver goes back to the left through two passives to pin p. Weave back to the right through the two passives and the pair from r, put up pin q, and continue the trail with these three passives.

Two pairs must be joined in for a leaf at z. Leaves are made using pairs from w, x, y and z. The other leaf is made with a pair from v and one from

u. A pin is put up at the top of the half stitch circle between the pairs of the centre leaf. It is covered with half stitch, and the right hand pair becomes the weaver, weaving to the right to work in the complete leaf from u/v. The half stitch circle will be completed bringing in, and leaving out all the leaf pairs. The other five leaves are worked, the trails completed, and a crossing of trails worked. The leaves on the left will join the curved trail, and the leaves on the right will pass through the trail to make plaits. Reference should be made to the open ring flower pattern and diagram **25b**.

The plaits are worked into the footside normally, and four plait crossings made when required. The plait is worked to pin f, which is put up between the plait pairs. The left hand pair of the plait and the trail crossing weaver from G make a tally. This tally is difficult to manage as the plait is not secure and it is helpful to pin the necks of the bobbins of the other half of the plait firmly by the thread while the tally is being made. The tally weaver is taken to the left, and twisted with the left thread of the tally. The centre and right threads are twisted and used to continue the plait from f.

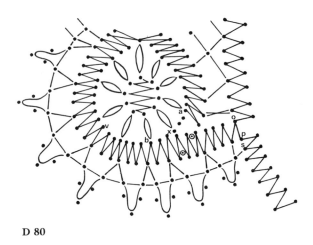

D 80

To complete the collar neatly   Refer to diagram **80**. Work the right hand trail as far as a. Work the left hand trail all the way to o; the last leaf to be brought in comes in at b. If all the pins are pressed into the pillow and the bobbins from the other trail laid to the left, this is straightforward to work. At o, the trail weaver links with the weaver from the footside, it then works to p. Cross the pairs on the footside (i.e. two passives and two weavers through the pairs from the headside trail). Take the weaver from the left of pin p, and weave a strip of cloth for approximately one inch, using the four pairs from the footside edge as passives. Tie the bobbins together in pairs, and cut off. The pairs from the trail that passed out to the right hand edge must be tied and cut off.

Press all pins into the pillow, and return to the curved right side trail. With the weaver as at pin a, continue the trail using the ringed pin-holes. Pins will be placed through the worked trail to these holes. Raise the pins as they are required for use, and work over the other trail as far as v. The last leaf is joined in at x, and then the trail is a simple cloth strip. Knot the ends and cut off. Tuck in the ends and any plait threads, overlap the trails, and sew together. On the footside, turn in the knots, fold the inch strip back to enclose the knots, and sew down.

To make the second half of the collar   Take a rubbing from the pricking and this will be a reversal of the piece made. Prick a pattern from the rubbing, and work the lace from centre front to back. The footside will be on the left side of the lace. The beginning is shown in photograph **42B**.

Collar No.2

Refer to diagram **81** and photograph **44**. The detailed diagram **82** will simplify the beginning. Prepare pricking **32** and bobbins.

To work the collar   Put up pin W, and lay two pairs vertically on either side of the pin. Enclose the pin, making a cloth stitch in front of and behind the pin. This is described in more detail in the previous pattern.

Take the right hand pair, hanging towards the front of the pillow, make a picot into pin x, and leave this pair hanging on the outside edge. Hang one pair on pin y. Put up pin Z, and lay two pairs vertically on either side of the pin. Take the left hand pair, weave through three pairs to the right in cloth stitch, twist the weaver twice, and work cloth stitch and twist with the outside pair. Put up pin o in position as footside pin. Ignore the outer pair as usual, work back through the three passive pairs, and continue as far as the tally.

Turn the pillow round so that the other ends of the vertical pairs are towards the worker. Plait the pairs from W and Z ready for the ninepin.

Turn the pillow back to the normal working position. Put up pin A and lay two pairs vertically to either side of the pin, then work cloth stitch and twist in front of and behind the pin. Put up pin b, and hang two pairs on the pin so that they fall to the right of the pairs from A. Take the left hand pair from b, and weave to the left through the two pairs hanging from A in cloth stitch. Take the right hand pair from b, and weave through the same two pairs to the left in cloth stitch. The pairs from A become inner footside passive pairs, and the pairs from b become the passives for the curved trail. Allow the pairs from b to lie across the pillow horizontally, and temporarily ignore them. Put up pin c, and lay two pairs vertically to the left of pin c. Weave the two threads hanging down into the working area through two pairs to the right in cloth stitch, put up pin d, and continue the inner trail on the footside. The weavers from each trail work together to make tallies at the appropriate holes.

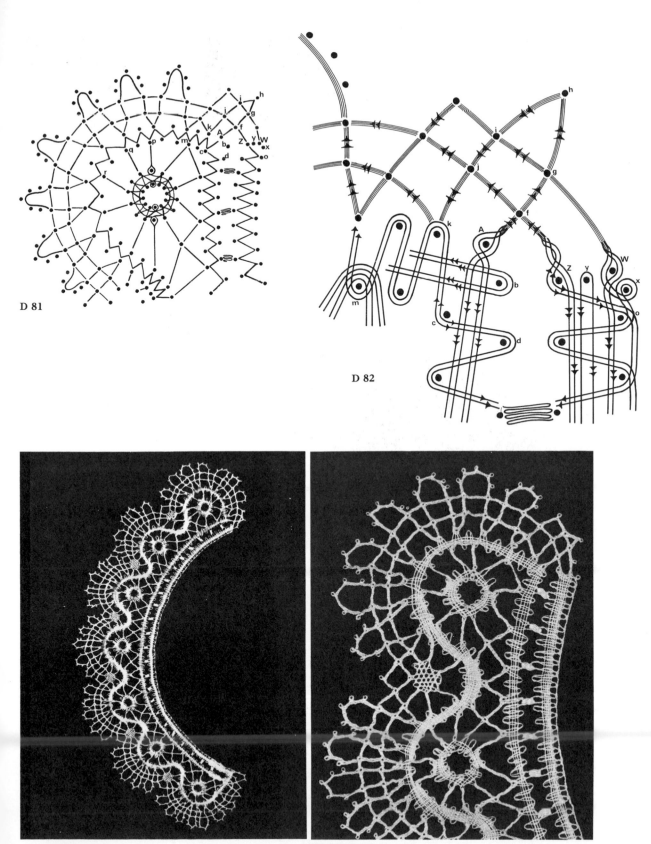

D 81

D 82

43   Collar no. 2

44   Beginning collar no. 2

Turn the pillow a quarter turn to the right so that the curved trail is in an easily worked position. Take the pair at c, and weave it through the two pairs from b in cloth stitch. (This pair was lying across the pairs from b, and has to be lifted into position to the right of the pairs from b, before work commences.)

Turn the pillow further round, and plait the pairs falling back from A to make the ninepin. The plait from A crosses the plait from Z at f, the plait from W at g, and makes a picot at point h. It crosses the plaits again at i and j, and is linked into the trail at k with the weaver from c. At m, four new pairs are introduced for plaits (refer back to page 108, diagram **71**). Also join in two new pairs at p, q and r for leaves. The centre of the pattern with the open ring has been described on page 72, diagram **52**.
To complete the collar   Study photograph **45**, and the method given for the previous pattern. The two footside trails are worked the full length, tied off, and the ends cut closely.

45   Finishing collar no. 2

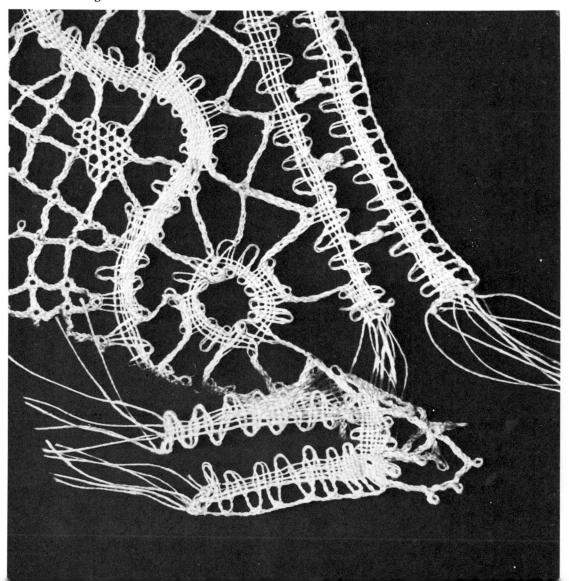

The curved trail is worked to the inner footside trail, a plait passes straight through it, and with the weaver from the curved trail works an overlap of the inner trail, quite independently of it, but using the same pins. The curved trail is continued with a new weaver and the corner pin used three times so that an overlap of the neck edge (footside) can be worked. The same pins are used, but there is no linking. The trails should be worked for an inch overlap. The ends are tied and cut off. Fold in the ends of the trails, tuck in any plait threads, and sew the trails together firmly.

To make the second half of the collar   Take a rubbing of the pricking. It will appear reversed, and make the pattern for the other half of the collar. Work with the footside on the left so that the collar is again worked from centre front to centre back.

BUTTERFLY MOTIFS

These and flower motifs are found among collections of old Bedfordshire patterns. They were used for insertion into pillow cases and table linen, and occasionally for dress adornment. Today they can be used with little adaptation for various forms of decoration – mounted under glass in trays or for pictures, or used as insertions, or even independently with a pin as a dress decoration.

Forethought is required. The method of working the butterflies will depend on the use to which the lace will be put. If it is to be used for insertion, strength to withstand frequent laundering is all-important; if it is to be mounted under glass, the finished appearance must take priority. For use as decoration requiring frequent but careful laundering, a slightly coarser thread may be used to withstand stiffening and handling.

Methods of working   The body is worked first. From old lace, it can be seen that pairs are joined on to the body, and the edge of the wing worked as a trail all the way round and back into the body. From this trail pairs are released for the centre of the wing and taken back in when not required. This gives a very uneven outline to the wing but a firm piece of lace.

When the trail returns to the body, the pairs are woven across the back and become the trail for the next wing. There are few joins and the result will withstand wear. However, if the lace is intended purely for decoration, the following way is recommended. It is securely ended off but not recommended for hard wear.

The body is worked first. Both sides of the wing are worked at the same time, the edge trail being started in the centre at the wing tip. Using this method it is easier to get a balanced plait arrangement in the middle of the wing, and the path of the plaits should be planned before beginning the work. To work a motif of any irregular pattern, the worker must possess a good understanding of techniques and the ability to adapt these to the various situations as they arise.

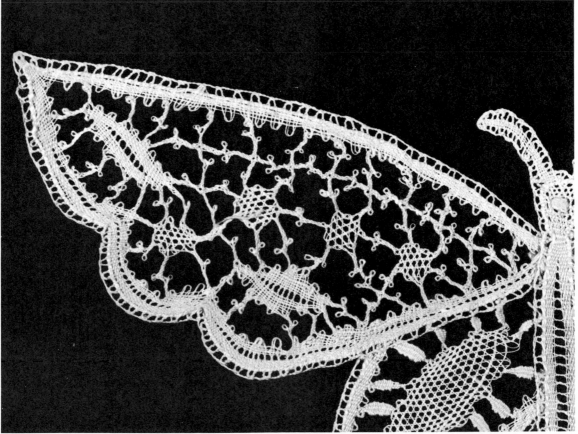

Top   **46a**   Butterfly motif no. 1
Above   **46b**   Butterfly motif no. 1 enlargement

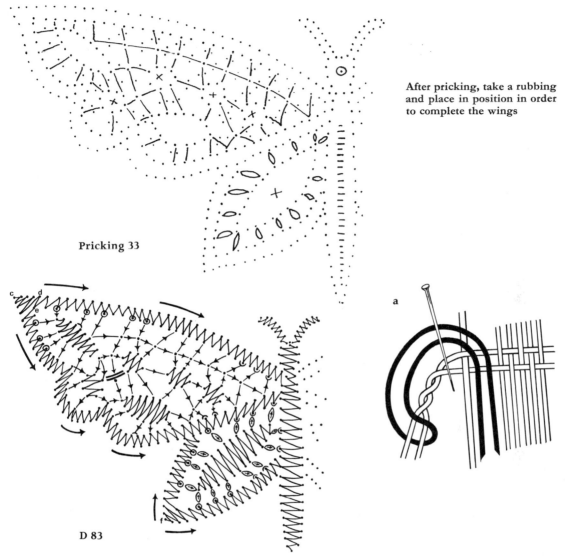

Pricking 33

After pricking, take a rubbing and place in position in order to complete the wings

D 83

Butterfly No.1

Prepare pricking 33. Refer to photographs **46A** and **46B** and diagram **83**.

To work the body   The body requires ten pairs of bobbins and one gimp pair. Put up a pin at the tip of one antenna and hang five pairs on it. Make a cloth stitch with the four right hand threads and twist all the pairs three times each. Take the second pair from the right to the left through two pairs in cloth stitch, twist the weaver three times, and work cloth stitch and three twists on the outside edge. Put up the footside pin inside two pairs, and work the length of the antenna with a footside on both sides. Work the other antenna similarly, and the weavers should meet at the centre pin, work cloth stitch and twist, put the pin and cover. The one pair becomes a passive and the other continues as weaver. Work to the outside edge.

Take a gimp pair and pass it through the seven centre pairs, but not through the weavers. The gimp threads will lie inside the weavers on each side, and will be used as passive threads in the lace. In each case the other half of the pair will be a thin lace thread. The head can be worked in half stitch, and, if desired, a raised tally may be worked in the centre. In each row of working the first and last pairs, which include the gimp threads, should be worked in cloth stitch. Twists on weavers are necessary to achieve a neat half stitch before and after these stitches. The body is worked in cloth stitch with a twisted weaver in the centre.

At the end of the body, throw out the gimps, and tie the weavers from each side around all the other threads. Knot the pairs together and tie the weavers around them a second time. Cut off the threads, and rejoin the pairs to begin the wing.

To work the larger wings   Put up pin c and hang seven pairs on the pin. Work cloth stitch and three twists with the left hand four threads. Twist all the pairs three times, take the second pair from the left and work to the right in cloth stitch through four pairs, twist the weaver three times, and work cloth stitch and three twists on the outside edge. Put up the pin inside two pairs.

Take a gimp pair and place it in position as described for the head. The gimp threads should lie as third from the left and fifth from the right. Continue with footside on both sides, introducing a new pair at each pin, until there are 11 pairs and the gimp pair.

Join in pairs as follows: work to the footside through the last passive pair which includes the gimp thread. Put up the footside pin to support the weaver before the stitch is worked, and twist the weaver three times. Put a new pair up and over the weaver, allowing it to fall inside the gimp thread. Refer to diagram **83A**. Complete the footside remembering that the pin is in position but the stitch must be made. After pin d, the weaver travels through four pairs only, pin e is put up and covered with cloth stitch and a weaver travels in each direction to continue the edge trails. The working of the wing should be possible following diagram **83** closely. The direction of all plaits is given. A ringed hole on the inner edge of the trail indicates that two pairs are joined in at the hole, and a hole capped with a semi-circle indicates that pairs must be discarded at the hole.

To join the edge trail to the body, remove the pin at the side of the body, and pull one half of the weaver through as shown in diagram **84**. Pass the other end of the weaver through the loop, pull them up tightly, and knot them together. Now weave to the other side and join the weaver to the body in the same way. Hook the passive pairs into the edge of the body, make them secure and cut off the threads.

To work the smaller wings   The small wing is worked following the photograph and instructions. It is started at pin f with 11 pairs and a gimp pair. One trail is sewn into the body and the other into the lower side of the large wing. Work the other half to match.

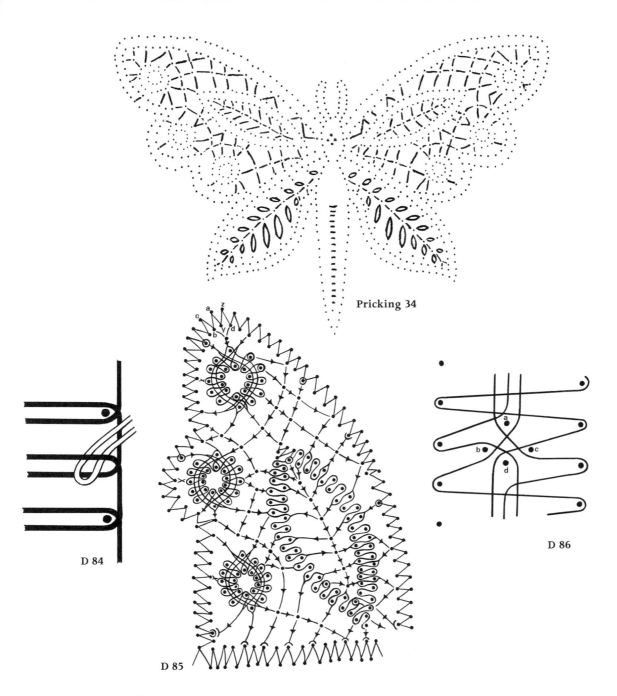

Pricking 34

D 84

D 85

D 86

Butterfly No.2

Prepare pricking **34**, refer to diagram **85**, and study photographs **47A** and **47B**. The body and antennae are worked in the same way as those in the previous pattern.

Working the decorative hole in the body Refer to diagram **86**. Work from the left side towards the centre and right side. Weave through the centre pair and on through one more pair. Ignore the weaver and the pair to the left of it, take the next pair to the left, and work that pair and the next to the left in cloth stitch. These four pairs make the hole. Twist the inner

47a Butterfly motif no. 2

two pairs three times each, put up a pin between them, and cover with cloth stitch and three twists. The outer pairs work out to the edges of the head, and back to the same position. They are twisted three times each and then worked in cloth stitch through the inner pairs to meet in the middle. Twist all four pairs three times each, and put up pins b and c to the outside of all four pairs. Work the centre pairs in cloth stitch and three twists, and put up pin d below the stitch. The outer pairs work out to the edges of the head and straight back to the centre in cloth stitch. They are worked together in cloth stitch, and one pair is left hanging unsupported while the other becomes the weaver.

The lower wings These are worked first, and the edges completed back to the body. The markings on the pricking indicate the leaf positions. A leaf is made near the point on one side, pairs are joined in for the centre plait, another leaf is made, and the pairs taken into the trail on the other side. The pairs are released for the next leaf. It crosses the centre plait, and another leaf is made and taken into the trail on the other side. Thus the lower wing is worked using very few pairs.

The upper wings These are begun at the tips, and the method of starting is similar to that on page 106. Put up pin a at the tip, and lay four pairs horizontally across the pillow behind the pin. Using the threads hanging

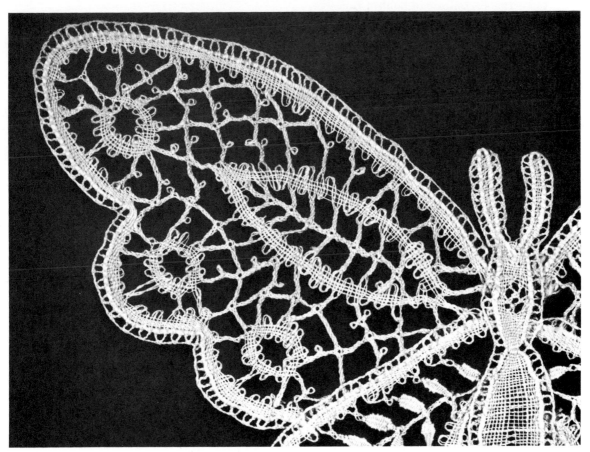

47b Butterfly motif no. 2 enlargement

to the right hand side of the pillow, make a cloth stitch. Twist the pairs three times, and also the threads in pairs to the left of the pillow three times. Now lay a gimp thread across the pillow below the pin, and then five pairs of bobbins. The pair to the left of pin a works through the six threads on that side in cloth stitch to pin b, and back to a footside stitch with the outer twisted pair at c. On the other side, the pair to the right of pin a works through the pairs on that side of the pillow to pin y, and back to the footside and twisted pair for pin z. At pins b and d, one pair is left out for the plait to the top of the ring.

Note that the rings are formed a little differently from those described earlier. The inner passives cross without a pin, and the ring weavers meet at the centre inner pin. For a method of taking pairs through plaits, diagram **53** on page 75 is frequently used. The small rings round the hole indicate that two pairs should be joined in, and holes capped with a semi-circle indicate that two pairs are thrown out at that pin. The working is straightforward, but requires care. There are no new techniques.

Note that if the butterfly is to be used as a dress trim, make a second body and sew it to the butterfly body with a little cotton wool as padding in the centre. A pin can be placed more readily in the thickness, and the result is more pleasing.

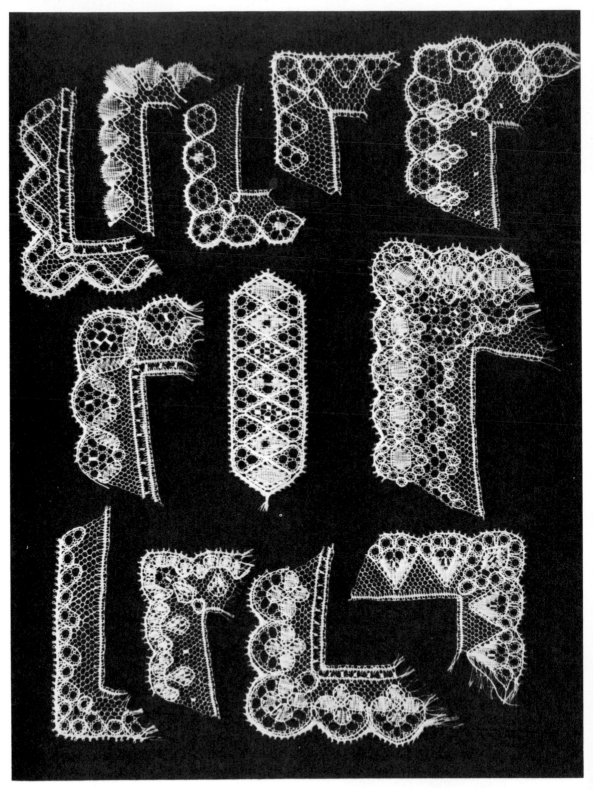

48   Bucks Point lace patterns

4 ❖ Bucks Point Lace

Bucks Point lace is an intricate lace recognized by the fine hexagonal net and honeycomb stitches. The net is worked in diagonal lines from the footside into the design which may be a simple shape or an elaborate floral pattern. The fine closely woven and twisted threads, the many effects produced by the variety and combination of stitches, together with the use of gimp threads, result in a lace of great beauty. The regular Torchon laces can be imitated readily by machine but the combination of the hexagonal net, the design and picots are still achieved only in the hand created article.

EXPLANATION OF TERMS AND TECHNIQUES USED
The prickings   In order to make any lace successfully it is important to have an accurate pricking. Bucks Point lace is so fine that it is not an easy task to make a good copy of the prickings, as explained on page 14. For the first few patterns it is possible to trace the holes on to paper and take a pricking from them, but soon the worker will find that an understanding of the way in which patterns are planned will help. The ground or net and the 'fillings' are based on rows of stitches worked in diagonal lines from the footside. In Torchon lace the angle of working is always 45 degrees, but in Bucks Point lace it may be at any angle between 52 degrees and 70 degrees from the footside; it varies according to the design and any adjustment made will alter the shape of the design, usually to its detriment. Refer to diagram **87**. To make an accurate pricking from the tracing, use a very hard sharp pencil and draw lines through the dots parallel to the footside. Place a straight edge diagonally across the pattern and prick the holes in on the intersections in the direction of working.

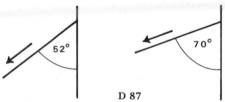

D 87

Edgings and corners The cottage lace makers who made lace for a livelihood worked on bolster pillows and worked the lace continuously round the pillow. Only more recently, with the revival of the craft and the making of lace as a leisure pursuit, have lace makers demanded corners to enable them to produce a clear, attractive piece of work for a definite purpose. The corners in Torchon lace are easy to design and work. The pattern is worked to the diagonal before the corner, the pillow turned through 90 degrees, and work continued on the next side. As Bucks lace is worked at a different angle and therefore this manoeuvre is not possible, a new feature must be introduced at the corner to separate the rows of ground which would otherwise converge and be unworkable. This will be discussed later, but the worker is advised to make half a dozen edgings to get a clear understanding of principles. The corners will then appear to be less difficult. For ease of explanation the corner instructions have been included with each pattern but they should be ignored until experience has been gained. Many prickings are given in two sizes. Originally all Bucks lace was very fine, but the coarser prickings will help the worker to follow the arrangement of holes and the direction of the threads.

Thread The following types and thicknesses are suggested as a guide. D.M.C. *Retors D'Alsace* is available in white ecru and black in the thicknesses given.

D.M.C. *Retors D'Alsace* no.30 suitable for coarser prickings when two sizes are given. Suitable for decorative strips and other patterns when there are 12 holes or less to 25mm on the footside.

D.M.C. *Retors D'Alsace* no.50 suitable for fine prickings when two sizes are given, and for other patterns with more than 12 holes to 25mm on the footside.

D.M.C. *Retors D'Alsace* no.60 suitable for very fine lace, including the kat stitch pattern (pricking 47) and the old prickings 56 to 65.

D.M.C. *Coton Perle* no.8 suitable for use as gimp with *Retors D'Alsace* no.30.

D.M.C. *Coton Perle* no.12 suitable for use as gimp with *Retors D'Alsace* no.50 and no.60.

D.M.C. *Cordonnet Special* no. 150 suitable for use for the coarser patterns, especially for practice.

FAN PATTERN
Prepare pricking **35** and 13 pairs of bobbins, one pair extra will be required for the corner. A single bobbin wound with gimp thread will also be needed. Refer to diagram **88** and photograph **49**. Hang two pairs on A1 and two pairs in order on B. Hang one pair on C to G inclusive, and allow the gimp thread to hang to the left of the pair on pin G. The gimp

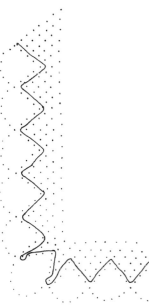

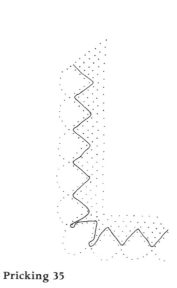

Pricking 35

D 88

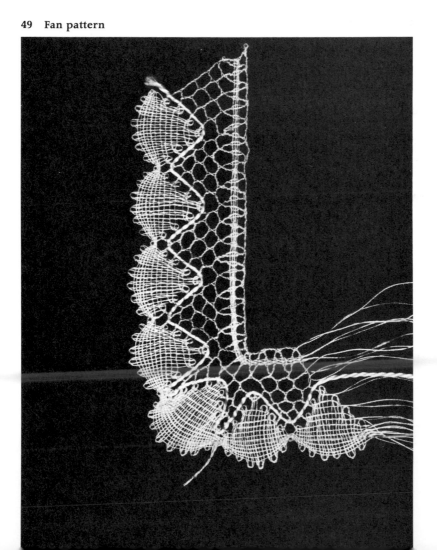

49   Fan pattern

should be supported on a pin slightly further back than the other support pins. Hang three pairs on H in order from left to right.

To begin   Twist the right hand bobbins on A1 three times, and cover pin A1 with cloth stitch and three twists. Cloth stitch and three twists is a stitch consisting of cloth stitch and three twists on each pair of bobbins. (Refer to diagram **12** on page 20, and the sequence is a, b, c, b, b, b.) Ignore the right hand pair and weave to the left through two pairs from B in cloth stitch. Twist the weaver three times, and work a ground stitch with the pair from C.

Ground stitch   Using two pairs, cross the second bobbin over the third, and then take the second over the first and the fourth over the third at the same time. Repeat this last move twice more. (Refer to diagram **12**, and the sequence is a, b, b, b.) It is important to think of this stitch as cross and three twists. Put up pin 2 to the right of both pairs. This is known as the *catch pin*. Take the left hand pair and the next pair which hangs from D and work another ground stitch. Put up pin 3 between the pairs. Do *not* cover the pin. Take the left hand pair and the pair from E, and work a ground stitch and put up pin 4. Work pin 5 with the pair from F, and pin 6 with the pair from G. If all the ground stitches have been worked accurately with three twists, the extreme left thread will have travelled from the footside pin. Check this by pulling the thread gently, and movement will be seen back to the footside. Remove the support pins C to G. B may be left in position a little longer as it supports the two passive pairs on the footside.

Whenever the footside has to be worked the full sequence is as follows: take the fourth pair from the outside edge, and work cloth stitch through two pairs towards the outside edge. Twist the weaver three times, work cloth stitch and three twists with the outside pair, and put up the pin inside two pairs. (In this case pin 7.) Ignore the outside pair and work cloth stitch back through the two passive pairs. Twist the weaver three times.

The catch pin is worked as follows   Take the weaver that has completed the footside sequence, and use it and the next pair to make a ground stitch. The catch pin is put up to the side of these pairs, the side nearest the passive pairs. (In this case pin 8, to the right of both pairs.)

Now take the left hand pair and work the diagonal row and pins 9, 10 and 11. Return to work footside pin 12 and catch pin 13. Work ground pins 14 and 15. Complete the next row 16, 17 and 18.

Note that rows of ground are *always* worked diagonally. They are worked from a point furthest from to a point nearer to the worker, and one stitch less has to be worked in each row.

The gimp thread   This lies between the cloth fan and the ground. It is passed between the threads of pairs 6, 11, 15 and 18. The gimp thread is always enclosed by twists. The pairs which have completed the ground are twisted already and the gimp is passed under the left thread and over the right. The pairs are twisted twice after the gimp.

To continue Take the left hand pair from H as weaver, work in cloth stitch through the other two pairs from H, and on through the pair from 6. Put up pin 19, and twist the weaver twice. Weave back through three pairs to pin 20. Twist the weaver, and work back through four pairs, three are already in the fan, and one pair from 11. Put up pin 21, and continue bringing in pairs at 23 and 25.

From pin 26 work back through five pairs to pin 27. One pair has been left out after pin 25 – the point of the fan. Always keep the same weaver. Working from 28 to 29 is through four pairs, and from 30 to 31 through three pairs. At pin 32 leave the weaver uncovered as it is easier to find so. Thus pairs hang from pins 25, 27, 29 and 31. Twist each pair twice, and pass the gimp thread through. It goes over the right hand thread and under the left hand thread. Twist each pair three times to enclose the gimp and prepare for the ground working.

Take the fourth pair from the outside edge, and work out to pin 1 for a complete repeat of the pattern.

The corner Complete the cloth fan, and work the footside stitch a. Refer

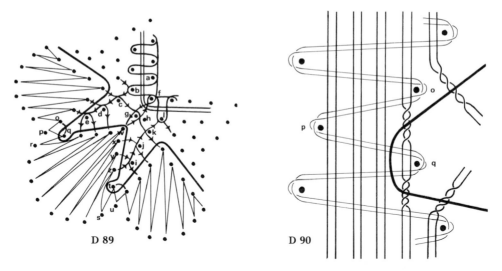

D 89

D 90

to diagram **89**. Work the catch pin stitch b, and ground stitches c, d and e. Work a footside pin at the corner at pin f and a ground pin at g. The cloth fan weaver is at p.

An extra pair must be introduced into the cloth. Bring one pair up round the weaver and let it fall inside one thread as described in diagram **83A** on page 125. Weave in cloth stitch to the right through four pairs. Pass the gimp thread to the left through the last pair from the fan and through the weaver from the cloth fan (diagram **90**). The weaver and the pair from o are both to the right of the gimp; work them together in cloth stitch, put up pin q, and cover with cloth stitch. Twist the right hand pair twice, and pass the gimp towards the right through the untwisted weaver and through the twisted passive from o. Take the gimp on to the right through two pairs from e, one pair from d, and one pair from g. Twist all the pairs after the gimp except the weaver. Weave to r, and continue the fan as far as s. Pass the gimp thread to the left through the pairs from w, x, y and z, and on through the next passive pair. Twist this passive pair twice before and twice after the gimp passes through. The fan weaver works from pin s through four pairs and the gimp thread is passed through the untwisted weaver. The weaver and passive are to the right of the gimp. Twist the passive and work a cloth stitch and pin t. Cover pin t and pass the gimp back to the right through the untwisted weaver and the passive which is twisted twice before and twice after the gimp. Weave to u. Pairs from w, x, y and z must be twisted three times to enclose the gimp.

The pillow must be turned to work the next side with the footside on the right. Pairs from w and g work a catch pin at h, and the footside is worked next, using the fourth pair from the edge, and the corner pin f is used a second time. The weaver from the corner as usual passes back through two passive pairs, is twisted and left waiting for the pair for the catch pin to be made available. The ground pins will be worked from the furthest point – from left to right – until the normal diagonal line is seen again. Use pairs from y and z to make a ground stitch, and put up pin i. Take the right hand pair and the pair from x, and work a ground stitch into pin j. Use the right hand pair and pair from h to work k.

Sufficient pairs are available for the next cloth fan. Pass the gimp through pairs from i, j and k. The extra pair in the fan should be removed. Put the penultimate pair of passives back across the work. Later they may be cut off. Work the fan completely, and take the gimp through ready to work the ground.

The first row of ground has the corner pin f as its footside pin and this has been worked already. Take the weaver from the footside which was left in position as fourth pair from the edge, and work a catch pin with the next pair to the left. Continue the diagonal row of ground.

Nook pins   The pins at p and q are nook pins; they occur frequently in floral designs. The general method of working is as follows: the weaver is passed round the gimp without twisting in order to keep the lace flat. The passive pairs are always twisted twice on either side of the gimp. Refer to diagram **90**.

SHEEP'S HEAD

This pattern introduces picots along a straight headside, honeycomb stitch and the use of a pair of gimp threads to enclose a part of the pattern. Prepare pricking **36** and 16 pairs of bobbins. Four pairs extra will be required for the corner. One gimp pair is required for the strip, and an extra pair for the corner. Refer to diagram **91** and photograph **50**.

To begin   Hang up bobbins in the same way as for the fan pattern. Choose the longest diagonal row of ground holes. This row has nine holes and

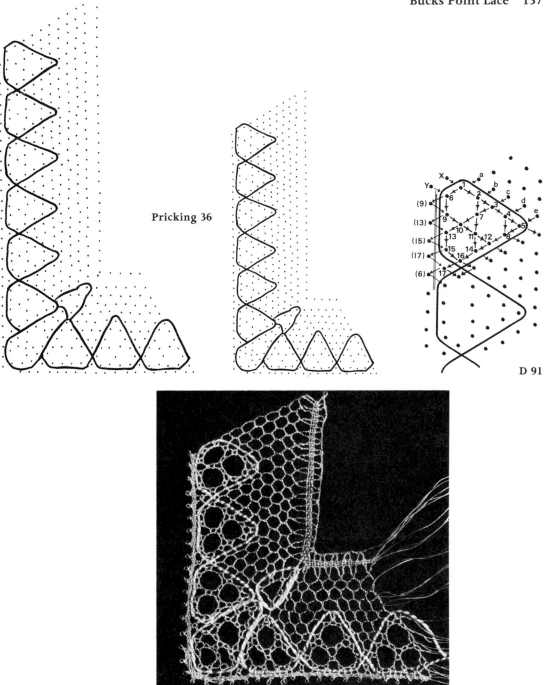

Pricking 36

D 91

50 Sheep's head pattern

leads into pin 1. At the footside indicate this row with a pin and hang two pairs of bobbins on it; it is the equivalent of A1. Now put up pins on the diagonal row *behind* the row to be worked. On the first pin put up two pairs in order, and one pair on each of the other pins. Refer to the previous pattern (diagram 88). The capital letters refer to support pins and the numbers refer to order of working.

Work the first row of ground — counting the footside pin, there are nine pins to be worked. Remove support pins. Work four more diagonal lines, each one stopping at the black line which indicates the gimp thread. Pairs should hang from pins a, b, c, d and e. Hang one pair on pins X and Y. Take the gimp pair and hang it on a support pin behind pin 1, and allow both threads to fall between the threads from a and X. Take the left hand gimp thread through pairs from X and Y, and twist the pairs twice after the gimp. Take the right hand gimp thread to the right through pairs from a, b, c, d and e. Twist these pairs twice each.

Honeycomb stitch   This is made using two pairs. Take the second bobbin over the third; and the fourth over the third and the second over the first at the same time. Repeat the second movement. (Refer to diagram **12** abb.) One honeycomb stitch having been made, the pin is put up and covered with a second honeycomb stitch. Honeycomb pins are always covered, and the stitches always have two twists.

Use the left hand pair from a and the pair from X to make a honeycomb stitch, put up pin 1, and cover. Use the right hand pair and the next pair to the right (from b) to work the next honeycomb pin 2. The right hand pair and pair from c work honeycomb pin 3. The pair from d is used for pin 4, and from e for pin 5. This row of honeycomb is continuous from pins 1 to 5. It is worked diagonally from the point furthest away to a nearer point. It can be worked from right to left or left to right as long as the hole furthest back is worked first. Remove pin X.

Use the pair from 1 and the pair from Y to work honeycomb pin 6. Use pairs from pins 2 and 3 for pin 7, and pairs from 4 and 5 for pin 8. The row of stitches 6, 7 and 8 are quite separate, this row has gaps between each stitch. Remove pin Y and ease the thread down.

Pin Y can be replaced and two more pairs hung on it in order. * Pass the gimp through the left hand pair from pin 6, twist the pair twice, and weave to the left through the two passive pairs hung up at Y. Make a double picot into pin 9. For double picots refer to diagram **38**, page 56. Remember that one picot consists of three twists, the threads being put round the pin, and three more twists. Take the picot pair back through the two passive pairs in cloth stitch, twist twice, pass the gimp through and twist twice more. ** The sequence * to ** is used regularly for each picot pin.

At pin 17 the pair will not travel back through the gimp as that pin is between the two heads. Take the weaver that has come through from picot (9), and use it and the pair from 6 to work pin 9. Complete the continuous row of honeycomb, pins 10, 11 and 12. The left hand pair from 9 works picot (13). Follow instructions from * to **. On return it works with the pair from pin 10 into pin 13. Pin 14 is the other honeycomb stitch in the gap row. Work picot (15) and the last continuous row of honeycomb at pins 15 and 16.

The honeycomb must be enclosed in gimp, pass the gimp to the left through pairs from 5, 8, 12, 14 and 16. The other gimp goes to the right through pairs from 15 and 16. Cross the gimps right over left. Take the pair from 15 for a picot at (17), and bring the pair back through the two passives but not through the gimp. The left hand pair from 16 works a honeycomb pin with this pair at 17. Make the picot at (6). Remove pin Y and ease the pairs down. One pattern is complete. The pairs at 17 and (6) come in for the next pattern as the pairs did from X and Y.

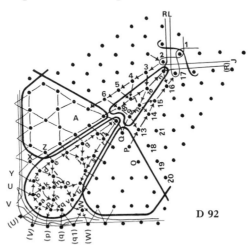

D 92

The corner Refer to diagram **92**. Complete the rows of ground leading into the last honeycomb head as far as possible. The fourth row has pin 1 as corner footside pin, pin 2 as catch pin, and pins 3, 4, 5 and 6 as ground stitches. Take the fourth pair from the footside edge, and work to the right through the two passive pairs only; when the corner has been turned it will become the new inner passive pair J. There is no fifth diagonal row of ground but a pair must be made available for the point of the honeycomb head.

Take the new gimp pair and place it horizontally across the pillow, taking one end through the right hand pair from 6 and through pairs from 5, 4 and 3. Enclose with two twists on each pair. Use pairs from 5 and 4 for honeycomb pin 7. Take the left hand pair from 7 and the right hand pair from 6 for honeycomb pin 8. Bring the left hand gimp thread towards the right through the left hand pair from 8. There are sufficient pairs to complete head A. As usual, cross the gimps below pin Z, and then continue with the gimp on the right through the five pairs from the head. The gimps lie together – there are no twists between, but two twists on each pair to enclose the gimp. Work pin X, and picot Y. Extra pairs are required for the corner and false picots are made. More details concerning the working and use of these are on page 141.

Hang two pairs on U, and twist the threads on either side of the pin three times each. Cover the pin with cloth stitch and two twists. Work the right hand pair in cloth stitch through two pairs to the right. Work the left hand pair in cloth stitch through one pair only. Take the third pair from the picot edge and work cloth stitch twice to the edge, make picot into pin V, and work back through one pair only. Hang two pairs on pin (U), make a false picot, and bring the right hand pair through three pairs to the right in cloth stitch. Bring the left hand pair through one pair only. Take the third pair from the picot edge, work two cloth stitches to the left, and picot into pin (V). Work back through three pairs in cloth stitch. Take the left hand gimp through pairs from X, Y, U, (U) and (V).

The corner honeycomb   This is worked at a different angle from the honeycomb in a straight strip. Use pairs from (U) and (V) to work honeycomb pin a. Use the right hand pair and the next pair to the right (from U) for pin b. Use the right hand pair and the next pair to the right (from pin Y) for pin c. The pair from pin X will work pin d, and so on to pin i. Use pairs from f and g for pin j, and from d and e for pin l, and from b and c for pin k. The left hand pair from l and the right hand pair from k work pin m, the pair from k and the left hand pair from m work pin n, and the right hand pair from m and the pair from l work pin o. The honeycomb may be completed using the pair from a and the left hand pair from n for pin p. The left hand pair at pin p passes out round the gimp, and through all the passives to make a picot at (p) and back through two pairs.

Four pairs were introduced for the corner, and gradually they will be removed. Discard the last pair worked through in cloth stitch by taking it back over the work, and allowing the bobbins to fall to the back of the pillow. Later the threads may be cut off. Take the right hand pair from p and the other pair from n, and work pin q. Take the left hand pair out to make a picot at pin (q). Bring it back through two pairs, and discard the last pair passed through. Take the right hand pair from q out to make a picot at pin (q1), and take it back through three passives to pin W. Use the left hand pair from i and the pair from h for pin r, use the left hand pair from r and the right hand pair from j for pin s, use the left hand pair from s and the left hand pair from j for pin t, and so on.

Take the right hand gimp, and pass it through pairs from i, r, s, t and u. Take the left hand gimp and pass it through two pairs from v and pairs from u, t, s, r and i. Twist these pairs twice to enclose the gimp. The left hand pair from v and the pair from (q1) work honeycomb pin W. Discard the middle pair of the three passives. The left hand pair from W works picot at pin (W), and works back through two passives. The middle passive pair is discarded. The left hand gimp is passed through pairs from W and (W) for the next head. Complete this head and enclose with gimp.

Return to the unfinished corner. The pair from Q passes through the gimp, and with the pair from pin 8 works pin 9. Pairs from 7 and 3 work pin 10. The footside passive marked R is twisted, and the right gimp passes through it. It is again twisted, and works pin 11 with the right hand pair from pin 10. The left hand pair from 10 and the right hand pair from 9 work pin 12. The right hand gimp passes through pairs from 11, 12 and 9, and the left hand gimp passes through the same pairs, 9, 12 and 11. The gimp threads are taken back out of the way, and later will be cut off, the three pair overlap being sufficient to achieve a neat and firm result.

The pairs from P and 9 work ground stitch and pin 13. The right hand pair from 13 and the left hand pair from 12 work pin 14. Pairs from 14 and 12 work pin 15, and pairs from 15 and 11 work pin 16. Find the passive pair R that was used at pin 11, and work it in cloth stitch through one pair to the right. It becomes the passive (R), and falls alongside J. The original passive L now falls to the right of the right hand pair from 16. Twist it three times, and use it to work pin 17 with the right hand pair from 16. Pin 17 is a catch pin, and both pairs fall to the left of the pin. Take the pair nearest the pin (the fourth pair from the edge), and work the footside using pin 1 again. The weaver returns through the two footside passives (R) and J, and is ready for use again.

Complete the ground for the next honeycomb head. Return to pin 13. The left hand pair from 13 and the pair from O work pin 18, and the diagonal row is completed with pins 19 and 20. Pairs from 14 and 18 work pin 21, and that diagonal row can be completed similarly. Continue until sufficient pairs are available for the head.

SHEEP'S HEAD DECORATIVE STRIP

When the Sheep's Head pattern is fully understood, the adaptation to a decorative strip with neat beginning and ending can be practised.

False picots are necessary to achieve the picot effect when joining in new threads. They are worked as follows: two pairs are hung on a pin, the threads each side of the pin are twisted three times each, and the pin is covered with a cloth stitch and two twists. This creates a corded or twisted effect round the pin. It is kept firm by the cloth stitch, and the two twists keep it distinct from the passive pairs. Two new pairs are introduced and normally only one is brought into the work from each picot pin.

To use the second pair the following method may be worked. Refer to diagram **93A**. A false picot is made at D, and the right hand pair works through all the passive pairs – usually only two (X and Y) – and round the gimp into the work at t. The left hand pair from D works through one pair only and becomes the passive Z. The third passive from the picot edge (Y) works through two pairs to the edge, makes an ordinary picot at e, works back through two passives (X and Z), round the gimp, and into the work at v.

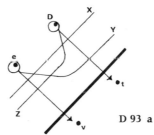

D 93 a

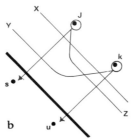

If picots are to be made on the other side of the work, refer to diagram **93B**, and reverse the above instructions. Make a false picot at J, and take the left hand pair through two passives (X and Y) to s. Take the right hand pair through one passive only (X) and it becomes passive Z. Take the third pair from the edge (Y) and work through two pairs (X and Z) to make a normal picot at k. Bring the pair back through to u.

The pattern　Prepare pricking **37** and 18 pairs of bobbins. One gimp pair is required also. Refer to diagram **94** and photograph **51**.

Make false picots at B, A and C. Referring to diagram **94A**, take the left hand pair from A through both pairs from B in cloth stitch. Take the right hand pair from A, and work through both pairs from C in cloth stitch. These pairs become the outside passive pairs. Work the left hand pair from C and the right hand pair from B together in cloth stitch to cross them, and they become the inner passives. The left hand pair from B works cloth stitch through one more pair to the right, and the right hand pair from C works through one more pair to the left. A gimp pair is passed through these two pairs and enclosed with two twists. They become the top two pairs for the cloth diamond, and work together in cloth stitch, pin r is put up and covered. The left hand pair hangs as a passive in the cloth and the right hand pair becomes the weaver.

There are two passive pairs outside of the gimp on each side and two pairs round a pin within the gimp for the cloth diamond. Make a false picot at D, and an ordinary picot at e. Refer to diagram **93A**. Repeat making false picots at F and H, and ordinary picots at g and i. Refer to diagram **93B** and make, on the other side, false picots at J, L and N, and ordinary picots at k, m and o. Pass the left hand gimp through pairs from D, e, F and g, and the right hand gimp through pairs from J, k, L and m. Work the cloth stitch diamond using the right hand pair from r as weaver. Remember to cover pin z with cloth stitch. Enclose the diamond with the gimps and cross them below z. Take the gimp on to the right through five more pairs – the two gimps will lie together and there will be no twists between – and on through pairs from N and o.

The honeycomb head is worked in the same way as the Sheep's Head although it is on the other side of the lace. Row 1 to 5 is the first row of continuous honeycomb stitches. Rows beginning at 6 and 13 are gap rows, and rows worked from 9 and 15 are continuous. Remember that the picot with the number enclosed in a bracket has to be worked before the

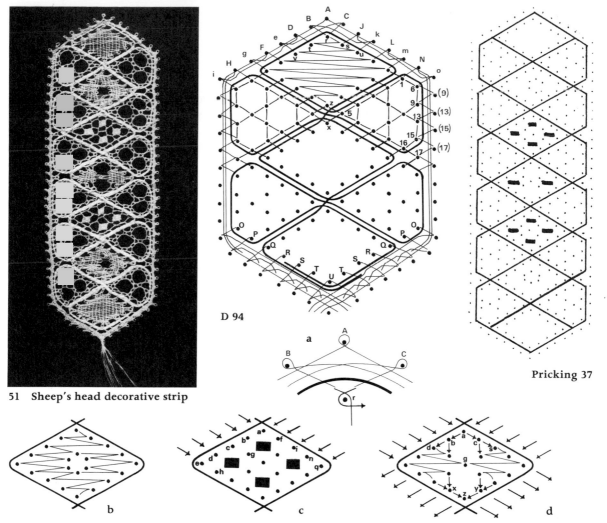

D 94

Pricking 37

51 Sheep's head decorative strip

a

b

c

d

honeycomb stitch with the same number. Take the right gimp through both pairs at 16, and to the left through the other four pairs from the head. It crosses the other gimp and continues through pairs from the left side of the cloth diamond, and through pairs from H and i. Complete the Sheep's Head on the left side of the pattern, referring to diagram **91** if necessary. Take the gimp back to the right to the centre, and cross it under the other gimp above pin x. Take these crossed gimps out in each direction ready for the next diamond.

A variety of patterns are given in the diamond shapes and choice is at the discretion of the worker.

Cloth diamond with hole Refer to diagram **94B**, and to the Torchon sampler on page 43.

Ground with tallies The method of making tallies or spots is described in the chapter on Torchon on page 47, and basically the method is the same. It is important at the end of a tally that the pair containing the tally weaver should be used only after the other pair, as its immediate use will pull the tally out of shape. Refer to diagram **94C** and work as follows.

Make ground stitches at a, b, c, d, e and f. Use the left hand from f and the right hand pair from b to make a tally. As there are three twists on each pair, the tally should be woven straight away, taking the second thread over the third and under the fourth. When completed, the tally weaver should be on the right. Twist the left hand threads and the right hand threads together three times each, and support the weaver in the right hand pair by placing the bobbin horizontally on the pillow until required.

The left hand pair and pair from c work pin g. The left hand pair from g and the pair from d work another tally. The weaver must be left on the right at the end of the tally. The left hand pair from the tally and the right hand pair from e work pin h. The next diagonal row of ground from i is worked normally, and the row beginning with pin n is similar to row f. The last row from q is a normal row.

Honeycomb and cloth   Refer to diagram **94D**. Pins a, b and c are honeycomb pins. Cloth diamonds begin at d and s. The diagram shows incoming and outgoing pairs. At g, the weavers work together in cloth stitch, the pin is covered, and the weavers return to their own diamonds. Pins x, y and z are honeycomb pins. Remember to twist twice the pairs coming out of cloth for honeycomb.

To complete the strip   Work the last cloth stitch diamond, and enclose it with the gimp threads. Overlap the gimps through three pairs on each side, and allow them to fall back out of the way of working. Later they will be cut off. Both sides are worked in the same way. Starting at O, take the pair out to do a picot and back through two pairs. Take the pair from P out to make a picot and back through two pairs. Discard the last pair worked through (i.e. the second passive from the picot edge).

Take pairs out from Q, R, S, T and U and discard one pair each time. When both sides have been worked, there will be three pairs hanging on each side – pass them directly through each other in cloth stitch so that they lie very flat. Take the outside pairs and cross them under the centre pairs, bring them round to the top, and tie them together tightly. Tie each pair of bobbins in the centre, then take the outside threads round the bundle once more, and tie. Trim all threads to leave a tassle.

Twisting of threads (to consolidate the number and position of twists in Bucks Point lace.) A gimp thread is always enclosed with twists, unless it passes through the weaver which is rarely twisted. There are two twists between gimp and honeycomb, and three twists between gimp and ground. If the gimp is passed through the pairs immediately after honeycomb or ground stitches no extra twisting is necessary – the twists that are part of the stitches are sufficient. When the stitches are to be made after the gimp has passed through the pairs, the twists must be made before the honeycomb and ground stitches are worked. There are two twists between cloth stitch and the gimp. These twists must always be made, after the cloth stitch and after the gimp has passed through. When

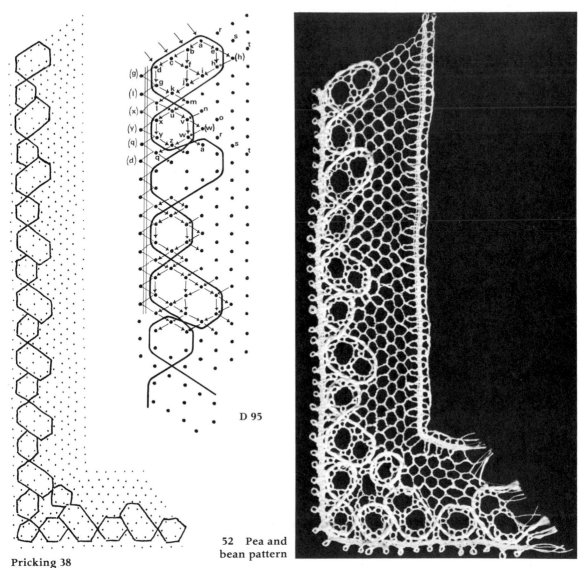

D 95

Pricking 38

52   Pea and
bean pattern

gimp threads lie together, there are no twists between them unless a particular effect is desired, usually only in the more elaborate laces. A weaver is twisted twice as it passes round the pin when a piece of cloth is being worked.

PEA AND BEAN PATTERN

In order to make a satisfactory corner design, the edging has the pattern reversed in the centre of each side. Arrange this when planning a piece to fit a rectangle of material. If a straight length is worked no reversal is necessary.

Prepare pricking **38** and 15 pairs of bobbins, also one gimp pair. One gimp pair extra will be required for the corner. Refer to diagram **95** and photograph **52**. The diagrams are intended to explain the arrangement of threads in the honeycomb, and to show the working of gimps and picots. They do not show all the rows of ground. The method of working ground was explained in the Fan pattern on page 134, and reference can be made to these instructions for all future patterns.

Beginning a pattern   It is advantageous to start with the second or third repeat on the pricking; the first set of pattern holes can be used for reference, and for the support pins which are later removed. In diagram **95** the first row of holes are the pin-holes to be worked, and the support pins must be put up in the row behind. The first row to be worked has the footside pin, the catch pin and four ground holes (i.e. six altogether), and the last stitch to be worked is at pin r. Two more rows of ground are worked, ending at pins s and t. Remember to remove the support pins to achieve a neat beginning.

The honeycomb   Now put up support pins for the honeycomb. Directly behind a, put up a pin to support temporarily the gimp pair. Diagonally behind a, b, c and d put up support pins with one pair on each. Take the left hand gimp thread through these four pairs, and the right hand gimp through pairs from r and s. The left hand pair from r and the pair to the left of it work honeycomb pin a. Complete the continuous row, pins b, c and d. Remove the support pins. Use the left hand pair from s and the pair from a to work pin e. This is the first pin in the gap row. Work pin f with pairs from b and c. Put up a support pin behind (g), and hang two pairs on it in order. These will be the passive pairs on the headside. The left hand pair from d works through these pairs to picot pin (g), and returns to complete the gap row by working pin g using the other pair from d. The gimp passes through the right hand pair from e, which passes into the ground, is twisted three times, and works ground pin (h) with the pair from t. The gimp is passed through the left hand pair, returns to the honeycomb, and works with the pair from e into pin h. The continuous row with pins i, j and k should be completed.

Cross the gimps below k. The pairs from g will work a picot at (l) and return through two passive pairs, a honeycomb stitch is worked with this pair and the pair from k into pin 1. The left hand pair works picot (x), and returns through two pairs only. Pass the left gimp through pairs from 1 and (x). Work three rows of ground to pins m, n and o. Pass the right hand gimp through pairs from m and n.

Honeycomb rings with six holes   These are found in many Bucks patterns, and are worked as follows. Two pairs enter the ring through the gimp from each side. Pairs from 1 and m work pin u. The left hand pair from u and pair from (x) work pin x, and the left hand pair from x works out to picot (y), and back to pin y, which is worked with the pair from x. The right hand pair from u and pair from n work pin v. The gimp passes through the right hand pair from v, which is twisted three times, and works ground pin (w) with the pair from o.

The gimp is passed through, and it returns to work pin w with the pair from v. The right hand pair from y and the left hand pair from w work pin z. Enclose the ring with gimps and cross them below pin z. The pair from y works picot pin (q), then works back through two pairs to work honeycomb pin q with a pair from z. The left hand pair from q works picot (d). The left hand gimp travels through pairs from q and (d), and the right hand gimp through pairs from z and w. A pattern is complete.

To begin the next pattern, work the three rows of ground ending at r, s and t. The pattern reversal is straightforward following the arrows on the diagram.

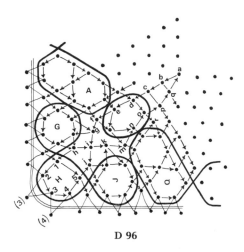

D 96

The corner Refer to diagram **96**, work honeycomb head A, and as much of G as possible. From the corner footside pin a, work catch pin b, and then c as usual. A new gimp pair is passed through the left hand pair from c and the two pairs to the left of it. Honeycomb pins d and e are worked. Pass the gimp through the left hand pair from e, and work pin f. Using the pair from ring G, work pin g, complete the ring, and work pins h and i. Complete ring H in the order indicated, and, after working pin j, work ring J, pin k, and complete the ring.

To complete the inner centre ring, work pin 1, bring the gimp through the left hand pair to work pin m, and then take it back through the same pair to pins n and o. This gimp is no longer required, and should be overlapped and cut off. The arrangement of the ground threads is seen in the diagram – rows of diagonal ground should be worked from p and q. The fourth pair from the footside at q uses corner pin a a second time, and work may proceed normally on the new side.

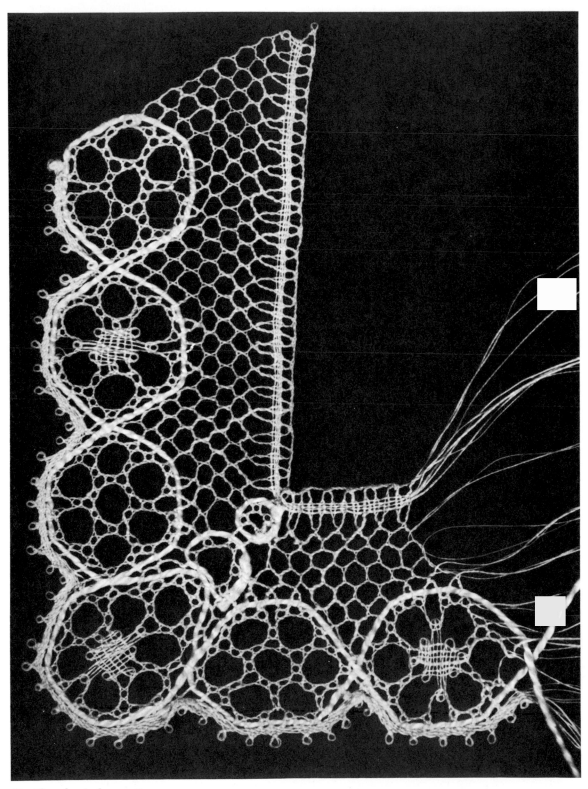

53   Church window pattern

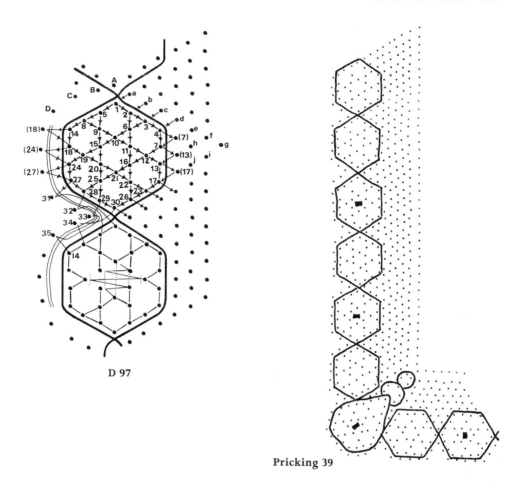

D 97

Pricking 39

CHURCH WINDOW PATTERN

In this pattern, which is also known as Plum Pudding, the picots are on a curve, and a method of working common to all similar patterns is given. Prepare pricking **39** and 18 pairs of bobbins, one gimp pair is also required. An extra two pairs and two gimp pairs are needed for the corner. Refer to diagram **97** and photograph **53**.

To begin the pattern   Select the longest row of ground stitches and put up the footside pin with two pairs on it ready to begin. This row has a footside pin, catch pin, seven more ground pins, and ends at a (nine pins altogether). On the row behind hang up pairs on support pins. If necessary refer to the instructions for the Fan pattern, page 132. Work seven rows of ground, ending at pins a, b, c, d, e, f and g. Hang a gimp pair on A, two pairs on each of B and C, and two pairs in order on D. Take the right hand gimp through pairs from a, b, c and d and the left hand gimp through pairs from B and C. Twist all pairs twice. When working the honeycomb head, note that all pins with brackets are worked before the same number pin without brackets.

Take the right hand pair from B and the pair from a to work pin 1, complete the continuous row with 2, 3 and 4. Pairs from B and 1 work pin 5, and from 2 and 3 work pin 6. The gimp passes through the right hand pair from 4 which is twisted three times and makes ground stitch (7) with the pair from e. The gimp passes to the left through the same pair which works pin 7 with the pair from 4. This completes the gap row. Remove support pin B. The right hand pair from C and the left hand pair from 5 work pin 8. Complete the continuous row as far as pin 13. Before pin 13 can be worked, work ground pin h using pairs from 7 and f, and ground pin (13) with pairs from 7 and h. Work the gap row and pins 14, 15, 16 and 17. Before working pin 17 ground pins i (with pairs from g and h), j (with pairs from (13) and i) and (17) (with pairs from 13 and j) must be completed. Remove support pin C.

To begin the picot heading   Take the left hand pair from 14, pass the gimp through, twist twice, work two cloth stitches, and make the picot at (18). Bring it back to work pin 18, and then complete the continuous row. From pin 18 the left hand pair works picot pin (24), and then pin 24. Complete the gap row with pins 25 and 26. The left hand pair from 24 works picot pin (27), and then pin 27. Complete the continuous row. Note that there are three picots worked with pairs taken from and returned to the honeycomb head. Enclose the head with gimp, crossing the threads below pin 30.

When working picots, the passive threads should lie flat in the curve and there should be no ugly hole at the deepest point. Work as follows. Pairs hang from 27, 28, 29 and the left hand pair from pin 30. Take the pair from 27 to picot pin 31, and back through two passive pairs only. In turn take pairs from 28, 29 and 30 to work picot pins 32, 33 and 34. It is in order for the pair from 30 to work picot pin 34, which is beyond the point, and return through two pairs. Hold this pair and count up the number of picots, which introduce pairs into the head, still to be worked. In this pattern only one pin still has to be worked. Take the pair being held, and work through one more pair in cloth stitch. This pair and the two passives to the right of it pass round the gimp for use in the head. This will leave three passives, and the third from the edge passes out through the other two pairs, works picot pin 35, and returns through the passives and round the gimp into the head. A complete pattern repeat has been worked.

This method is applicable to most patterns and should be learnt and understood. The general principle is as follows: In turn all pairs are worked through all the passives to make picots and are worked back through two pairs only. The last pair works back through the two passives, and on through sufficient pairs to make picots for the pattern. These picots are worked by taking the third pair from the edge and working out to the picot pin and back through the passives as far as the pattern. If the gimp thread is brought through each pair as it becomes available, there is less likelihood of mistakes being made.

Mayflower   This occurs in different kinds of honeycomb fillings, and consists of a cloth stitch diamond worked within the honeycomb. Before working the mayflower the basic stitch arrangement must be fully understood. In order to work the mayflower the pins should be worked in the following order – referring to numbers on the previous head – 1, 2, 3, 4; 5, 6, 7; 8, 9; 14, 18. Pairs from 9 and 6 make a cloth stitch to begin the diamond, and the right hand pair becomes weaver and works from pin to pin as follows: 10, 11, 15, 12, 19, 16, 20 and 21. Pairs are taken in at 11, 15, 12 and 19; and left out after 12, 19, 20 and 16. Pin 21 is covered with a cloth stitch. All pairs leaving the cloth diamond are twisted twice each. The honeycomb is completed in the following order: 24, 25; 13, 22, 17, 23, 26; 27, 28, 29, 30.

Catch pins   In photograph **53** it can be seen that the ground stitches to the right of the head are worked differently after the first pattern repeats. Whenever there are vertical rows of holes with ground one side of the gimp a catch pin may be used for neatness. Referring back to diagram **97**, the gimp passes through the pair from 4, is twisted three times, and works a ground stitch with the pair from e. Pin (7) is put up to the left of both pairs. Take the gimp through the left hand pair, twist it twice and work pin 7. The same method is used at pins (13) and (17). In the Pea and Bean pattern it could have been used for pins (h) and (w) (diagram **95**, page 145).

The corner   Complete the head immediately before the corner, also the sequence of picots to give three pairs for use in the corner head. Refer to

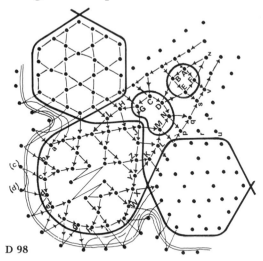

D 98

diagram **98**. Work the footside, and corner pin z. A new gimp is introduced through the pairs that would normally work the catch pin, instead they work honeycomb pin A inside the circle. Take the gimp through the next ground pair to the left and work honeycomb pin B. The left hand pair is released, and the gimp passes through it so that it is available for the next ring. Pass another new gimp through this pair and the next three pairs to the left (i.e. two from ground and one from honeycomb). The middle pairs work honeycomb pin C, and the right hand pairs work pin D. The right hand pair passes round both gimps to work pin E. Working pin F will complete the ring; enclose it with gimps, overlapping them below E and F. They are discarded. The left hand pairs inside the gimp work pin G, and from that pin the left hand pair goes to work the ground pins H and I. The right hand pair from G also leaves the ring to work pin J later. The honeycomb head must be worked completely before any further ground or honeycomb ring stitches can be made. At (c) make a false picot and work picot (d). At this stage the worker learns to assess the number of pairs required, and which pairs to use for the head.

It is obvious that the pair from G needs to work pin J, and the gimp will be taken to the right through all pairs including the pair from G. The seventh and eighth pairs to the left work pin a. Three pairs are required on the left to work honeycomb, and a false picot was made to provide the extra pairs. Pass the gimp through these three pairs. Work the honeycomb continuous row to the right from a. Work gap row b. Work the first two pins in continuous row c, and pins d and e. Work the mayflower and complete the honeycomb, ending at pin j; enclose with gimp. Two pairs joined in at the false picot are no longer required and should be discarded in the passive pairs, as in the decorative strip. From the diagram note that pairs from Z and Y work pin K. Pin L is worked before the ring can be completed. Pairs from L and J work pin M, and the ring is completed at N. Follow the diagram directional arrows to work the ground required for the next honeycomb head, remembering that the first continuous row of honeycomb must be worked before pin p.

HONEYCOMB, CLOTH AND FOUR PIN BUDS PATTERN
This pattern has the hexagon of honeycomb, a cloth diamond with one pin outside the gimp, and four pin honeycomb buds. Prepare pricking **40** and 25 pairs of bobbins, also one gimp pair. Four pairs extra and two gimp pairs are required for the corner. Refer to diagram **99** and photograph **54**.

Begin by working the diagonal row of ground ending at pin a, work five more rows of ground to have pairs available for the four pin buds. Hang the gimp pair on A and one pair on B, C, D, E, F, two pairs in order on G and two pairs on K.

To work the four pin bud in honeycomb stitches   Take the right hand gimp through pairs from a and b, and the left hand gimp through pairs from B and C. Pairs from a and B work pin 1, from 1 and C work pin 2, from 1 and b work pin 3, and from 2 and 3 work pin 4. Bring the right hand gimp to the left through pairs from 3 and 4, and the left hand gimp to the right through pairs from 4 and 3, and c and d. Work the bud labelled e, and enclose with gimps. Use two pairs from e and pairs from f and g to work bud h. Leave the left hand gimp hanging and take the right hand gimp to

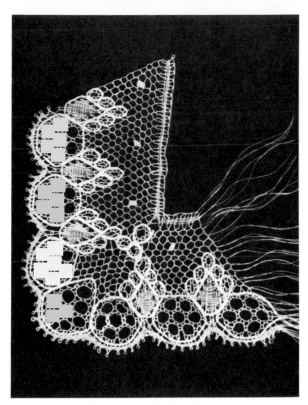

54   Honeycomb, cloth and four pin buds pattern

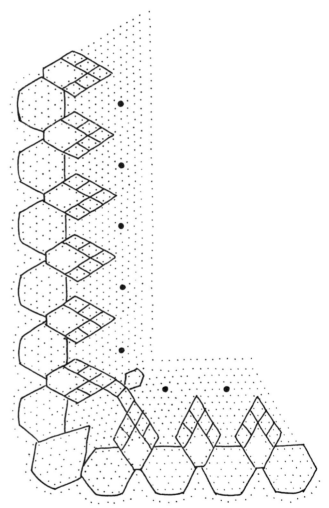

Pricking 40

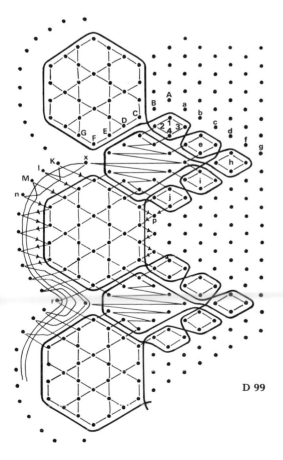

D 99

the left through the pairs from the three buds, and on through pairs from D, E and F.

Working the cloth diamond   Pairs from D and 2 begin the cloth diamond. To work pin x, take the gimp through the weaver, twist the weaver twice, and work cloth stitch through pairs hanging from G. Put up pin x, and work back through these pairs which become passives on the headside, pass the gimp through and complete the diamond. Bring the gimp round the diamond, cross it under the other gimp, and take it through two pairs from h. The other gimp (now on the left) passes through two pairs from the diamond in order to have pairs available to work the four pin bud i.

Cross the gimps and work four pin bud j. The left hand gimp is hanging, and the right hand gimp passes through two pairs from bud j and three pairs from the cloth diamond. Make a false picot at K, bring one pair through the two passives from x, work picot 1, and bring that pair through too. Make a false picot at M, and a normal picot at n. Take the gimp through these four pairs.

The honeycomb head   This is worked in the same way as the Church Window pattern. Note that the first catch pin at p is worked with a pair from j.

The use of pairs for picots is affected by the position of x. Work the four pairs out for picots, and back through two pairs as usual. Before the picots for the next head can be completed the weaver from the diamond must work pin x. Then bring the pair from r through all the passive pairs and work the other picots as usual using the third pair from the outside edge.

The corner   Written explanation becomes increasingly confusing as the lace becomes more difficult, and the number of pairs is increased. Diagram **100** should be studied carefully. The directional arrows explain the way

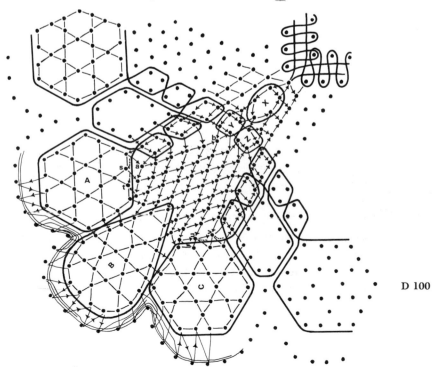

D 100

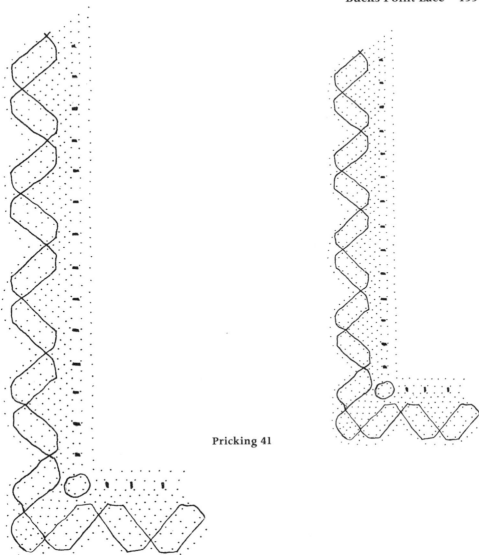

Pricking 41

of working. When A is being worked, the pairs enter the corner ground filling and do not return to the honeycomb. Pairs are introduced over the gimp for pins s and t, and will be no longer required after pins u and v. They can be carried alongside the gimp and discarded. Honeycomb rings X and Y, each with its own gimp pair, must be started before the ground filling. The first row of ground is worked from a to b, and immediately ring Y can be completed and the gimps crossed for Z. All the ground filling will be worked before C.

RAM'S HORNS PATTERN

The variation on the footside is sometimes known as cucumber foot. It is useful to add interest or increase the width of any pattern, however the arrangement of holes is different from the normal footside. Prepare pricking 41 and 18 pairs of bobbins, also one gimp pair. An extra four

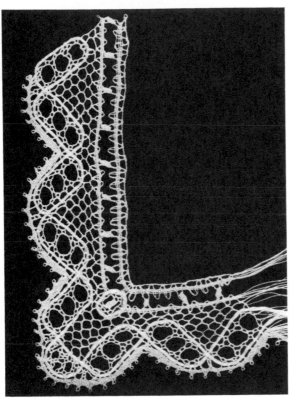

55   Ram's horn pattern

D 101

pairs and one gimp pair will be required for the corner. Hang two pairs on A1, and two pairs in order on B and C. Hang one pair on D, E, F and G. Refer to diagram **101** and photograph **55**.

To work cucumber foot   The pairs on B and C are passive footside threads. Twist the pairs, and cover A1 with cloth stitch and three twists. Work through the two passive pairs as usual, and put up pin 2 to the right of the weaver. Using the pair at D3 as weaver, work to the right in cloth stitch through two pairs from C, and put up pin 4 to the left of the weaver. The weavers at pins 2 and 4 work a tally, and the tally weaver is twisted with the right hand thread ready to work back to the footside later. The other two threads are twisted together, and they work back through two passive pairs to the left in cloth stitch. Twist the weaver three times, and make a ground stitch with the pair from E. Put up catch pin 5 to the right of both pairs. Work ground pins 6 and 7 and remove support pins E, F and G.

Take the pair immediately to the left of catch pin 5, and work to the right in cloth stitch through the two passive pairs. Put up pin 8, and work back through the two pairs to catch pin 9 and ground stitch 10. Again take the pair nearest to the passive pairs and work through them to pin 11, then back to catch pin 12 and pin 13. The fourth pair from the edge (this comes from the tally at 2) works the footside pin 14. The weaver works back as usual to become the fourth pair from the edge. Pin 15 is put up, and the weaver returns to footside pin 16. There is no link with the rest of the pattern. Continue as far as pin 19 when another tally is worked. Remove support pins B and C.

Referring to diagram **102**, it is seen that a footside is worked independent of ground and linked only with tallies. To the inside of it is a second footside with catch pin linking it to ground, however this footside lacks the straight edge and is joined to a straight edged footside with tallies.

To work the pattern   Hang up a gimp pair on G, and pass it through six pairs hung up on support pins for the honeycomb. Pass the right hand gimp through pairs from 7 and 10. Hang two pairs in order on a support pin behind g for passive pairs. Work in letter order on the diagram from a to u. Cross the gimps below pin r, and work six rows of ground to lead into the next piece of honeycomb. This is worked from a to r, and the gimps cross below r. The working sequence for picots from J to R is normal. Pairs from m, n, o, p, q and r work out to the edge, make a picot and return through two pairs only. Beyond O, there are three picots which send pairs directly into the honeycomb. Therefore the pair which has worked picot O continues through three pairs more (five in all) in cloth stitch. The third pair from the edge works out to picots P, Q and R, and each time comes back to the honeycomb. One pattern repeat is complete.

The corner   Refer to diagram **103**, and work honeycomb A. Make false

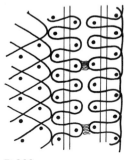

D 102

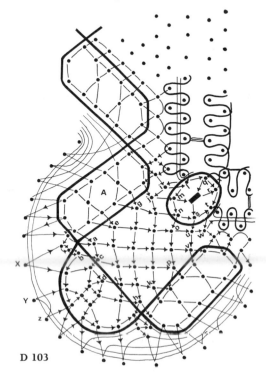

D 103

picots at X and Y, and a picot at z. Note the direction of rows of ground in the corner – rows are worked from a, e, g and j. Shorter rows are worked from o, and u. Close reference to the diagram shows the direction of working. For guidance, note that the ground is worked from pin a, and the honeycomb from pin b. When pin b has been worked the ground a, c is worked. The honeycomb is worked to d, and then the diagonal row of ground e, f, to release the pair for the honeycomb below d. Diagonal g, h is worked, and the honeycomb completed. Pin i is worked, and the ground row j to k.

The honeycomb ring   This is worked as follows, passing a fresh gimp through the pairs when necessary as indicated in the diagram. The left

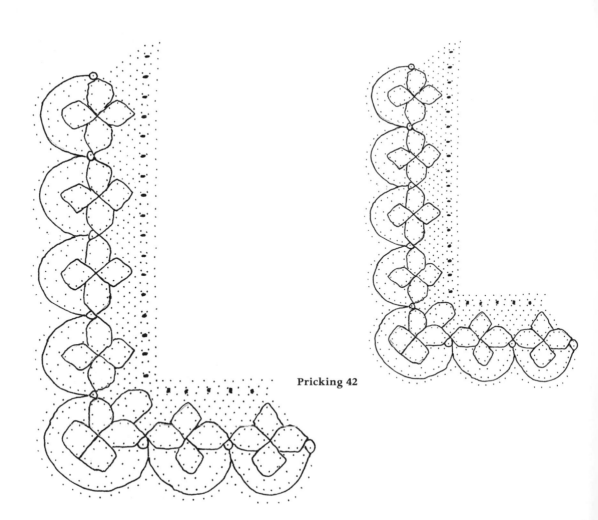

Pricking 42

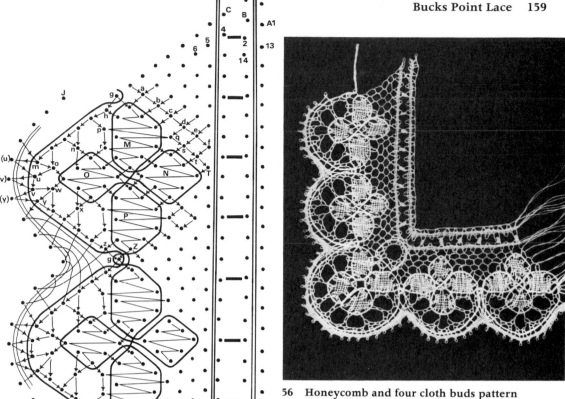

56   Honeycomb and four cloth buds pattern

hand passive pair and the right hand pair from i work pin 1. The left hand from 1 and the next pair to the left work pin m. The left hand pair from m and the next pair work pin n. Complete the ground row o to p.

The right hand pair of passives from the inner footside is carried with the right hand gimp. The corner footside weaver and the right hand pair from 1 work pin q. The right hand pair from m and the left hand pair from q work a tally. The pair from q and the half tally work pin r, and the right hand pair from r works the corner footside pin a second time. The pair from n and the other half of the tally work pin s. The right hand pair from s and the left hand pair from r work t to complete the ring. Enclose the ring, overlap the gimps and discard them. Diagonal ground row u to v can be worked, also pin w using pairs from t and u. The right hand pair from w becomes the weaver, and works to the right through the pair from t and the pair carried with the gimp. Continue the new side normally.

PATTERN WITH HONEYCOMB AND FOUR CLOTH BUDS
Prepare pricking **42** and 24 pairs of bobbins. One gimp pair and one single gimp bobbin are also required. One gimp pair extra is needed for the corner. Refer to diagram **104** and photograph **56**.

Set in the cucumber foot as in the previous pattern, and work rows of ground from a to catch pin f. The first few numbers are given for guidance but more ground stitches in each row are worked. From f work through the passive pairs and return the weaver pair ready for the next catch pin. Support the single gimp from pin J, and behind g hang up two pairs, taking the gimp to the right through these pairs and working honeycomb pin g. Take the gimp back to the left through both pairs. The pin supporting the gimp should be left until several pattern repeats have been worked, but the other support pin removed at once. Hang up six pairs on support pins behind the honeycomb, and take the gimp through to the left. Using the pair from g to begin the continuous row, work from h to m. Remove support pins, and hang up two headside passive pairs and work gap row stitches n and o.

Four cloth buds   These are worked consecutively M, N, O, P, and, to achieve a neat centre, the one gimp enclosing each of the buds N and O. Hang the gimp pair on a support pin so that it falls into the work between g and a. Pass the left hand thread through pairs from g and h, and the right hand thread through pairs from a, b and c. Work the cloth ring M. To work pin p, take the weaver out and twist it twice, work a cloth stitch and two twists, put up pin p, cover and take the weaver back into the cloth. Pin r is worked similarly. Take the weaver out to pin q, work a ground stitch with the pair from d, and put up catch pin q to the left of both pairs. Take the left hand pair back into the cloth. Complete the cloth and enclose with gimps, crossing them at the bottom of the ring.

Work ground pins s and t, and catch pin T. Take the right hand gimp thread through the three pairs from M and through pairs from s, t and T. Work cloth diamond N. Take the gimp to the left through the six pairs to enclose the diamond, pass it over the other gimp, and on through the next six pairs (i.e. two from M, one from r, two from n, and one from o). Complete the cloth diamond O, and bring the gimp back to the right through the six pairs from the diamond, under the other gimp, and through three pairs from N. The left hand gimp passes through *two* pairs from O. Before working P, one more row of ground is worked using the pairs from N. Also the picots and honeycomb stitches u, v, w and x must be completed. P is worked in the same way as M. The pair from v makes picot (y), and returns to honeycomb stitch y. The honeycomb row is worked to z. The gimp passes through all honeycomb pairs, including both pairs from z and the left hand pair from Z.

The other gimps cross below Z, and the left gimp passes to the left through the left pair from Z and the pair from z. Pin g is a honeycomb pin with the pairs from z and Z. The two gimps to the right of the pin cross the left gimp, and then the single gimp passes through the left hand pair from g. The other gimp passes through the right hand pair from g – this pair is between the gimps ready for the cloth bud. For gimp arrangement refer to diagram **104**.

The corner   This is less complicated than most. The weaver from the

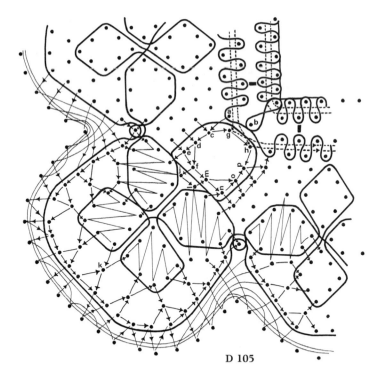

D 105

inner footside at catch pin a passes through two passive pairs in cloth stitch as usual, and works cloth stitch and three twists with the weaver from the corner footside at pin b. Put up pin b, cover it, and work out to the same corner pin a second time. Introduce a new gimp, and take it through pairs as required following diagram **105** closely.

The pair at catch pin a and the pair to the left of it work honeycomb pin c; continue to the left and work pins d, e and f. The pair at c works with the next pair to the right (i.e. the left passive pair on the inner footside) for pin g. The right hand pair stays alongside the gimp until it returns as a passive after the corner. The left hand pair works with the other passive at pin h. The right hand pair will return to its use as a passive after the corner is turned. Refer to the dotted lines on the diagram.

The honeycomb and cloth buds are worked in a straightforward manner, but care and frequent reference should be made to the diagram to ensure the use of the correct pairs. Note that the pair used at j must be left hanging until required for re-use at 1. Also note the use of pairs at k. After k has been worked, the pillow can be turned to work the rest of the corner more easily, and the new side. Only when the cloth buds are worked can the honeycomb circle be finished by working m, n, o and p. Enclose the ring with gimp. The arrows on the diagram explain the use of pairs in the ground, and the dotted lines show the use of the passive threads on the inner footside.

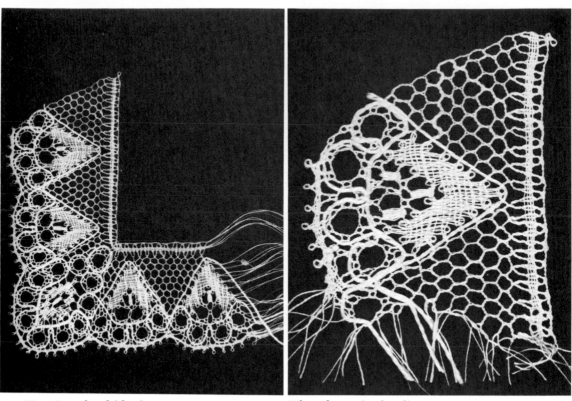

57a   Open headside rings

57b   Alternative heading

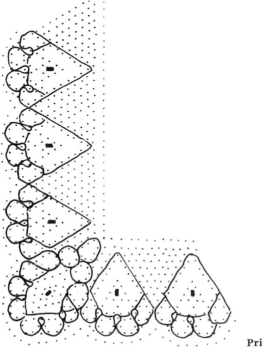
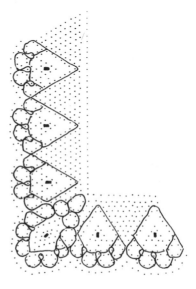

Pricking 43

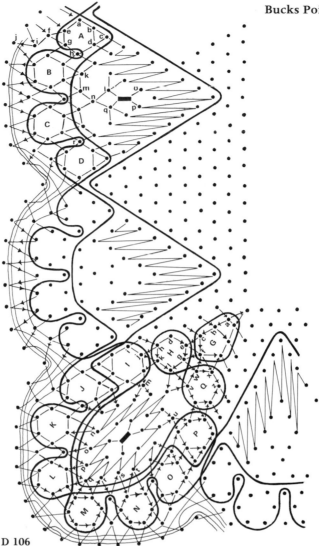

D 106

TWO OLD BUCKS LACE PATTERNS

The next two patterns have an identical arrangement of holes on the headside, but the interpretation is quite different. See prickings **43** and **44**, photographs **57a** and **b**, and **58**. Sometimes the ink markings on old patterns are no longer legible and the method of working is at the discretion of the worker. In the first pattern the circles are worked in honeycomb, and in the second, in cloth stitch.

Pattern No.1

Prepare pricking **43** and 21 pairs of bobbins. A single gimp bobbin and a gimp pair will also be required. Refer to photograph **57a** and diagram **106**. Work the footside and ground so that ten pairs of bobbins are available to begin the honeycomb ring and cloth from the right.

Working the honeycomb circles   Hang four pairs on support pins to come in on the left as indicated by arrows. Hang up the single gimp and the gimp pair on separate pins behind a, and allow them to fall between the pairs from the ground and the pairs on the left. Take the single gimp through the three pairs from the ground from left to right. Pass the right hand gimp of the pair through the same three pairs, and the left hand gimp through two pairs to the left. Work honeycomb ring A, noting that pin c is a honeycomb pin within the ring, but pin f is a honeycomb pin outside worked with a pair from a support pin. In order to keep an uninterrupted curve on the centre gimp, the left hand gimp has to pass round pin h. This is achieved by passing the left hand gimp through the pairs required for the stitch from g and d, the honeycomb stitch is made, the pin covered, and the gimp taken back from right to left through the same pairs. Pin i is a honeycomb pin worked with the pair from f and a pair brought in from the left. Two passive pairs are hung up, and the pair from i goes out to the picot pin j. The left hand gimp passes through two pairs from i and j to provide the pairs for ring B. The centre gimp passes through pairs from c, d and h.

Follow the diagram, and work the first half of the cloth stitch as far as pin p. Work ring B, and pins k, l, m and n. Work ring C. Pairs from l and o make a tally, and release pairs for q and p. Complete the cloth stitch. Work ring D, taking the left hand gimp to the right through the pairs required for pin r, and then back through these two pairs and one more. The use of pairs for picots and the crossing of gimps is clearly shown on the diagram.

The corner   Refer to the corner on diagram **106**. Follow the directional arrows and work the rings in the order given from G – the pins are worked from a in order. In ring G, work pins a, b and c. Begin H with another gimp and pin d. Work pin e, and in G work f, taking the pair back for g. G cannot be completed as pin f has to be used a second time. Continue to L, and before completing L the cloth diamond outline and tally should be worked. As the pairs leaving the honeycomb for the cloth have to return to the honeycomb, an extra pair is joined in at each of pins n, o and p, and left out after pins r, s and t. At q, the pin is used twice, in the working of both rings L and M. Work M, N and O and begin P. Work Q, beginning at pin v, and pins w and x, using pin f a second time. Complete G and P, and then Q, which is completed at z.

Pattern No.2
Prepare pricking **44** and 21 pairs of bobbins, also one gimp pair. Refer to diagram **107** and photograph **58**.

Work from the footside rows of ground for the cloth bud A. The weaver has to pass outside the gimp to maintain a close even cloth bud; the pin-holes between gimp and picots are worked in honeycomb, and in order to keep the tension firm, cloth stitch and two twists may be worked before and after the pin. When the weaver enters the ground, it is neater to use a catch pin stitch, putting the pin to the gimp side of both pairs. The weaver may pass from the cloth, round the gimp, and through the

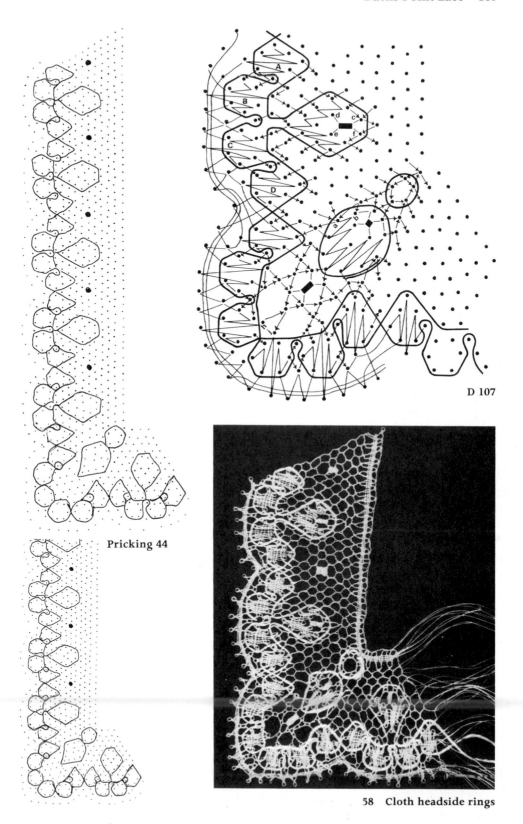

D 107

Pricking 44

58   Cloth headside rings

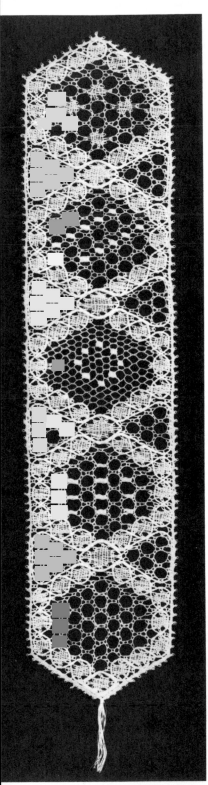

59   Decorative sampler

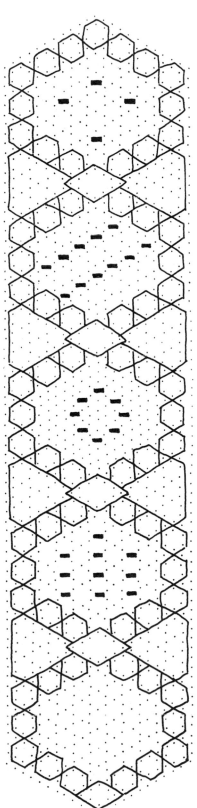

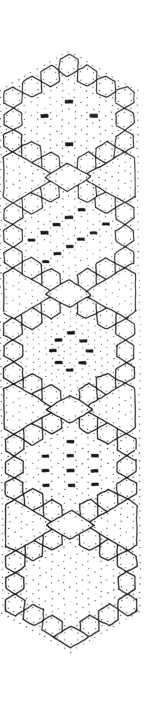

Pricking 45

passives to the picot. Special care must then be taken to ensure that the tension is good before the weaver returns to the cloth.

Note. A weaver works out to make picots infrequently; only when the pins are vertically arranged in cloth, and a close even result is required. The diagram explains the method of working, pin c is honeycomb, and pairs from c and d work a tally. Pin f is honeycomb. In the corner at a, the right hand of the three pairs works cloth stitch through the two pairs to the left, pin a is put up, and the weaver goes back through three pairs to b. The left pair from a can be used for a ground stitch. Extra gimp pairs are required for the circles. An extra pair is joined in at h and carried with the gimp from j as it is no longer required.

DECORATIVE SAMPLER

Refer to photograph **59** and diagram **108**. Prepare pricking **45** and 26 pairs of bobbins and two gimp pairs. All the techniques found in this sampler has been used in previous patterns. To begin, refer to the Sheep's Head decorative strip on page 141.

To work the following refer as follows:

Cloth buds entering honeycomb and making picots on page 160, photograph **59**.
Honeycomb with mayflower on page 182, photograph **60A**.
Honeycomb with tallies within rings on page 182, photograph **60B**.
Ground with tallies on page 143, photograph **60C**.
Honeycomb with tallies on page 182, photograph **60D**.
Honeycomb on page 144, photograph **60E**.

To complete the sampler refer to the decorative strip on page 144.

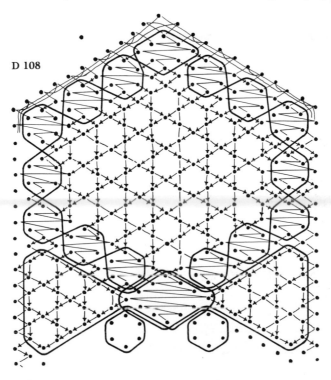

D 108

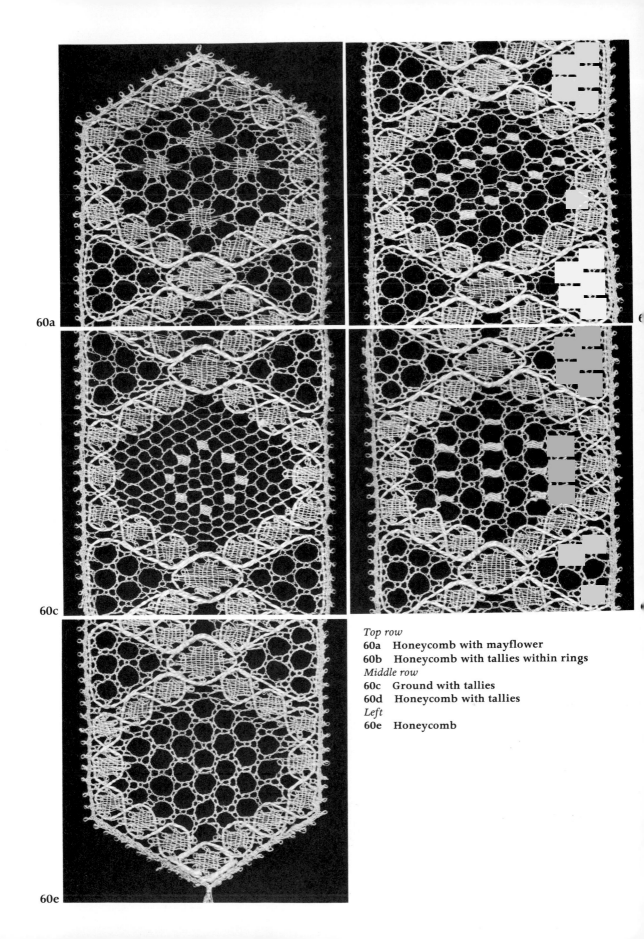

60a

60c

60e

Top row
60a Honeycomb with mayflower
60b Honeycomb with tallies within rings
Middle row
60c Ground with tallies
60d Honeycomb with tallies
Left
60e Honeycomb

RING OF HONEYCOMB BUDS WITH CLOTH CENTRE PATTERN

This is an attractive old pattern that is worked quite regularly. See photograph **61**. Diagram **109** gives the necessary instructions, and diagram **110** clarifies the use of the three pairs of gimp where they meet around a centre four pin bud. Prepare pricking **46** and 30 pairs of bobbins. Four gimp pairs will also be needed. The corner needs several extra pairs joined in as required, and taken out by carrying alongside the gimp and then throwing out.

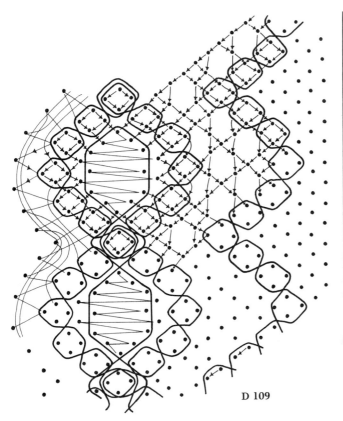

D 109

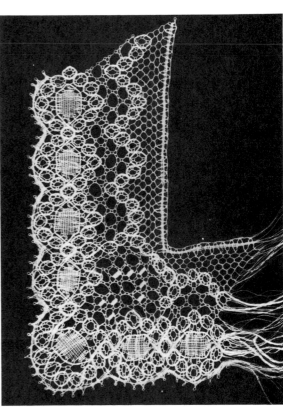

61   Ring of honeycomb buds with cloth centre pattern

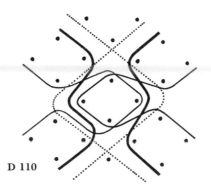

D 110

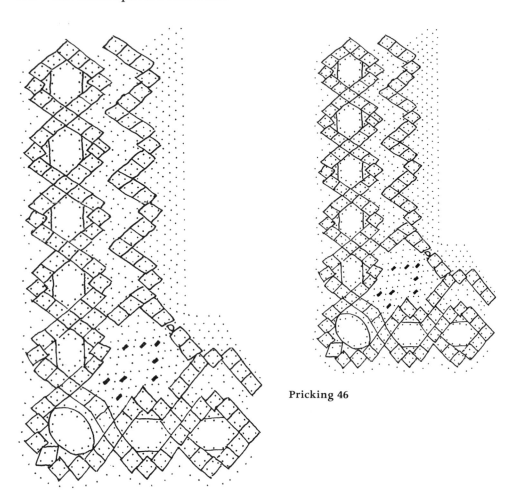

Pricking 46

KAT STITCH PATTERN

Kat stitch is also known as wire ground, and lace with this stitch is usually made in black thread. It was popular during the Victorian era, and should be quicker to work than the ordinary point ground. Black lace usually has any solid parts worked in half stitch, but half stitch is rarely found in white point lace. See photograph **62**.

Prepare pricking **47**, and 27 pairs of bobbins, also one gimp pair. Refer to diagram **111**. Hang up three pairs on A 1 and two pairs in order on B to H inclusive.

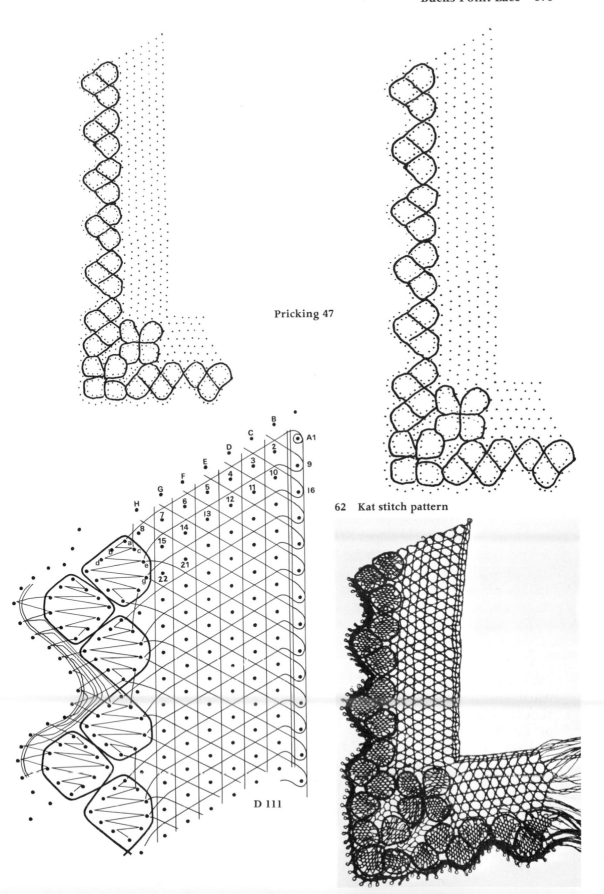

Pricking 47

62   Kat stitch pattern

D 111

To work Kat stitch   Twist the two right hand bobbins three times, and work cloth stitch and twist through the other two pairs on A1. Continue with this pair, which is third from the right side edge, through the next two pairs from B with cloth stitch and twist. Put up pin 2 to the right of the weaver (i.e. between the last pairs worked), but do not cover the pin. Use the weaver to work through two more pairs (from C), and put up pin 3 to the right of the weaver. Continue across the row, working through two pairs and putting up the pin, until pins 4, 5, 6, 7 and 8 are in position.

Working from left to right and without any pins, cross the pairs between the pins with cloth stitch and twist. To the right of pin B there are three pairs, but work the two pairs nearest B in cloth stitch and twist. To work the footside pin, take the third pair from the edge and work cloth stitch and twist twice to the outside edge. Put up pin 9 inside two pairs, ignore the outer pair, and work cloth stitch and twist round the pin. Remove pin B.

To continue the kat stitch, take the weaver which is the third from the right, work cloth stitch and twist twice, and put up pin 10 to the right of the weaver. Work cloth stitch and twist twice, and put up pin 11. Continue as far as pin 15.

The difficulties encountered in a Kat Stitch pattern only arise when the ground is linked into the pattern. In this pattern the problems are few as the pattern is regular and the line between ground and pattern is straight. Use gimps as required.

The diagonal weaver from A is in line with pin a. A vertical pair has to be introduced to enter half stitch at c, so hang this pair behind the work, and take the weaver through it, round the gimp, and into a. The Kat stitch weaver from pin 9 has worked across to the left of pin 15. Work through one more pair, which is the vertical pair through which all threads pass travelling in and out of the half stitch. It enters the half stitch at e, and leaves immediately, passing back through the same vertical pair. The weaver to the left of 21 works through two more pairs, and pin 22 is put up. The weaver enters the half stitch at g, and leaves immediately. Complete the first half stitch bud, and enclose with gimp. The right hand pair from the bottom hole works through one pair in cloth stitch and twist to lie ready for the next row of Kat stitch ground.

Work the second half stitch bud, introducing the passives on the head-side before making the first picot, and leaving pairs out for picots. The first and third buds are worked in the same way. The picot heading should be worked altogether when the rest of the pattern repeat is complete.

The corner requires extra pairs, and these are joined in when required to keep sufficient pairs in the half stitch and to maintain the straight weavers and vertical threads. Pairs no longer required are carried with the gimp and discarded. Extra gimp pairs should be introduced as required, and later discarded. The important consideration is the appearance of the finished lace.

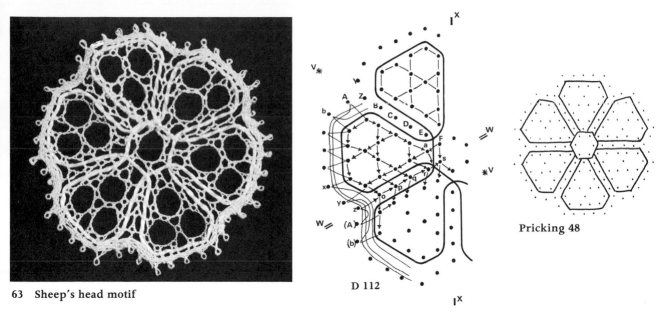

63 Sheep's head motif

D 112

Pricking 48

CIRCULAR MOTIFS

The attractive old circular patterns are usually most elaborate, but for the experienced worker with plenty of time they are well worthwhile. Simple motifs useful for small doilies, for decoration and for mounting under glass for paperweights or trays are quick to make and require only a basic knowledge of Bucks point laces. They require comparatively few bobbins and are easy to design.

The patterns consist of six triangular heads about a centre point. An understanding of the method of designing will facilitate the working. Refer to the first motif, photograph **63**, and the Sheep's Head pattern on page 136. The lace is worked at an angle of 60 degrees from the footside. If six heads are placed about a centre point a small motif results. Begin by marking a six pin honeycomb ring on to a grid at 60 degrees. Divide the sheet into sections by joining opposite points of the ring through the centre and extending the lines outside the centre ring. The stitches on these lines fall between sections and can be honeycomb or ground. The pattern is placed within each section, and the picots arranged as necessary.

Sheep's Head Motif

Refer to diagram **112** and prepare pricking **48**. Join the balance marks on the diagram and work out the position of them on the pricking, if necessary indicate them in another colour to avoid confusion. Place the edge of a cover cloth along the line labelled X. This line is in the same position as the footside in a straight edging.

Make a false picot at A, and a normal picot at b. Take the pairs from both picots through two passives hung up at Y. Hang a gimp pair on Z and pass the left hand gimp through these two pairs. Hang pairs on B, C, D and E, and two pairs on F. Enclose pin F with a honeycomb stitch. Take the right hand gimp through five pairs (i.e. from B, C, D, E and the left hand pair from F). Work the honeycomb Sheep's Head completely, and bring the left hand gimp towards the centre through all the pairs except the pair from a. Work picots x and y. Make a false picot at z, and bring one pair through the passives to work the honeycomb pin o. Continue working pins p, q and r. The pair from a is not required, and should be placed alongside the gimp and eventually discarded. Take both gimps through the right pair from r. This pair and the pair from F work pin s. One section of the motif is complete.

Move the extra cover cloth so that the edge now lies along line V, and turn the pillow so that the 'footside' line is vertically on the right. Take the third pair out to make picot (A) and then repeat using the third pair for picot (b). Take the right hand gimp to the left through pairs from r, q, p, o, (A) and (b). The other gimp passes to the right through one pair from s. All pairs are now available to work section two. As a false picot was made at z there will be a pair extra in the headside, and this will make the picot to begin the row which is worked when the head is complete. Again, the pair at the point of the Sheep's Head has no further use, and is later discarded. Move the extra cover cloth to the line W and continue until the six sections are complete.

It will be necessary to push the pins from the earlier sections down into the pillow so that the last two sections can be worked. A piece of clear plastic film placed over the pin heads and held in position by cover cloths will make the working easier.

Motif No.2

See photograph **64** and the Church Window pattern on page 149. Prepare pricking **49** and refer to diagram **113**. The Church Window pattern has been adapted, and honeycomb stitches used instead of ground. The gap row falls on the line between sections. This is advantageous as no pair leads into the centre, and therefore no pair is discarded. The general method is the same as for the previous pattern.

Hang up two passives for use in the heading. Make false picots at A and L, and picots at (i) and (n). Pass the gimp through the four pairs from the picots, and through four pairs hung up on the right for use in the honeycomb head. Hang up three more pairs behind for use at e, f and g. Work in letter order the pins from a to z and Z. After pin o, work a mayflower. Enclose the head with gimps, and cross them below u. Work picot pins 1 to 7 inclusive. Hang up a single gimp and an ordinary pair to the left of it behind pin 8. Pass the gimp through this pair, and the pair from g, and work honeycomb pin 8. Take the gimp back through the left hand pair. Work gap row pins 9 and 10.

Take the right hand gimp through the pair from u, and the left hand gimp through the pair from Z. Work honeycomb pin u and enclose with gimp. Take the gimp through the pairs for the next section. Move the extra cover cloth to the next position.

Motif No.3

This is an adaptation of the first old Bucks pattern on page 163. It is worked in the same way as the previous motifs. Refer to photograph **65** and diagram **114**.

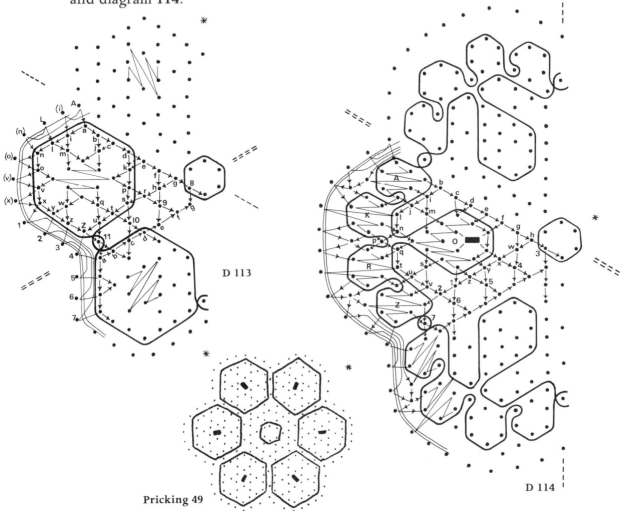

D 113

D 114

Pricking 49

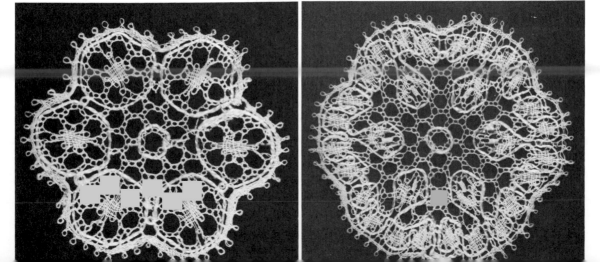

64   Church window motif

65   Old Bucks pattern motif

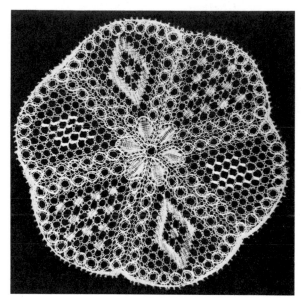

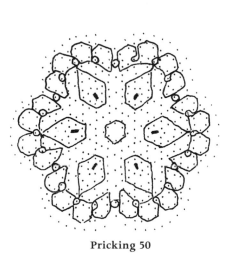

Pricking 50

66   Circular large mat no. 1

Prepare pricking **50** and work the pins and rings strictly in letter order. The rings are marked with capital letters, and should be started immediately after the pin of the preceding small letter has been worked. The ring is worked as convenient.

After pin z has been worked, work in numerical order pins 1 to 7. The picots are worked as required. Turn the pillow to complete six sections.

Circular Mat No.1

This is designed and worked in the same way as the small motifs. See photograph **66** and pricking **51**. The honeycomb rings and the picots are placed on the outside edge more for appearance than ease of working. The worker must endeavour to achieve a neat edge and close passive pairs by using available pairs when convenient, and joining in extra pairs when necessary. Between each section is a row of honeycomb stitches. Three different arrangements are shown for the sections but the worker may prepare a pricking using one design for all sections if preferred.

The top pin for each ring must be correctly ascertained. A line drawn from the top to the bottom hole in each ring should lie parallel to the positioned extra cover cloth – see previous motifs. This is vital to the success of the pattern.

To begin, place an extra cover cloth to the side of the section to be worked and parallel to the line YY. Line XX indicates the row of honeycomb immediately before the section to be worked. The first ring to be worked in each section is marked on the pricking with an asterisk. The rings along the diagonal to the cloth diamond are worked in order. Refer to diagram **115A**. A false picot is made at A and a normal picot at (b), and these provide pairs for the first ring. At least four pairs of headside

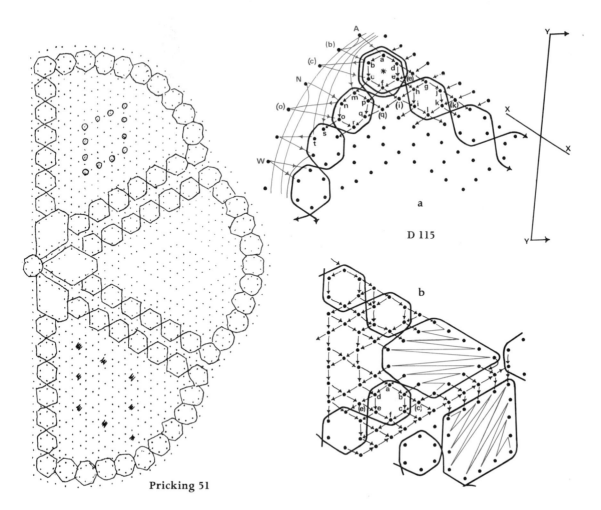

D 115

Pricking 51

passives will give a firm beginning and will be useful for honeycomb rings when picots do not fall in a convenient position. The diagonal row of honeycomb XX can be used for support pins. Work the ring with two gimp pairs round it in letter order. Pins (e) and (i) are worked as honeycomb pins. Cross one pair of gimps for use in the next ring to the right. Work top pin g and continue to l. The remaining rings are worked in the same way using the pins between the rings but no others.

On the headside, as no picot pin is available for pin m, the inner passive works this pin. This use of the passive helps to keep the passive pairs neat and close to the gimp. It was done regularly in the pattern on page 169. A false picot will introduce a pair for pin n, although there are already three passive pairs. Later, the inner pair will be required at pin s. The false picot at pin W will serve as a reminder that both pairs may be brought in from the same pair if required.

Work the continuous row of honeycomb from (q) towards the centre, and the cloth diamond can be completed. Refer to diagram 115B. The pair hanging from the point of the diamond is carried with the gimp (as in the

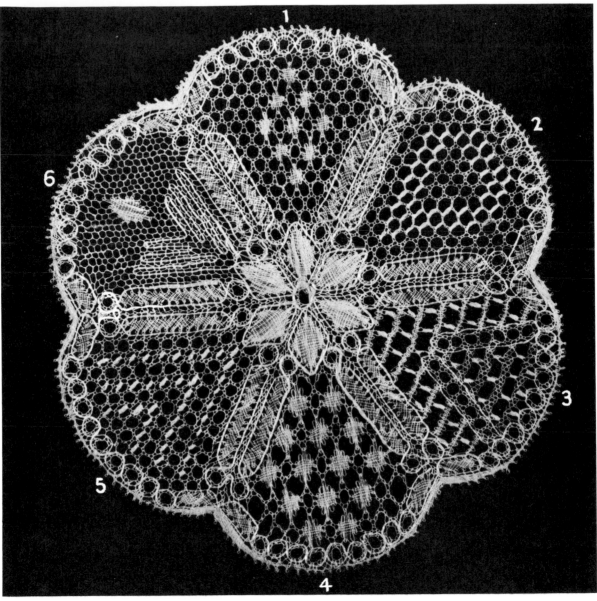

67 Circular large mat no. 2

first motif), and the first stitch inside the centre gimp ring is worked with the pair from the continuous row between sections, and a new pair introduced for the purpose. This can be done only when the section is complete.

The fillings are variations of basic honeycomb, and the filling is worked completely before working the rings from the centre to the headside. Follow the directional arrows, and work the ring nearest the centre in letter order. Complete the other rings in the same way, and use double gimps on the final rings which are common to the diagonal row and the headside. The pillow is turned and the extra cover cloth moved to the next position. Work the row between sections.

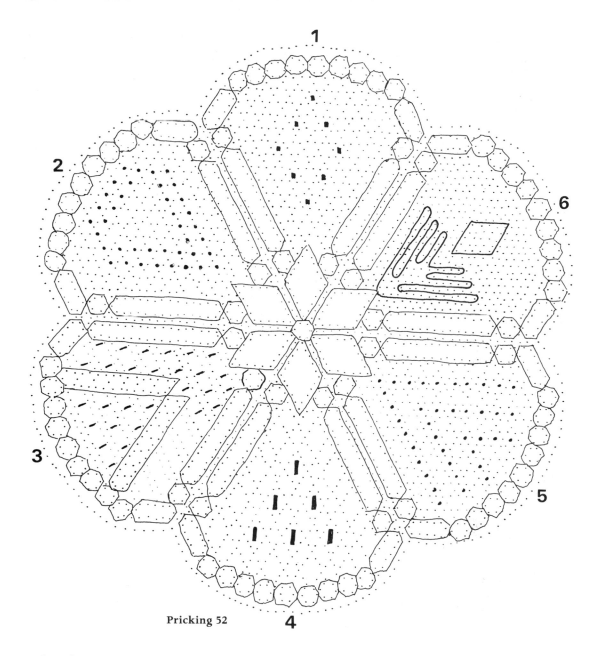

Pricking 52

Circular Mat No.2
This is given as a sampler of different stitches but may be pricked according to the wishes of the worker. Refer to photograph **67** and pricking **52**.
Refer to the description of stitches and fillings on the following pages:

1 Honeycomb with mayflowers, on page 182.
2 Honeycomb with tallies in place of honeycomb stitches at the points of the diamonds, on page 182.
3 Vertical rows of cloth or half stitch with tallies, on page 183.
4 Honeycomb with four pin sided mayflowers, on page 183.
5 Honeycomb with tallies within the rings, on page 182.
6 Ground with gimp and tallies, on page 181.

PRINCIPLES OF LACE DESIGN

Workers who wish to enjoy the more advanced old patterns, or who wish to adapt or design Bucks Point lace, require a good basic knowledge of practical lace making, and an understanding of the way in which patterns are made. Many patterns, particularly the narrow edgings are quite geometric in design, but many have the beauty of flowers and scrolls which run freely through the lace. However, all Bucks Point patterns have a geometric basis. The angle between the footside and the diagonal row of ground is somewhere between 52 and 70 degrees. Refer to diagram **87** on page 131. Usually all the stitches with the exception of cloth are worked at the same angle. Occasionally, there may be a slight variation in the honeycomb in an old pattern.

The appearance of the lace depends to a large extent on the choice of angle. Many narrow edgings are worked at an angle of 52 to 55 degrees, whereas the wide, elaborate patterns are usually worked at 70 degrees. In lace made at the angle of 70 degrees, the cloth work is very close; it will be

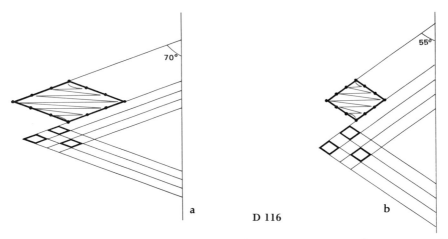

a   D 116   b

more even at 55 degrees. Refer to diagrams **116A** and **116B**. Notice also, the change in the shape of the four pin buds, the sharp pointed buds are unattractive unless the lace is very fine. The coarser the lace and thread, the more obvious any defects become.

On pages 217 and 219 there is a selection of grids and ground dots. Often it is helpful to plot a pattern very much enlarged, similar to the diagrams in this book, and the grids on pages 216 and 218 are for that purpose only. When using the grids, ground dots or prickings, it is important to anchor the tracing paper firmly so that an accurate copy can be made. Of course, a pattern may be put on tracing paper over the grid, and then only the dots required are marked in. For the student interested in making her own grid, diagrams **117A**, **117B** and **117C** explain the method. The distance apart of the marks on the base and upright must be the same. It is suggested that 2.5mm is suitable for the less experienced worker, and 1.5mm is better for those who wish to use fine thread.

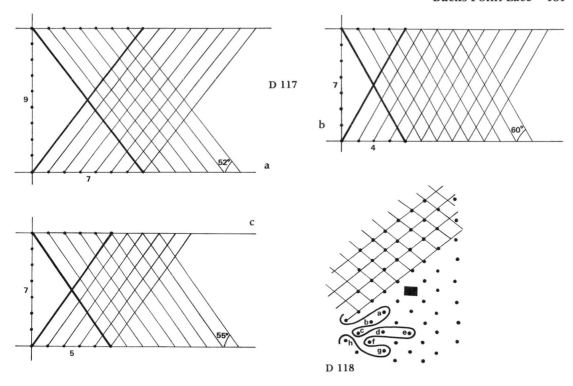

D 117

D 118

Ground   See diagram **118**. Instructions are given for working ground in the Fan pattern on page 134. The holes are spaced evenly at the required angle. Tallies occur in ground, and are worked instead of a ground stitch. When pricking a pattern with tallies, leave a space without a hole, and mark with an ink dot to indicate the position. Working instructions are on page 143.

Gimp threads in ground provide added interest, but require clear thinking to achieve the correct design. The diagram explains the working. The gimp passes through pairs leading into a and b, and through the diagonal pair to a. Work ground pin a and pin b, take the gimp back through the pairs from a and b, and on through the diagonal pairs entering c from right and left. Work pin c, and take the gimp back through both pairs from c and the next pair from b. Work the next row of ground as far as d, pass the gimp through the diagonal pair and work pin d, and continue. There are twists on both sides of the gimps, sometimes as part of the stitch, and sometimes added. However, there are no twists between the gimps which lie together. Ground stitches are used throughout.

The footside   See the same diagram. The holes for the footside are in line with the diagonal, although very often they are dropped slightly to allow space for the passive pairs. It is good practice to add the footside row of holes after the rest of the ground has been pricked, and work along a straight edge.

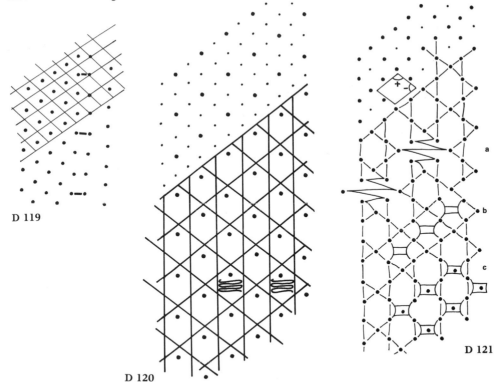

D 119

D 120

D 121

Cucumber foot This is a variation on the footside, and diagram **119** explains the method of pricking. It is tedious and inaccurate to prick in the centre of a grid rather than on the dots of intersections. It is sometimes easier to prick in the footside and catch pin rows, then carefully lift the grid, replace it in the correct position, and continue pricking. The second and third vertical rows must be exactly opposite each other and *not* diagonally opposite. If one vertical row of holes is missed out, the effect is right but the distance apart is too great for neat tallies.

Kat stitch ground The method of pricking is shown in diagram **120**. Only alternate diagonal and alternate vertical rows are pricked. The working is given on page 170. The tally in Kat stitch is worked using the two straight pairs, and only a clear understanding of the direction of threads makes the working possible. The tally is worked at the same time as the row of independent stitches. It is worked before the left hand side pairs are worked, and after the right hand pairs are crossed. This gives the straight pairs together.

Honeycomb is plotted on ground pins. See diagram **121**. The method of working continuous and gap rows has been described on page 138. When patterns are not geometric, it is more difficult to find the diagonal lines on which to base the working. In order to identify them, look for diamond shapes with the obtuse angle at the top. Honeycomb was often called 'five pin', and this referred to the five pins in the 'X' indicated on the diagram.

Variations include mayflower, the cloth diamond – a, in the diagram.

Instructions are given on page 154. Tallies may be worked inside rings – b, or in place at holes at the points of the diamonds – c. Methods of working these are on pages 167 and 189.

Honeycomb and mayflower A different arrangement of the holes for honeycomb is shown in diagram **122**; this is found in old patterns and is very attractive. When fitted into geometric patterns for practice (pricking **52**) it is necessary to carry any unwanted pairs of bobbins alongside the gimp until required again. One problem is to start this filling in an irregular situation, when the cloth diamonds are incomplete. The pinholes are then worked in honeycomb stitches.

Work the gap row in preparation for the cloth diamonds. Begin and work pin a as usual, and pins b and c. At pin d, no pair enters the cloth, the weaver is given extra twists and travels back through the three pairs in the mayflower. The same happens at e, and one pair is brought in at each of f and g. After f and g, pairs are left out. Nothing is left out after h and i, these pins complementing pins d and e. Pairs are left out after k and j, and the last two pairs enclose pin l. Arrows show the use of pairs, refer to diagram **122**.

Pin chain may be used when there are two consecutive pin-holes and no pairs to come in. The honeycomb stitch is worked, the pin put up, another stitch worked, and another pin put up and covered.

Vertical rows of cloth or half stitch and tallies The method of pricking is in diagram **123**, and an opportunity to try the stitch is found in the

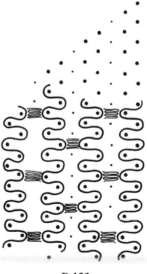

D 123

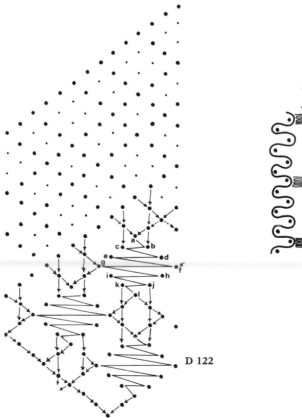

D 122

circular sampler on page 179. The weavers work through two pairs to form vertical strips of cloth or half stitch, and the weavers from each strip meet and work a tally at intervals indicated on the pattern. This is very similar to cucumber foot.

Pin chain and tallies   Diagram **124** illustrates the method of making the pricking, which, when seen in a pattern, appears as widely spaced holes. Every hole is worked in honeycomb stitch, pin, honeycomb stitch as follows. Work pins a and b. Take the inner pairs, make a tally, and then work pins c and d. The right hand pair from d with a left hand from e make a tally to g and h. Similarly, the left pair from c and the right hand pair from f make a tally to j and k. The inner pairs at k and g work a tally, and so on. Sometimes the tallies are not as close together as illustrated lower in the diagram.

Nook pins   Full instructions are given on page 136, and in diagram **90**. However, the nook pin may lie deep in the cloth, and the gimp has to be taken through any number of cloth passive pairs. See diagram **125**. Occasionally, the weaver passes through the gimp, is twisted, and taken back through without the nook pin stitch. See diagram **67** on page 103 for the method of twisting.

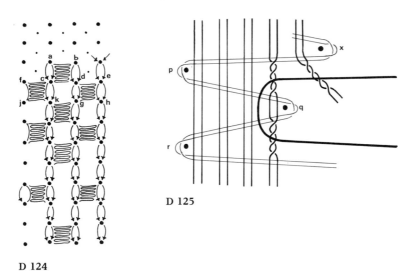

D 125

D 124

CORNERS

Apart from the truly beautiful wedding handkerchiefs, corners are seldom found in old Bucks Point patterns. It was the practice of the lace maker to produce yards and yards of edging, which were mitred or gathered when necessary. The lace maker of today wishes to enhance the finished article with an attractive corner that is part of the design, and this is no easy task in Point lace. Diagrams **126A**, **126B** and **126C** on page 186 give one example of a way in which a corner may be created for a simple pattern. When studying the diagrams refer to the following points:

1   Use a mirror to assess the possibilities in the design, as described on page 37.

2   Always make a complete break in the diagonal ground from the catch pin to the design. In the Church Window pattern on page 148, honeycomb rings are used. In the Kat stitch pattern on page 171, the four half stitch buds are repeated across the corner and in the pattern on page 169 the normal design has been used in a slightly different form and brought down to the footside.

3   The pattern design has to be rearranged to cope with the curve and the change in the direction of the lace. Regular geometric patterns with a definite line of cloth stitch are difficult, and a new idea must be introduced to 'fill' the corner. The ring of honeycomb buds in the pattern on page 162 is a typical example. To retain the solidarity of the pattern, and to form a definite link with the design, cloth is introduced in a different form inside the ring. In the pattern given here more tallies are included to give weight to the design.

4   The picots should be taken almost to the corner point, and pleasantly spaced and rounded. A curve which reduces the corner will look unattractive. The picot line is dependent upon the rest of the design.

5   The filling stitch – usually some variation of honeycomb – must be worked at the correct angle from the footside. This is explained in detail overleaf, when the method of making is discussed referring to pattern.

6   Cloth stitch is usually worked with the passive threads lying parallel to the footside, and the weaver at right angles to it. If the cloth stitch is worked throughout in this manner the direction of the threads will always appear the same. However, at the discretion of the worker, the cloth in the corner may be worked with the weaver running parallel to the corner diagonal.

7   The most important consideration is the appearance of the finished lace, and good lace can only be achieved when the correct thread arrangements and the right line is maintained. Extra pairs may be joined in, preferably with false picots, or over the cloth stitch weaver. If necessary they may be joined in over a gimp thread, but this is inclined to spoil the gimp line. Pairs should be discarded when no longer required, either in the passives in the headside, or in other cloth work. They may be carried alongside the gimp and then discarded as soon as they are securely anchored – usually after one inch of gimp has been used. If they are fastened together with a rubber band around the bobbins there is less chance of mistakes.

8   Certain patterns have a directional design, and it may be necessary to reverse the pattern direction on the straight edge so that the corner can be symmetrical. See the Pea and Bean pattern on page 145.

For details of the method for making the corner for a pattern, see photograph **68**, and diagrams **126A**, **126B** and **126C**.

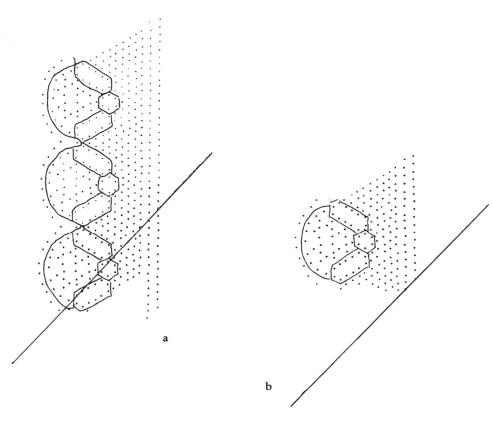

a

b

D 126

c

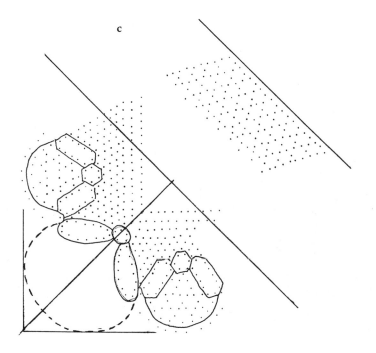

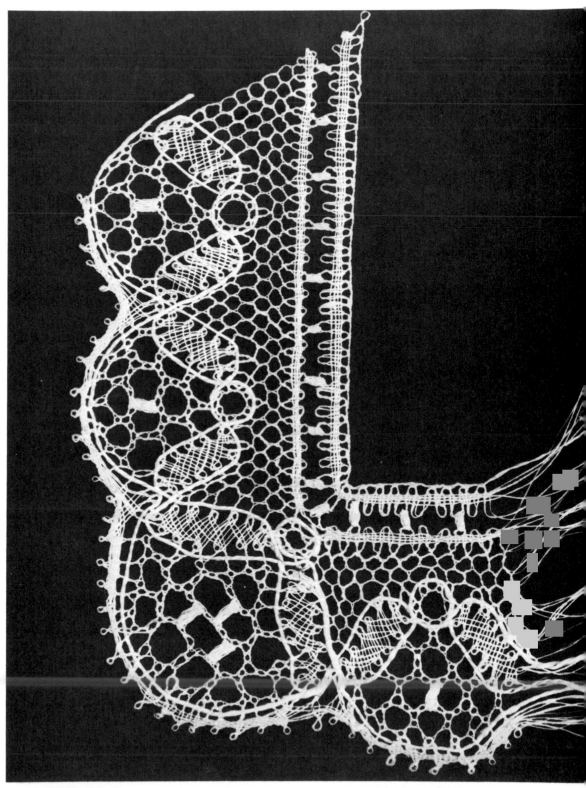

68   Buttercup pattern

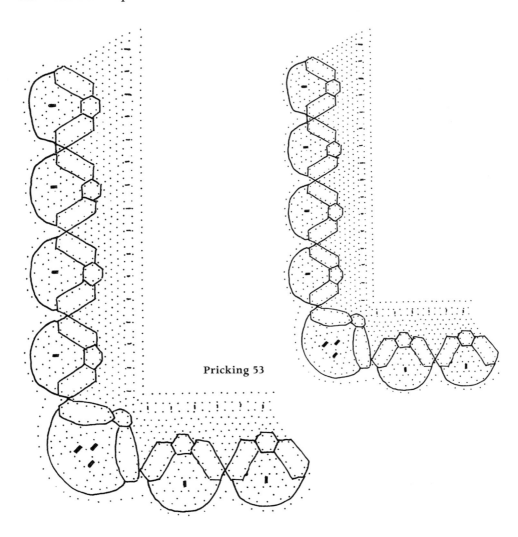

Pricking 53

A   Use a mirror to decide on the form of the corner. Decide which pin hole will fall at the corner footside, and mark in the true diagonal at 45 degrees through this hole.

B   Through four thicknesses of paper, prick in every hole that will be in the finished pricking. Leave adequate space to plan the corner design. Through the corner pin-hole cut on the diagonal at 45 degrees, reverse one piece, and fit them together, using Sellotape on the back of the paper. Draw in the design and mark in the pin-hole positions, refold the paper on the corner line through the double sheets, and prick in the holes. Unfold the paper and mark in the gimp lines. If the corner is symmetrical, a better result will be obtained if the holes are pricked at the same time. Be sure to put holes on the fold in afterwards to avoid double pricking.

C   Decide on the line of the picots and plan the filling stitches to come out towards this line.

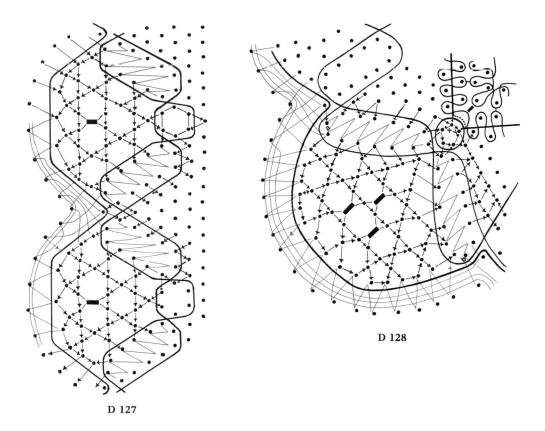

D 127

D 128

D   In order to establish the correct position of the stitches within the corner take the corner diagonal (i.e. the true corner at 45 degrees), and draw a line through it at right angles to it. This line is the equivalent of the footside, and should be used to set the honeycomb in position. Prick a section of honeycomb from the straight pattern on to clear film and mark in the footside position. Place the film over the pricking at the correct angle and try to match the holes on either side of the centre corner line. Prick in the holes.

E   Finally decide on the position of the picot holes, working out an even arrangement and relating them as far as possible to the honeycomb stitches.

F   Transfer to card for use.

To work the pattern prepare pricking **53** and refer to diagrams **127** and **128**. Both a gimp pair and a single gimp are required, the latter remaining near to the headside passives throughout. In the corner begin at pin x, using the left hand inner pair and the pair to the left of it. The ring is worked in an anti-clockwise direction, and cannot be completed until both cloth ovals are worked. At pin y, the ring is completed, and the passive pair returns to its normal position. The other passive pair is carried with the gimp. The first cloth oval is worked from a, and the second from b, at some pins two pairs enter or leave the cloth work.

TWELVE PATTERNS WITH PHOTOGRAPHS AND PRICKINGS

These are arranged in order of difficulty; the first seven have instruction diagrams. All are old Bucks Point patterns.

69   Old Bucks patterns

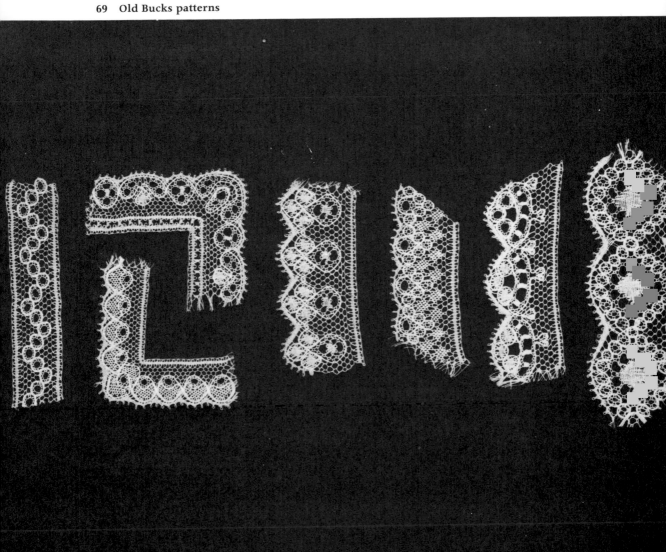

Pattern No.1

The footside instructions on page 134 apply to both the right and left hand sides of the lace. Refer to photograph **70**, pricking **54**, and diagram **129**.

70   Old Bucks pattern no. 1

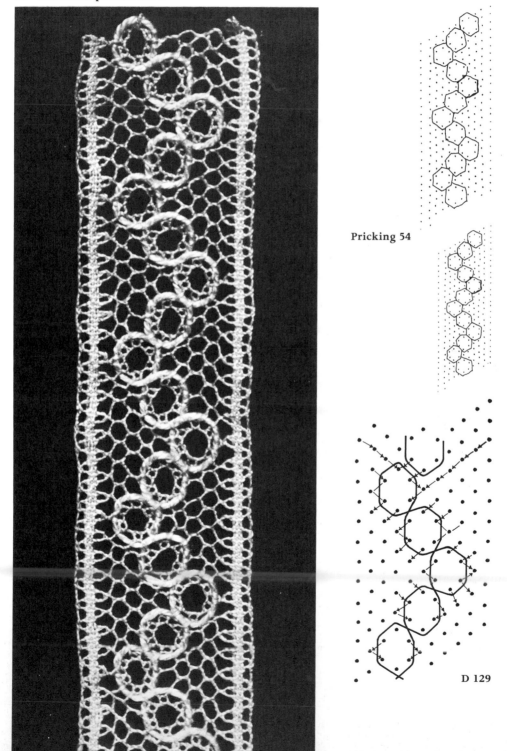

Pricking 54

D 129

Pattern No.2

This is an old pattern from Downton, near Salisbury, and is unusual in that there are diamonds of half stitch in the ground. See photograph **71**, pricking **55** and diagram **130**.

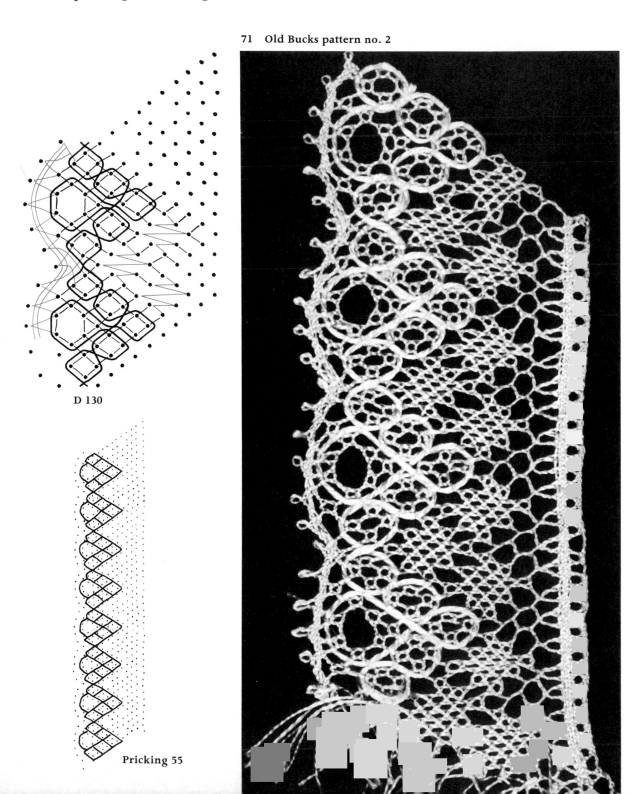

71   Old Bucks pattern no. 2

D 130

Pricking 55

Pattern No.3

This pattern may be interpreted in a variety of ways, but was found worked as shown. The cloth arrangement within the honeycomb is unusual. See photograph **72**, pricking **56**, and diagram **131**.

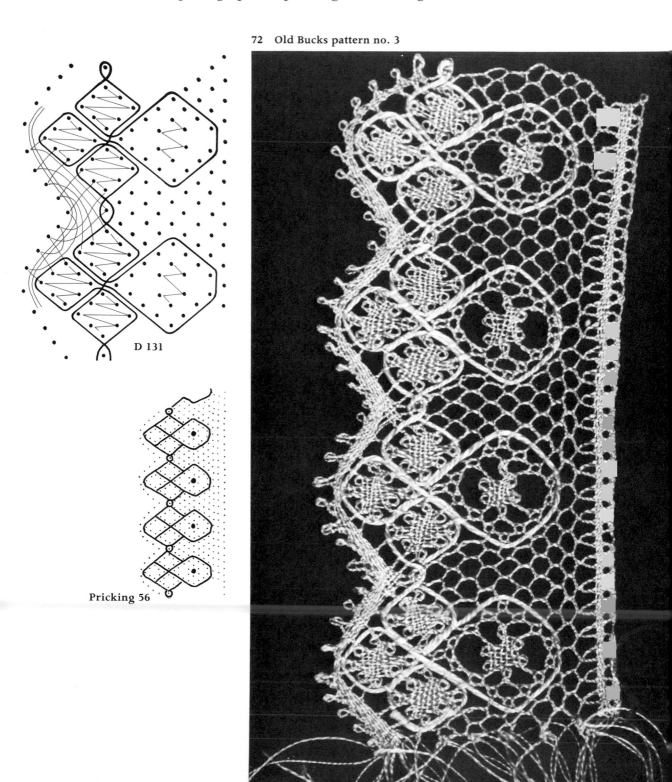

72   Old Bucks pattern no. 3

D 131

Pricking 56

Pattern No.4
A very pleasing regular pattern that is quick and easy to work. See photograph **73**, pricking **57**, and diagram **132**.

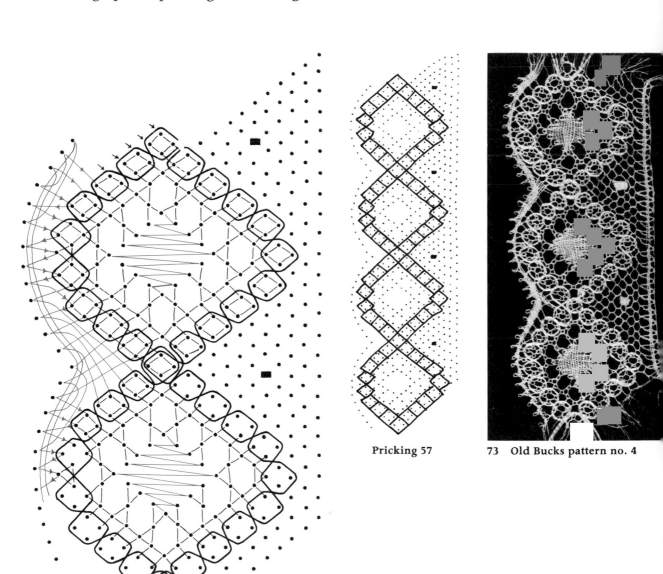

Pricking 57

73   Old Bucks pattern no. 4

D 132

Pattern No.5
Cucumber foot in fine lace is attractive, and provides a wider lace without
too much ground. See photograph **74**, pricking **58**, and diagram **133**.

74   Old Bucks pattern no. 5

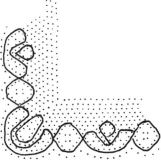

Pricking 58

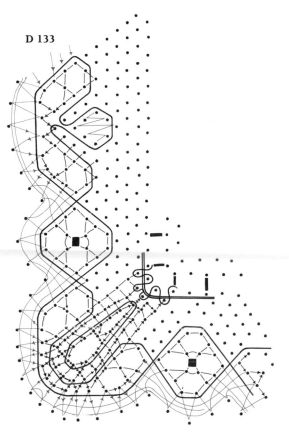

D 133

Pattern No.6

The half stitch semicircle is rarely found in white lace and possibly the pattern was originally in black. It is very suitable for black lace. See photograph **75**, pricking **59**, and diagram **134**.

75   Old Bucks pattern no. 6

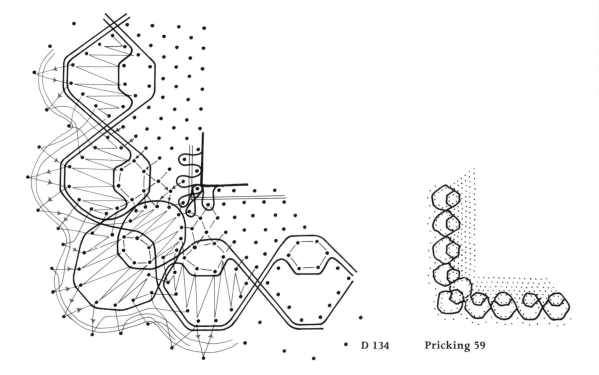

D 134   Pricking 59

Pattern No.7

This is more difficult and each repeat does not necessarily have the same holes as the previous one. Diagram **135** acts as a guide only. See also photograph **76**, and pricking **60**.

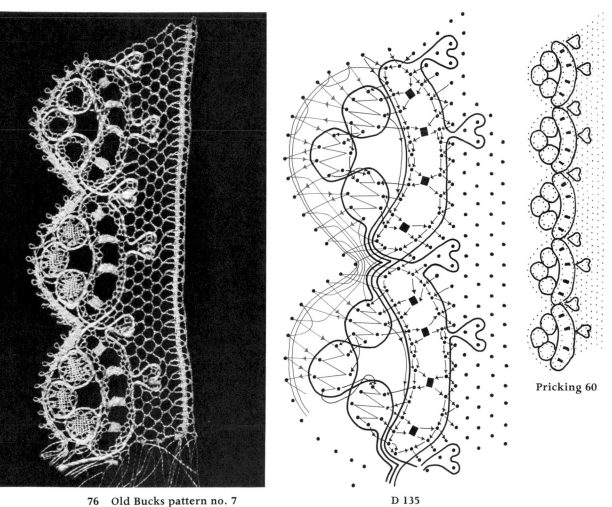

76 Old Bucks pattern no. 7

D 135

Pricking 60

Pattern No.8
This pattern is very easy – no instruction diagram is necessary. See photograph **77**, and pricking **61**.

77   Old Bucks pattern no. 8

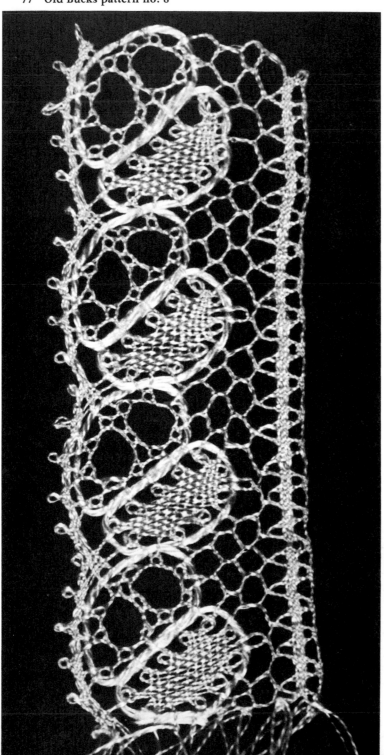

Pricking 61

Pattern No.9

The work has been started at the corner in order to avoid a join in the ground. Notice the angle of the honeycomb in the corner, and the double gimp threads. The gimp thread in the cloth is kept in position by nook pins. See photograph **78**, and pricking **62**.

78   Old Bucks pattern no. 9

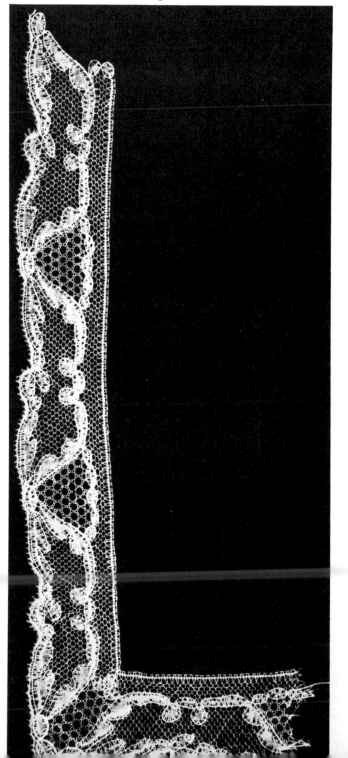

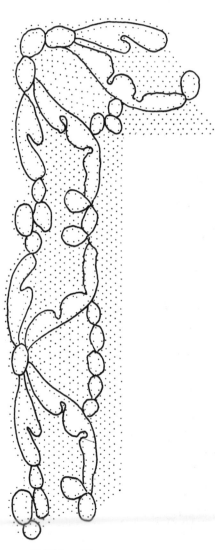

Pricking 62

Pattern No.10

Fine Point lace pattern with an asymmetrical design. There are several possibilities for a corner design without reversing the pattern. See photograph **79**, and pricking **63**.

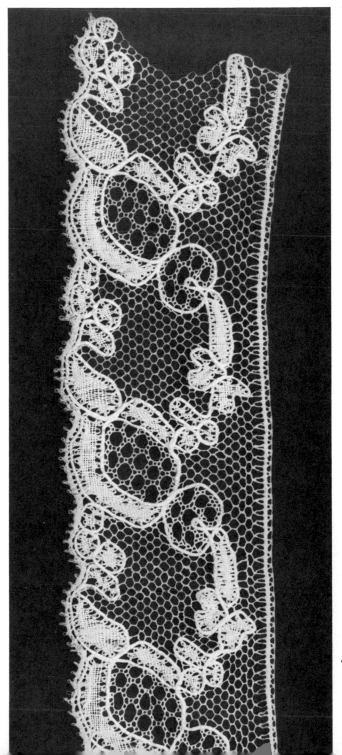

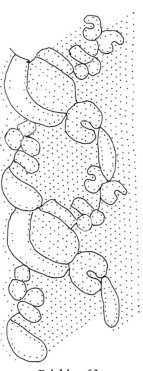

Pricking 63

79   Old Bucks pattern no. 10

Pattern No.11

The holes in the cloth are emphasized by gimp, and a pair is carried inside the gimp to work honeycomb stitches with the weaver; a cloth stitch may be worked if preferred. This pattern has been started at the corner to avoid a join in the ground. See photograph **80**, and pricking **64**.

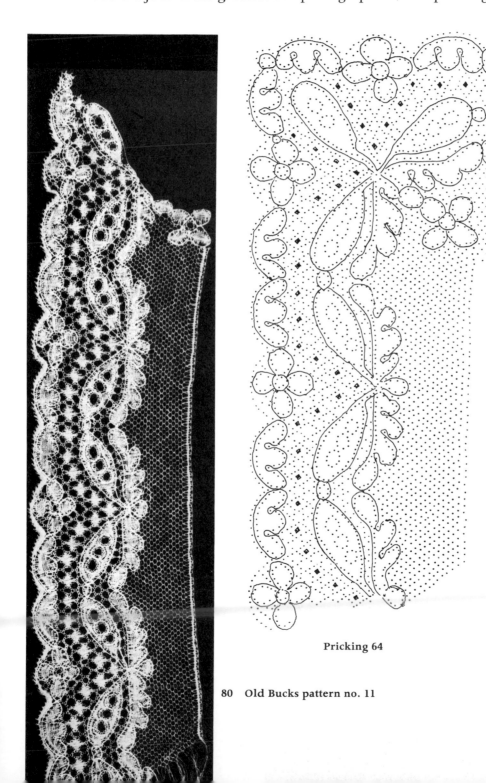

Pricking 64

80   Old Bucks pattern no. 11

Pattern No.12

Before beginning the lace, plan the arrangement of the gimps and make a diagram. The holes in the cloth have no gimp, and so avoid special emphasis on this feature. See photograph **81**, and pricking **65**.

81   Old Bucks pattern no. 12

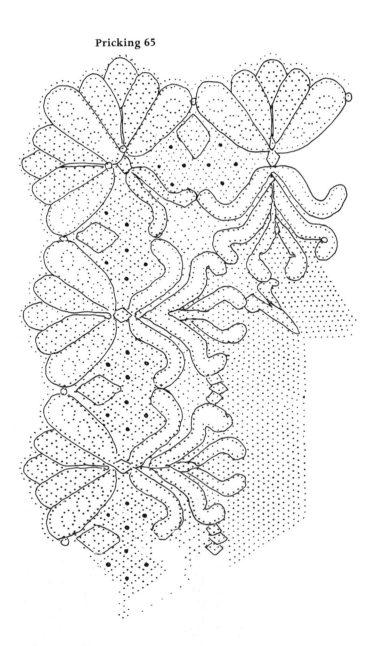

Pricking 65

5 ❖ Braids and trimmings for modern use

Trimmings for upholstery, lampshades or dress can be designed and worked according to the decoration required. The range of threads available in a variety of weights, textures and colours lends itself to experiment and an exciting opportunity to create original patterns. The application of old techniques for modern use is a fascinating pastime, and when well planned should be quick to execute and bold in design. Frequently only one predominant feature is necessary and the background threads may be the same colour as the fabric on which it is to be used. A selection of ideas is given, but it is hoped that these are for example and interest and that the worker will gain experience and design her own. Very simple ideas are effective – see photographs **82A** and **82B**.

 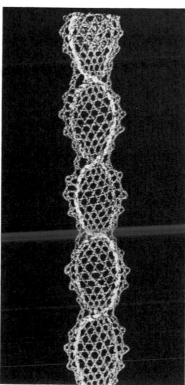

82a and 82b
Simple braids

FRINGE

A fringe is worked on to a cloth braid which may be inserted between two pieces of material, or edge-stitched into position. A weaver and sufficient pairs to fill a braid are necessary and two extra pairs for the fringe. Any soft thread, silk or mercerized cotton, is satisfactory. The example in photograph **83** is worked in mercerized cotton with a six-stranded silk used for the fringe. Prepare pricking **66** – the distance apart of the holes depends on the thread used. Using the threads mentioned above, a grid of 10 squares to 20mm was used.

Referring to the pricking, hang the weaver on a pin at a, and work through sufficient pairs in cloth stitch to make a firm strip to b. Support two pairs for the fringe on c, and take the weaver through these pairs in cloth stitch. Make a cloth stitch with the fringe pairs, and put up pin b to the left of both fringe pairs, but to the right of the weaver. Take the weaver to the right through the two fringe pairs and through the braid pairs to d. Take the fringe pairs round a pin put up at e. Continue.

RAISED GIMPS

A cord or chain effect may be achieved over cloth stitch by using thick threads, usually in contrasting colour. Sufficient pairs are required to make a very close braid so that the raised threads are prominent, also two thick threads for the cord or four for the chain. See photograph **83**.

Cord   Refer to diagram **136A**. Take the weaver from the left to the centre of the braid in cloth stitch (i.e. through half the pairs). Pass both weaver threads over the first thick thread and under the second. Cross the thick threads right over the left, and then weave to the end of the row. Working back to the left, pass the weaver threads under the first thick thread and over the second. Cross the thick threads right over left. Complete the row and continue.

Chain   Refer to diagram **136B**. The diagram shows clearly the working.

STRAIGHT BRAID A

See photograph **84** and diagram **137**. Select threads in contrasting colour and texture, and make pricking **67**. For guidance the sample shown was worked on a grid of eight squares to 25mm, and no.8 pearl cotton was used. Add holes as indicated within the squares on the working diagram in order to facilitate the beginning. Colours used were (b) blue, and (s) silver. Blue lines on the diagram indicate the blue threads and black indicate silver. When more than one pair is hung on a pin place in order from left to right. On pin Aa hang (s) (b), and on B, C, D, E and F hang (b) (s).

Work cloth stitch and twist with pairs on Aa, take the (b) pair to the left to work with (s) from B in half stitch, put up pin b, and cover. Continue the diagonal row, use the (b) pair from B to work half stitch, pin c, and

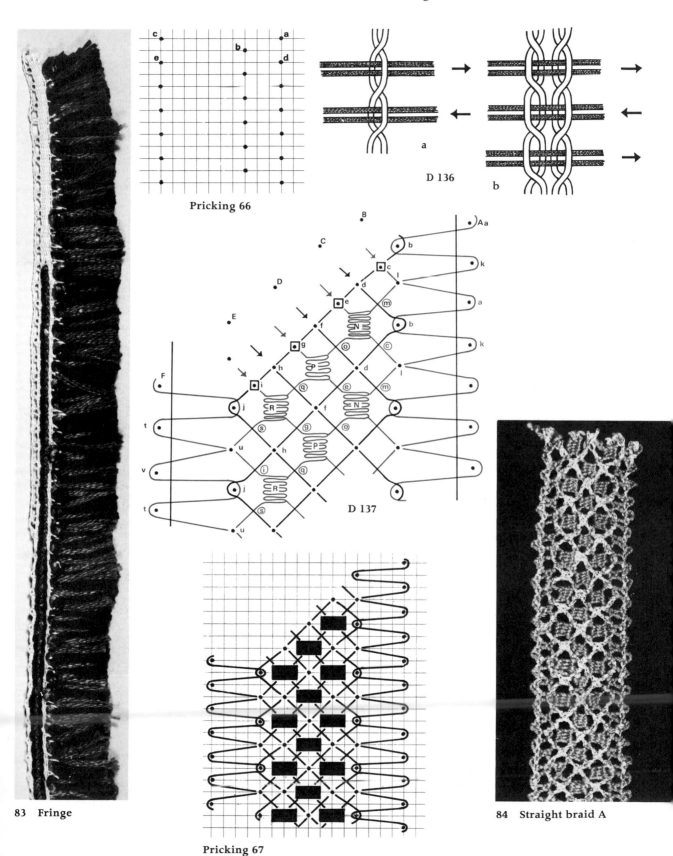

Pricking 66

D 136

D 137

83   Fringe

Pricking 67

84   Straight braid A

cover. Bringing in a pair at each pin, work pins d, e, f, g, h and i with half stitch, pin and cover. Remove support pins B to E. Work cloth stitch and twist with the pairs on F and use the (b) pair and the diagonal (s) pair from i to work cloth stitch and twist, pin j, and cover. With the two right hand pairs, work cloth stitch and twist, pin k, and cover. The inner (b) pair from k works with the next (b) pair in half stitch pin l and cover. *Without* a pin the left hand pair from l works cloth stitch and twist with the (s) pair to the left of it at m. The pairs from e and m work a tally N. Leave the tally weaver at the right hand side of the tally, and take the left hand pair from the tally through the next (s) thread without a pin at o. The diagram shows the continuation of the pattern and the order of working. For guidance, the pattern is repeated with letters in blue. Note that letters inside circles indicate that the stitch is made without a pin.

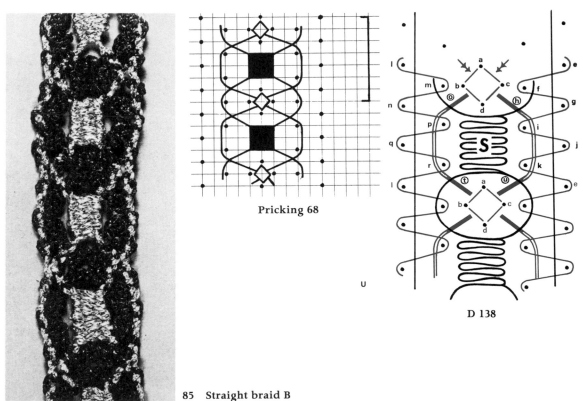

Pricking 68

D 138

85   Straight braid B

STRAIGHT BRAID B

Refer to photograph **85**, and prepare pricking **68** and threads. Again (b) blue is indicated on diagram **138** in blue and (s) silver is in black. Hang up pairs on support pins and work rose ground unit abcd. Hang two pairs on l and two pairs on e, and work cloth stitch and twist so that the (s) pairs are the edge passives. The weaver from e works cloth stitch and twist, pin f, and cover with the (s) pair from a support pin. Work pin g and then cross the (s) threads through the two pairs from cd. The weaver from g works to the left through pairs from h. Continue with pins i, j and k. Similarly work from l to r following the diagram. The (s) pairs make tally S and then pass through the (b) pairs from k and r at u and t. The pattern is repeated beginning with the blue letters abcd. Ringed letters indicate that no pin is used.

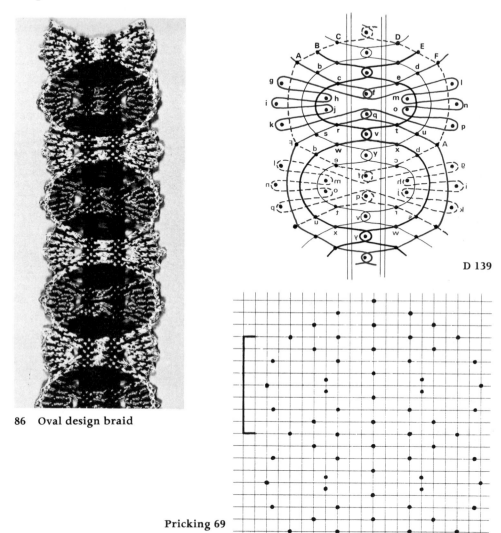

86   Oval design braid

D 139

Pricking 69

OVAL DESIGN BRAID

See photograph **86** and diagram **139**. Prepare pricking **69** and threads in three colours. The method of working may be elucidated by close reference to diagram **139**, the braid being worked in letter order. Pins b, c, d and e are worked as half stitch, pin and cover. Pins f to p are worked as cloth stitch and twist, pin and cover. Pins r, s, t, u, w and x are worked as half stitch, pin and cover, but v and y are worked with cloth stitch and twist, pin and cover. A and F are half stitch, pin and cover. For the pattern repeat, the letters are in blue, and the second colour does the weaving.

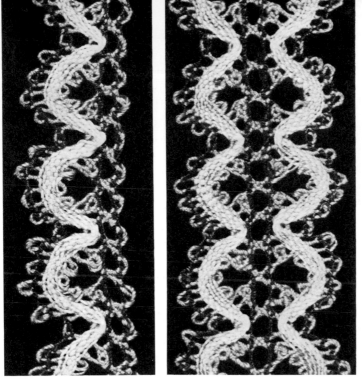

Pricking 70 A

87a Single-headed scallop braid

87b Double-headed scallop braid

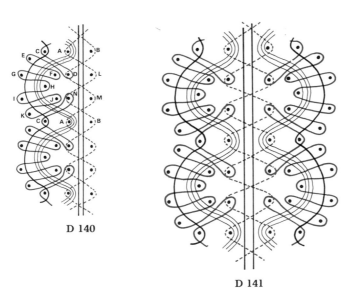

D 140

D 141

SCALLOP BRAID

See photograph **87A** and **87B**, also diagram **140**. The colours may be arranged according to diagram and photograph. On the diagram the blue lines are the weavers, the thin black lines are the trail pairs, and the thick black lines are the passive pairs. Refer to the footside arrangement on page 78. Prepare pricking **70A**.

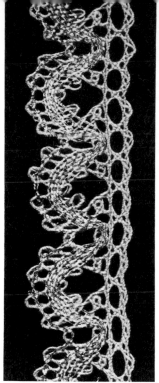

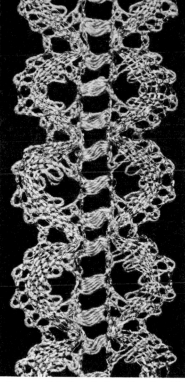

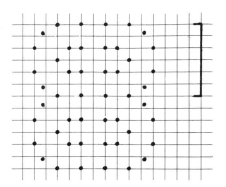

Pricking 70 B

88a Single-headed scallop braid

88b Double-headed scallop braid and a tally used to cross weavers

Hang two pairs at B and C, and five pairs in order at A. At pin A, work the left hand pair through the other four pairs on that pin with cloth stitch. Work cloth stitch and twist to cover pin B, and cross the weavers between the passive pairs with cloth stitch and twist. Cover pin C with cloth stitch and twist, and work through three trail pairs in cloth stitch only. Bring the left hand weaver through its passive pair, work the two weavers in cloth stitch and twist, and cover. Work the left hand weaver to the left through the three passive pairs in cloth stitch, twist the weaver once, and work cloth stitch and twist on the outside edge. Put up pin E and cover.

Work pins F, G, H, I, J and K, and back towards N. Work pin L, and cross the weavers with cloth stitch and twist. The left hand weaver works with the trail weaver into pin N. Work pin M, cross the weavers, and work out to pin B on the right. The other weaver passes through its passive pair, and through the three trail pairs to A. The trail weaver works out to C. A pattern is complete, it is essential to follow the diagram. In the pattern the trail is worked in cloth stitch, but all other stitches are cloth stitch and twist.

. . .

Pricking **70B** and diagram **141** explain the working of the double-headed scallop braid. Photographs **88A** and **88B** show the braid with other threads and a tally used to cross weavers.

DIAMOND AND SCALLOP BRAID

This pattern is similar to the Torchon pattern on page 39. Photograph **89**, pricking **71**, and diagram **142** explain the method of working.

89   Diamond and scallop braid

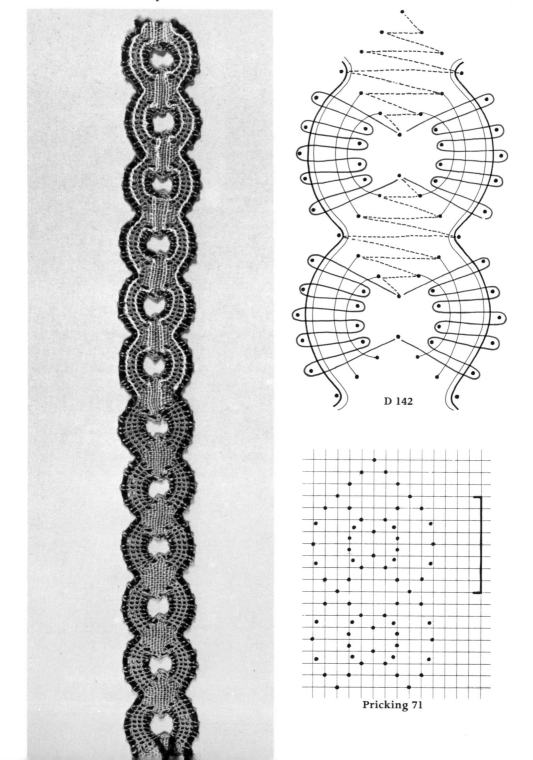

D 142

Pricking 71

PLAIT CROSSINGS
These are very useful and instructions are in the chapter on Beds lace for four and six plait crossings. The eight plait crossing is described below. See photographs **90A** and **90B**.

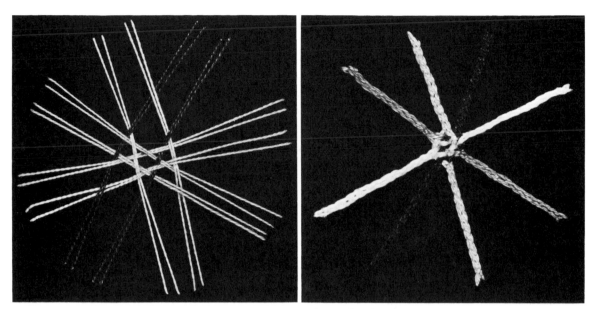

90a, 90b   Eight plait crossing

Eight Plait Crossing
Use the four plaits as eight pairs, using each pair as if a single bobbin. Use the centre four pairs to work a half stitch. Make a half stitch with the right hand four pairs and then with the left hand four pairs.

Return to the centre four pairs and work a half stitch. With the right four pairs work a half stitch, and then with the left four pairs. Put up a pin in the centre. Make a cloth stitch with the centre four pairs. Find the right hand four pairs, and cross the centre pairs left over right. Find the left hand four pairs, and cross the centre pairs left over right.

Appendix

GRIDS

These should be pricked on to parchment, transparent film or pricking card in order to have more permanent and accurate copies.

A   4 squares = 25mm.
B   8 squares = 25mm.
C   25 squares = 25mm.
D   10 squares = 25mm.
E   12.5 squares = 25mm.
F   4 pin-holes to each 25mm on footside (at 60 degrees from footside).
G   12 pin-holes to each 25mm on footside (at 60 degrees from footside).
H   16 pin-holes to each 25mm on footside (at 60 degrees from footside).
I   4 pin-holes to each 25mm on footside (at 55 degrees from footside).
J   12 pin-holes to each 25mm on footside (at 55 degrees from footside).
K   16 pin-holes to each 25mm on footside (at 55 degrees from footside).

SUPPLIERS OF LACE-MAKING EQUIPMENT, MATERIALS AND BOOKS

United Kingdom

Alby Lace Museum
Cromer Road
Alby
Norfolk
NR11 7QE

E. Braggins & Sons
26–36 Silver Street
Bedford

Stephen Cook
'Cottage Crafts'
6 Woodland Close
Flackwell Heath
Buckinghamshire
HP10 9EP

Leonie Cox
The Old School
Childswickham
Near Broadway
Worcs
WR12 7HD

English Lace School
Honiton Court
Rockbeare
Near Exeter
Devon

J. & J. Ford
October Hill
Upper Way
Upper Longdon
Rugeley
Staffordshire
WS15 1QB

Frank Herring & Sons
27 West Street
Dorchester
Dorset
DT1 1UP

Honiton Lace Shop
44 High Street
Honiton
Devon

D.J. Hornsby
149 High Street
Burton Latimer
Kettering
Northants
NN15 5RL

All branches of
John Lewis

Lambourne Valley
Cottage Industries
11 Oxford Street
Lambourn
Berks
RG16 7XS

Mace and Nairn
89 Crane Street
Salisbury
Wiltshire
SP1 2PY

The Needlewoman
21 Needless Abbey
off New Street
Birmingham

Dorothy Pearce
5 Fulshaw Avenue
Wilmslow
Cheshire

Bryn Phillips
'Pantglass'
Cellan
Lampeter
Dyfed
SA48 8JD

Jack Piper
'Silverlea'
Flax Lane
Glemsford
Suffolk
CO10 7RS

Peter and Beverley Scarlett
Strupak
Hill Head
Coldwells
Ellon
Grampian

J.S. Sear
Lacecraft Supplies
8 Hill View
Sherrington
Buckinghamshire

Sebalace
Waterloo Mills
Howden Road
Silsden
W. Yorks
BD20 0HA

A. Sells
49 Pedley Lane
Clifton
Shefford
Bedfordshire

D.H. Shaw
47 Zamor Crescent
Thruscroft
Rotherham
S. Yorks
S66 9QD

Shireburn Lace
Finkle Court
Finkle Hill
Sherburn in Elmet
N. Yorks
LS25 6EB

Stephen Simpson
Avenham Road Works
Preston
Lancs

Christine and David Springett
21 Hillmorton Road
Rugby
Warwickshire
CV22 5DF

Valley House Crafts Studios
Ruston
Scarborough
N. Yorks

George White
Delaheys Cottage
Thistle Hill
Knasesborough
N. Yorks
HG5 8LS

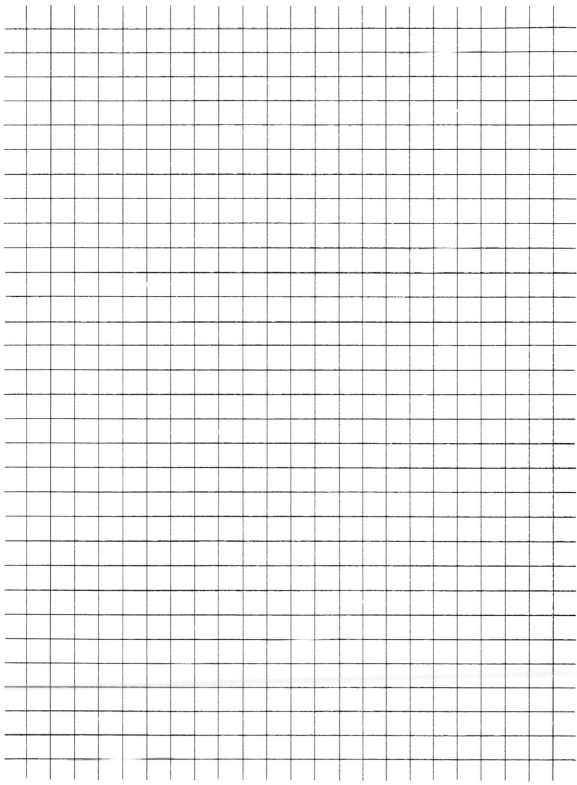

A

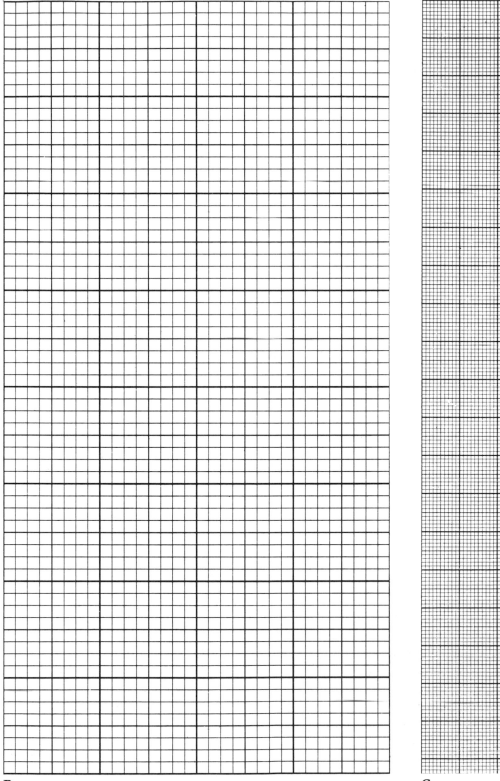

B   C

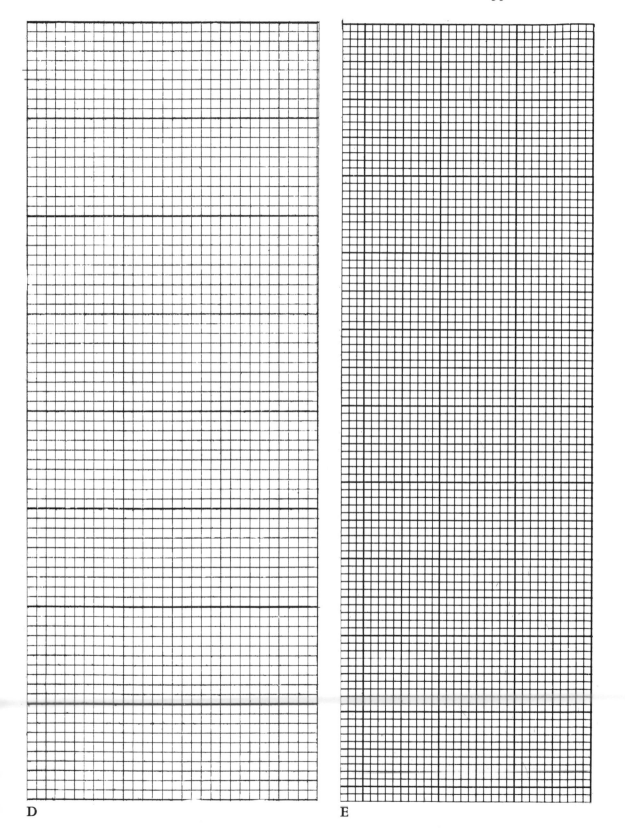

D

E

F

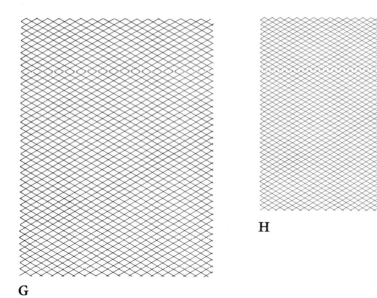

G

H

I

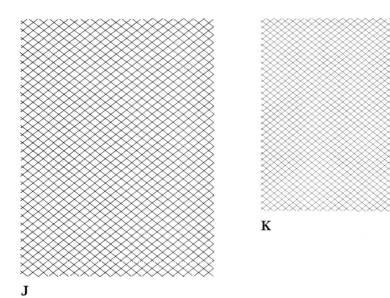

J

K

Index